RAMAYANA

The Timeless Hindu Epic About Good Over Evil

Swami Divyananda

GRAPEVINE INDIA

Published by

GRAPEVINE INDIA PUBLISHERS PVT LTD

www.grapevineindia.com
Delhi | Mumbai
email: grapevineindiapublishers@gmail.com

Ordering Information:
Quantity sales: Special discounts are available on quantity purchases by corporations, associations, and others.
For details, reach out to the publisher.

First published by Grapevine India 2023

CHAPTER I:
THE CONCEPTION

THE LARGE kingdom Kosala, to the north of the Ganga, was made fertile by the river Sarayu. Its capital was Ayodhya, which was constructed by Manu, the great monarch of the Solar Dynasty. From the capital city of Ayodhya which meant something which cannot be subjugated by war, King Dasaratha controlled the kingdom. He had fought for the Devas, and his fame had spread throughout the three worlds. He was on par with Indra and Kubera. Kosala's people were content, cheerful, and moral. A powerful army guarded the region, and no attacker could come close. It had forts with moats around them as well as extensive defensive facilities, and true to its name, Ayodhya defied all enemies.

Dasaratha had eight smart ministers who were always ready to advise and carry out his directives. Vasishtha, Vaamadeva, and other Brahmanas were great sages who taught dharma and performed ceremonies and sacrifices. Taxes were low, and crime was punished proportionately. The king's brilliance shined like the rising sun, surrounded by the brightest advisors and statesmen.

Many years flew past. Dasaratha had one sorrow in the middle of all this prosperity: he had no son.

One day in early summer, he contemplated sacrificing a horse to produce offspring. He sought the guidance of his religious teachers and had sage Rishya-Sringa execute the Yagna. The Yagna was a spectacular celebration attended by many of the rulers of the day. Yagna were not easy to accomplish. The location and construction of the sacrificial platform had to be meticulously planned and carried out in accordance with the rules. There were professionals whose advice was sought to arrange things. It involved constructing a new camp city capable of housing tens of thousands and providing hospitality and entertainment for the invitees, who included the land's princes and sages. When all preparations were complete, the ceremonies were carried out exactly as prescribed by the Shastras.

While Ayodhya prepared for the yagna, a great calamity troubled the heavens. A meeting of the Devas, in other words the heavenly beings, took place in heaven. The Devas complained to Lord Brahma that Ravana, king of the Rakshasas/demons, was bringing them immense agony and hardship because he was drunk on the power provided to him by Brahma's blessing. They made a plea to Brahma, "Ravana is beyond our ability to subjugate, conquer, or kill. In the safety of your boon, he has grown cruel and insolent, mistreating everyone, including women. You are our only hope, and it is up to you to design a way to kill Ravana and end his oppression."

Brahma knew he had granted Ravana the boon he had sought, making him impervious to Devas, Asuras, Gandharvas, and other such beings. Ravana, however, was too arrogant to ask for protection from humans. All the Gods were delighted and turned to Vishnu when Brahma revealed this fateful omission. The Devas completely surrendered to Vishnu, begging him to be born as a man and put an end to Ravana and his misdeeds. Vishnu accepted and assured the Devas that he would be born as one of King Dasaratha's four sons, who was presently undertaking a progeny sacrifice.

In Ayodhya the yagna began and as the ghee was thrown into the fire, a majestic figure emerged from the flames, radiant like the noonday sun and bearing a bowl of gold. The figure addressed King Dasaratha by name and said: "The Devas are pleased with you and are answering your prayer. The gods have sent you payasam for your wives. You will be rewarded with sons if they drink this wonderful nectar."

Dasaratha received the bowl with much enthusiasm and gave the payasam to his three wives, Kausalya, Sumitra, and Kaikeyi. He instructed Kausalya to drink half of the payasam and gave Sumitra the other half. Kaikeyi drank half of what was left, and the rest was given to Sumitra again. Dasaratha's wives were overjoyed, and before long, all of them were expecting moms.

Dasaratha's sons, Rama of Kausalya and Bharata of Kaikeyi, were born over time. Sumitra had twins, Lakshmana and Shatrughna, after drinking the heavenly payasam twice. The sons are traditionally thought to be parts of Vishnu in proportion to the amount of payasam consumed by their respective mothers. As a result, Rama was half-Vishnu.

Dasaratha's four sons received all of the training expected of princes. Rama and Lakshmana were particularly loyal to one another, as were Bharata and Shatrughna. Dasaratha was pleased to see his four boys grow up to be strong, virtuous, brave, and beloved, as well as possessing all other princely traits.

CHAPTER II:
RAMA LEAVES HOME

ONE DAY, when the King was contemplating the marriage of his sons, ushers hurried in to inform him that the famous Sage Vishvamitra had arrived to meet him. Vishvamitra was revered by all as the most powerful of the rishis. Vishvamitra was a king who had become a Brahmarishi after undergoing extraordinary tapasya.

Vishvamitra's arrival in Ayodhya was unexpected, yet King Dasaratha climbed down from the throne and walked a few steps respectfully to greet the sage. He welcomed Vishvamitra in the same way that Indra would greet Brahma, and touching his feet, he exclaimed, "I am exceedingly blessed among men. Your presence can only be attributed to the merit of my forefathers. You were born a king and have become a Brahmarishi through tapas. And you have come to seek my presence. Is there anything I can do for you that is within my power? If that's the case, give me a command and I'll follow."

Dasaratha's remarks filled Vishvamitra with joy, and his countenance lit up. "O King, your words are befitting of you," he said. "What else could you say if you were born into the Ikshvaaku family and had Vasishtha as your Guru? You said 'yes' before I even asked. This makes my heart sing.

I'm currently making a sacrifice. Maareecha and Subaahu, two mighty Rakshasas, contaminate it as it nears completion. They defile the sacred fire with impure blood and flesh. We may curse and destroy them like other rishis. That, though, would be a waste of all of our tapas. Our problems will be solved if you send Rama, the eldest of your warlike sons, with me. He will grow into a regal figure under my care. He will undoubtedly defeat these Rakshasas, and his fame will become renowned. Give Rama to me only for a few days. Please do not turn down my plea. You need not be concerned about Rama's safety. You will achieve immortal fame in all three realms. I'm sure Vasishtha and your ministers will agree with me."

Dasaratha shook from dread and worry. He was forced to choose between allowing his beloved son to be slaughtered by the Rakshasas and incurring Vishvamitra's wrath.

Dasaratha stood speechless for a few moments, as he was surprised and perplexed. But, as he recovered from the shock, he urged the guru not to press his demand, saying, "Rama is not yet fully sixteen years old. How is he going to combat Rakshasas? What is the point of sending him with you? It is not acceptable for me to send a mere boy to battle them when I am present and my army is ready to march. How can a young boy safeguard you and your yagna? Tell me everything I need to know about your adversaries. I will accompany you at the head of my troops to do your bidding and meet your requirements. Please inform me about these desecrators."

Vishvamitra told King Dasaratha about Maareecha, Subaahu, and Ravana, their master. And he demanded once more that Rama accompany him.

Dasaratha insisted on his refusal. "I shall die if I am separated from Rama," he declared. "I and my soldiers will accompany you. Why does it appear that the task proposed is difficult even for me. How will my son handle it? I'm afraid I can't send him. If you please, I have my troops ready." Vishvamitra was furious at his attempt to retract his hasty words. The King's arguments and pleas were like pouring oil on the fire of his rage. "This behaviour is unbecoming of your lineage," the elder said. "Please tell me whether this is your last word. I'll return the way I came. Long may you live with your family, having deviated from the road of truth!"

The earth trembled, and the gods feared the implications of the sage's fury.

"It ill befits you, King, to refuse after having promised once," Vasishtha said softly. "You can't do it if you're from the Ikshvaaku line. If you fail, you will forfeit the merit of all your tremendous gifts and actions. Send Rama with the sage, as well as Lakshmana. You do not need to be concerned about their safety; while they are safeguarded by Vishvamitra, no Rakshasa can harm them. You have no clue how powerful Vishvamitra is; he is tapas in human form. He is the bravest of the brave and the wisest of the wise, and he is a master of all weapons. When he was king, the gods granted him control over all weapons. You may be wondering why he desires the princes. He can take care of himself and his yagna , but he has come here to request your assistance for the sake of your sons. Do not be hesitant. Send him with your sons." After hearing the intelligent Vasishtha, Dasaratha understood things clearly and decided to send Rama and Lakshmana.

The two princes were then brought before the sage. The King, the Queen-Mothers, and Vasishtha bestowed their blessings on them and dispatched them with Vishvamitra.

The inhabitants of the sky spread flowers and created a nice breeze. Sounds of good fortune were heard. The two lads strode boldly on either side of the Sage, bow in hand. They moved, each like a three-headed snake with a raised hood, with swords of victory hanging from their waists and bows and quivers perched on powerful shoulders.

CHAPTER III:
RAMA SLAYS THE MONSTERS

VISHVAMITRA and the two princes spent the night by the Sarayu River. Before retiring, Vishvamitra imbued upon the princes two secret mantras, Bala and Atibala, which had the power to protect them from fatigue and harm. They arrived in Anga Desa at Kaamashrama. "This is the place where Lord Shiva was long engaged in austerities," he explained after presenting the princes to the rishis there. Manmatha, the stupid God of Love, pointed his arrow toward Shiva and was incinerated by his fury. As a result, this location is known as Kaamashrama."

They were the rishis' guests that night, and the next morning, after performing the normal rites, the sage and his students started on their journey and arrived at the Ganga. The rishis prepared a raft for them to cross the river.

The princes heard a noise in the middle of their journey and questioned Vishvamitra about what it could be. He said that the sound was the river Sarayu flowing into the Ganga. The princes silently paid their respects at the confluence of the two holy rivers. After crossing the Ganga, Vishvamitra and the princes proceeded through a deep forest made terrified by the resounding roar of wild creatures.

"This is the Dandaka jungle," Vishvamitra explained. "What today is a desolate forest was once a thriving nation. Once upon a time, Indra was tainted by sin after killing Vritra and was thus exiled from the world of the Devas. The Devas assigned themselves the duty of purifying Indra. They brought sacred river water and bathed him to the accompaniment of chants. The rivers that cleansed Indra seeped into the earth and nourished it, making the land extremely productive. People lived happily here for a long time until Taataka (wife of Sunda, a Yaksha (nature-spirits/ semi-gods)) and her son Maareecha wreaked havoc and turned it into the horrible wasteland it is now. They're still in the woods. And no one dares to go inside for fear of Taataka. She has the strength of a herd of elephants. I've brought you here to rid the forest of this formidable foe. There is no doubt that you will slay this monster who is causing problems for the rishis."

Rama, who was listening, asked the sage, "You say she is a Yaksha. I've never heard of Yakshas being extremely powerful. Furthermore, how can a woman acquire such strength?"

"You are raising a significant question," Vishvamitra responded. "Her strength is the result of a boon bestowed by Brahma. Suketu was the name of a Yaksha who dwelt there. Having no children, he performed tapas and received a boon from Brahma: 'You will get a lovely daughter of tremendous physical power, but no son.' Taataka, Suketu's beautiful and strong daughter, married Sunda, a Yaksha, and their child is Maareecha. Sunda once died as a result of Sage Agastya's curse. Taataka and Maareecha were provoked by this and rushed on the sage who cursed them to be monsters feeding on the carcasses of men. Taataka has thus transformed into a hideous beast. Since then, she and Maareecha have been harassing the people of Agastya. Do not be afraid to destroy her because killing a woman is against Kshatriya dharma. The responsibility of kings is to punish evil, whether male or female. Many women have been executed for their crimes. As a result, don't be afraid."

"Our father desires that we obey you without inquiry," Rama said to Vishvamitra. "We will kill Taataka on your orders and for the sake of the greater good." After saying this, he strung his bow and twanged it till the forest echoed to its harsh note and the wild creatures fled in fright in all directions. It reached Taataka quickly, overwhelming her with awe at the audacious intruder who dared to enter her realm. Raging with fury, she dashed in the direction of the sound and leaped on Rama. The fight began.

The prince first considered chopping off the monster's limbs to save her life. But Taataka struck with ferocity, ascending into the heavens and raining stones on Rama and Lakshmana. The fight continued, and Vishvamitra warned Rama not to put off administering the monster's fatal blow.

"She does not deserve sympathy," he remarked. "The sun is going to set, and remember that Rakshasas become stronger at night. Kill her as soon as possible." Rama decided to kill Taataka and pierced her chest with a lethal arrow, causing the large, ugly creature to fall, lifeless.

The Devas rejoiced, and Vishvamitra, overcome with delight, embraced and blessed Rama.

Taataka's death lifted the curse on the forest, making it more visually appealing. The princes spent the night there before proceeding to Vishvamitra's ashrama the next morning. Vishvamitra summoned Rama to his side the next morning, blessed him, and added, "I am quite glad indeed." How can I repay you for everything you've done? I will teach you how to use all of the astras." Vishvamitra then offered Rama the heavenly astras he had gained via tapas. He taught him how to wield, handle, and recall the many divine weapons, and Rama passed on his wisdom to Lakshmana.

As they continued on their trek, Rama pointed to a large hill with a beautiful forest on its slopes and inquired, "Is that where we have to go? And who are the villains who are impeding your yagna? And what should I do to exterminate them?" Rama was ready to battle and gain the sage's favour.

"That's where we're headed," Vishvamitra said. "It is known as Siddhashrama. It was here that Narayana and subsequently Kashyapa practised tapas, which resulted in God's incarnation as Vaamana. I reside in this holy location. And it is here that the Rakshasas appear to hinder our worship and austerities. Your presence here is to put an end to this evil."

"So be it," Rama responded.

The entrance of Vishvamitra and the two princes was cause for celebration at the ashrama, and the rishis welcomed them with water and fruit. Rama advised Vishvamitra that he might start preparing for his yagna right away, and Vishvamitra took the vows that night.

The princes went to Vishvamitra early the next morning and enquired when the Rakshasas were anticipated so that they could prepare for the impending bout. Vishvamitra was under a vow of silence and could not respond, but his juniors, the rishis, advised the princes that they should be attentive for six nights and days to protect the sacrifice.

The princes stood guard for six days and nights, fully armed. On the sixth day, Rama said to Lakshmana, "Brother, now is the time for the adversaries to come. Let us be cautious." Even as he spoke, flames erupted from the sacrificial fire, for Agni, the God of Fire, was aware that the Rakshasas had arrived. A huge roar could be heard from the heavens as the rites were being performed.

Rama raised his eyes to see Maareecha, Subaahu, and their supporters ready to pour impure stuff on the sacrificial fire. The army of Rakshasas was like a vast black cloud in the sky. "Look, Lakshmana," he said, aiming the Maanavaastra at Maareecha. It did not kill Maareecha, as intended, but it launched him a hundred yojanas near the sea, wrapped in invincible force. Rama killed Subaahu with the Agneyastra, and the two princes then destroyed the Rakshasa army. The sky had brightened up again.

Vishvamitra was overjoyed with the completion of his yagna. "I owe everything to King Dasaratha," he remarked. "You have kept your promise, princes. I admire your strength. This ashrama has transformed into a bright spot because of you."

After their morning prayers the next day, Rama and Lakshmana returned to Vishvamitra and requested further commands.

Sage Vishvamitra was well aware of the reason for Rama's birth. He was aware of the abilities of the weapons he had given to Rama. However, when experienced, the fact is more than just an expectation. Sage Vishvamitra was overjoyed, and his face shone like a flame. He suddenly remembered the service he still had to perform for Rama. This was the prince's wedding to Sita.

"We intend to continue to the kingdom of Videha where, in the capital city of Mithila, Janaka, the famed philosopher king, intends to commit a major sacrifice," the rishis assembled there told Rama. "All of us are going, and it would be great if you and your brother could join us. The Prince of Ayodhya should witness the magnificent bow in Janaka's court."

So it was resolved, and Rama and Lakshmana travelled to Janaka's city with Vishvamitra.

CHAPTER IV:
SITA

JANAKA, Mithila's king, was an ideal ruler. He was a renowned companion of Dasaratha, who dispatched ministers to Mithila to summon King Janaka when he prepared his yagna for progeny.

Janaka was not only a courageous monarch, but he was also as knowledgeable about the Shastras and Vedas as any rishi. Janaka was thus worthy to be the father of Sita, who was to be Vishnu's wife when he appeared on Earth in human form. Janaka ploughed the designated place once, wanting to execute a yagna. As usual, he did everything himself. Janaka noticed a stunningly gorgeous infant among the shrubs as the field was being removed and levelled. Janaka was childless and welcomed the infant as a gift from the goddess Earth.

He rushed to his beloved wife, holding the infant in his arms, and said: "Here's a hidden treasure for us. I discovered this child on the yagna site, and we will surely adopt her as our own." And she gladly agreed. Sita was the child raised by King Janaka and his beloved queen.

Janaka was heartbroken, having to part with Sita when she reached marriageable age. Despite his best efforts, he was unable to select a prince worthy of Sita. Many monarchs came to Mithila seeking Sita's hand, but none of them was good enough in Janaka's opinion. The King deliberated for some time before making a choice.

Varuna, the god of sky and oceans, once gave Janaka Rudra's bow and two quivers after being satisfied with a yagna performed by him. That was an ancient heavenly bow that no ordinary person could move. He saved this as a treasured heirloom. Janaka issued this announcement because only a highly remarkable man could be regarded worthy of Sita: "Sita, my daughter, shall be given in marriage to the prince who can lift, bend, and string the bow of Shiva which Varuna gave me and to none other." Many princes who heard of Sita's beauty travelled to Mithila only to be disappointed. None of them could complete the task.

The rishis from Siddhashrama, led by Vishvamitra, were making their way to Mithila on bullock carts. The animals and birds in the ashrama attempted to follow Vishvamitra, but he politely asked them to remain behind.

They arrived at the Sona River in the evening. Vishvamitra recounted the history of the location to Rama and Lakshmana while they slept for the night. They continued their journey in the morning, crossing another river, and arrived at the Ganga by lunchtime.

They bathed in the holy river, and the rishis prayed to their forefathers. They improvised an ashrama, performed pujas, and cooked their food there.

Vishvamitra blessed the princes when they finished their meal. “The sun is going down,” he said. “Let us perform our evening prayers in the Ganga waters, which your ancestor delivered to our earth.”

CHAPTER V: AHALYA

AFTER A DAY at Visaala, Vishvamitra and his companions set off toward Mithila. On the trip, not far from Mithila, they came across a beautiful ashrama that appeared to be abandoned. "Whose is this ashrama with ancient trees? Why is such a gorgeous dwelling deserted?" Rama inquired about Vishvamitra.

Vishvamitra responded, saying: "This ashrama is cursed. Sage Gautama lived here with his wife Ahalya, spending his days in peace and holy meditation. One day, while the sage was away, Indra, filled with unholy desire for the beautiful Ahalya, entered it disguised as Gautama and approached the lady with urgent solicitation. She was not deceived by the impersonation. But the vanity of her beauty and her pride that it had won her the love of the lord of the celestials, she lost her judgement and yielded to his desire.

"When the sin was committed, seeing its heinousness and her betrayed husband's great spiritual fire, she informed Indra of his dreadful risk and urged him to leave. Indra fled in a guilty panic, but he ran into the rishi, who was just returning from his ablutions, clad in wet garments and emitting spiritual radiance. The pretence was futile in the face of such all-seeing intelligence, and Indra bowed in desperation and flung himself at the mercy of the rishi. The sage cursed him as he looked at him with rage and contempt.

"The sage then turned to his erring wife and prescribed a long penance for her, saying, 'Living on air, you shall stay here, unseen by anyone. After a long time, Dasaratha's son will pass this way. When he sets foot in this ashrama, you will be freed from the curse. Welcome him as a guest. You will then recover your lost virtue and get back your beauty.' The sage then left his violated ashrama for the Himalayas to engage himself in austerities there.

"Let us enter the ashrama; you will bring redemption to Ahalya and rekindle the light in her, as the sage predicted," Vishvamitra remarked to Rama. The curse was lifted as Rama entered the ashrama, and Ahalya stood before them in all her splendour. After lying hidden between leaves and creepers for many years and keeping her pledge, she now gleamed like the moon rising from the clouds, a flame erupting from smoke, and the sun's reflection in rippling water.

Rama and Lakshmana touched the feet of the sage's wife, who had been purified through penance. She greeted the holy princes with all the traditional hospitality customs. A shower of flowers descended from the heavens as Ahalya, purged of guilt, shined like a goddess; at the same time, the sage Gautama returned to the ashrama and reconnected with his remorseful and purified wife.

CHAPTER VI: RAMA WINS SITA'S HAND

ALL PREPARATIONS for Janaka's yagna were finished, and numerous rishis and Brahmanas from various kingdoms had arrived in Mithila. Vishvamitra and the princes were greeted warmly. Satyananda, Janaka's preceptor, was the first to honour Vishvamitra. Janaka followed him. "I am truly blessed that you should attend my yagna," the King responded to the sage.

Janaka asked Vishvamitra, pointing to Rama and Lakshmana, "Who are these god-like youths who resemble each other and hold their weapons with the proud ease of seasoned warriors? Who is their contented father?"

Vishvamitra informed Janaka that they were King Dasaratha's sons. He described how they had defended his yagna and vanquished the Rakshasas. "They have come here to behold, if they may, the mighty bow of Rudra in your palace," the sage said. Janaka cheered as he realised the significance of Vishvamitra's comments. "The Prince is welcome to view the bow," he continued. "If he can string it together, he will earn my daughter's hand in marriage. Many princes saw this bow and returned, unable to even move it. I will be overjoyed if this prince succeeds where so many others have failed, and I am forced to give Sita to him as a result." Janaka then directed his men to deliver the bow, which was safe and sacredly stored in an iron box. It was transported on an eight-wheeled vehicle and pulled like a temple chariot during a celebration. "Here," Janaka explained, "is Rudra's bow, which my forefathers and I adore. Let Rama see this bow."

Rama came out to the iron bow case after gaining permission from Vishvamitra and the King, while all eyes were riveted on him in hopeful expectancy. Opening the box, he lifted the bow as if it were a garland of flowers, and placing one end of it on his toe, he bent and strung it and drew the string back with such tremendous power that the great bow cracked with a thunderclap. A shower of flowers descended from heaven. Janaka declared, "My beloved daughter will marry this Prince. Send your swiftest messengers to Ayodhya to deliver the news to Dasaratha and invite him," Vishvamitra instructed Janaka.

Janaka's emissaries arrived in Ayodhya three days later. They saw King Dasaratha, who sat on his throne like Indra, and told him, "Sage Vishvamitra and King Janaka have sent you pleasant news. Your son, who came to Mithila, won our princess Sita by satisfying the condition for her hand in marriage. He not only strung Rudra's bow, which no one had ever lifted, but he twisted its tough pride till it snapped. King Janaka looks forward to your gracious approval of the marriage, as well as your attendance and blessing at the festivities. May it delight you to begin your journey for Mithila with your entourage."

Dasaratha, who had dispatched Rama with Vishvamitra with an anxious heart despite the sage's guarantee, was overjoyed when he heard the good news. He informed his ministers to get ready for the journey, and the next day he travelled to Janaka's capital.

Dasaratha and his companions arrived at Mithila and were greeted warmly. After the exchange of courtesies, Janaka told Dasaratha, "My yagna will soon be done. I believe it is ideal to have the marriage as soon as the yagna is done," he said, seeking his consent. "You are the bride's father, and it is up to you to order things as you see fit," Dasaratha said.

Soon after, at the allotted hour, King Janaka spoke to Rama, "Here comes my daughter, Sita, who will always travel the path of dharma with you. Take her hands in yours. She will always walk beside you like your own shadow, blessed and dedicated."

King Janaka, therefore, married Sita to Rama in an auspicious manner.

CHAPTER VII: PARASURAMA'S DISCOMFITURE

VISHVAMITRA left the two kings and headed to the Himalayas after successfully returning to Dasaratha at Mithila, the princes entrusted to him at Ayodhya, and after attending the wedding celebrations.

King Dasaratha returned to Ayodhya with his retinue. There were ill omens along the route, and Dasaratha was worried. He asked Vasishtha what they meant. Vasishtha said that there was no reason to be concerned because, while the birds in the air warned of impending problems, the animals on the ground guaranteed a pleasant outcome.

As Dasaratha and Vasishtha were speaking, a violent storm broke out; trees were uprooted; the earth quaked; and clouds of dust rose and blocked the sun, creating all-encompassing darkness. Everyone was terrified. They soon discovered the cause of the peculiar occurrence. The awe-inspiring figure of Parasurama, the sworn enemy of Kshatriyas, stood before them, a bow on one shoulder, a battle-axe on the other, and an arrow blazing like lightning in his hand. His face shone with fiery brilliance. The son of Sage Jamadagni instilled fear among the Kshatriyas, many generations of whom he had wiped out.

Dasaratha's entourage of Brahmanas said to one another: "Because his father was murdered by a monarch, Parasurama vowed to exterminate the Kshatriya race. We dared to believe that his furious rage had been satisfied by the blood of the countless kings he had slaughtered. He has resumed his heinous campaign." They did, however, honour him with the traditional presentation of water. Parasurama addressed himself to Rama after hearing it: "I've heard of your prowess, Dasaratha's son. I was startled to discover that you strung the bow in King Janaka's court and drew the string till the bow snapped. Here is my bow, which is identical in every way to the one you shattered. You will be worthy of my war if you can string this bow."

Dasaratha was upset by this turn of events and pleaded that his son Rama be spared from the trial. He told Parasurama: "You have the title of Brahmana. We've heard that, satisfied with your vengeance, you've returned to tapas, as is your custom. Is it proper for you to betray your pledge and seek to harm a young prince who has done you no wrong and who is dearer to us than life?"

Parasurama heard him without looking at him and addressed himself entirely to Rama, as if the rest didn't exist: "Viswakarma originally created two identical bows. One was handed to Rudra, while the other was entrusted to Vishnu. This is the one Vishnu was given. Shiva's bow is supposed to have been strung and bent to breaking point by you. String this Vishnu bow if you can; if you do, it will be proof of your ability and might, and I will then honour you by fighting with you."

Rama spoke to him in a respectful but forceful tone: "Jamadagni's son! You were vengeful since your father was murdered by a king. That is not your fault. But you cannot dismiss me because you have humiliated others. Please hand over your bow."

He then seized the bow and arrow from Parasurama. He drew the string after stringing the bow and placed the arrow to it. He smiled as he addressed Parasurama: "This powerful Vaishnava arrow on the string cannot be returned casually. It must have destroyed something. Tell me, should it impair your locomotor abilities or should it swallow the fruits of your tapas?"

The brilliance on Parasurama's countenance disappeared when the son of Dasaratha strung the bow of Vishnu, and he stood, no longer the warlike conqueror, but a self-subdued rishi, because the purpose of the Parasurama avatar had passed.

To the Prince of Ayodhya, Parasurama responded mildly: "I know who you are. I don't regret that you put an end to my arrogance. Allow me to serve you all of my tapas. But, due to my pledge to Kaashyapa, I am unable to remain in his kingdom and must return to the Mahendra Mountains before the sun sets. Allow me to employ my locomotion power for this solitary purpose. Subject to this, let the arrow you've attached to the bow consume all of my tapas-earned power."

So speaking, Parasurama proceeded around the Prince in solemn circumambulation and then left.

The people of Ayodhya were overjoyed to learn that Dasaratha and the royal princes were returning to the capital. The city was decked out in flowers and sparkled like the deva-lok.

For twelve years, Rama and Sita lived peacefully in Ayodhya. Rama had given his heart to Sita. It was difficult to tell whether their love increased as a result of their qualities or as a result of their physical beauty. Even without words, their hearts spoke. Sita sparkled like Lakshmi in paradise as she rejoiced in Rama's affection.

CHAPTER VIII: FESTIVE PREPARATIONS

DASARATHA adored all four of his boys, but Rama was his favourite. And the latter deserved it for his royal traits and devotion to dharma. Queen Kausalya, like Aditi, the mother of the gods, was proud to have a son like Rama.

Rama's beautiful body and virile beauty, strength, courage, purity of his heart, flawless life, his compassion, the sweetness of speech, tranquilly, deep wisdom, and statesmanship were all revered by the people, who eagerly awaited his accession to the throne.

Dasaratha was aware of his subjects' admiration for Rama and relished their expectation. As a result, considering his old age, he desired to crown Rama as Yuvaraaja and entrust him with the de facto governance of the realm. He convened the Raaja Sabha after informing his ministers of his desire. The Raaja Sabha was attended by Rishis and wise men, city leaders, and monarchs from adjacent regions. Dasaratha stood and addressed them once everyone was seated in their proper places.

His strong male voice filled the large auditorium like the sound of a trumpet or the roar of rain-bearing clouds. His features sparkled with a princely brilliance. His remarks were meaningful and enchanted everyone who heard them.

"Like my forefathers, I have cared for this kingdom as a mother does for her child. My body is now old and infirm. As a result, I would like to select my eldest son as Yuvaraaja and shift the burden of responsibility to him. I hope to spend the remainder of my life in the forest, following the holy custom of my forebears. Rama is more than capable of taking on the role of king. He is a master of administration and statecraft, and he is unrivalled in valour. I have no reservations about transferring this trust of sovereignty to him, and I hope that this honoured assembly will allow me to do so."

Shouts of jubilant approval came from the large gathering, and the assembled princes and administrators said in unison, "So be it."

"You agree with my suggestion but give no justification," the King said again. This will not suffice. Let the enlightened persons explain why they agree."

Then other people stood up to explain Rama's merits and suitability to reign. Hearing these accolades about him filled the King's heart with gladness.

Finally, the entire assembly rose and exclaimed, "Let there be no delay. Let Rama be designated as Yuvaraaja."

The King said that he was delighted and would immediately carry out their demands. "This is the fortunate month of Chaitra, the season when the trees in the forest are covered with blossoms," he added, turning to Vasishtha, Vaamadeva, and the other holy men and guardians of the sacred rites. "Make all necessary arrangements for Rama's anointing, revered elders."

The assembly was relieved to hear such swift directions. Sumantra, the minister in charge of the home, proceeded to fetch Rama as directed by the King. Rama approached his father, completely unaware of what was going on.

When he learned of the decision to make him Yuvaraaja, he meekly accepted, saying, "I am duty obliged to carry out your orders, whatever they may be."

"You are a good prince, beloved of the people," Dasaratha stated as he blessed Rama. "Allow your civility and consideration to grow in tandem with your opportunities to do good, earning you eternal glory." Rama then returned to his home.

Sumantra had just returned home when he called to say that his father wanted to meet him. When asked why Sumantra couldn't say; all he knew was that he had been ordered to find the prince right away. "The King must have taken counsel over the coronation ritual and probably met with some difficulty," Rama reasoned. "But whatever happens, it will be for the best." Rama was not eager to assume authority but looked at it as only a duty to be done. He was ready to take it up if the King wished him to. But if the King wanted him to give it up, he was willing to do so. Rama went to his father in this mindset.

"I am elderly; I have loved my life as a man and a monarch," the King replied to Rama, who sat next to him on the throne. I have completed all of my obligations to my ancestors. There is nothing else I can do.

"My only ambition is to place you on our fathers' throne. I experienced nightmares last night. Those who can see into the future warn me that a great sadness, even death, may befall me very soon. As a result, I'd like the coronation to take place tomorrow. You and Sita should fast tonight in preparation for tomorrow's anointing. Lie down on a bed of darbha grass and rely on trusted and alert companions to keep you safe. It appears to me that the current period when Bharata is absent is ideal for your installation. Not that I don't believe Bharata is the soul of virtue in thought and behaviour, and that he is committed to you, but men's minds are changeable and susceptible to unforeseen influences."

So the King decided that the coronation should take place the next day and informed Vasishtha of his decision. Bad nightmares were added to the list of grounds for scheduling the coronation on the same day.

Rama left his father's house and headed to Kausalya's chambers to inform her of the news and ask for her approval. But the Queen had already received the news. Sumitra, Sita, and Lakshmana were all present, as was Kausalya, who sat in ceremonial white, praying for the son.

Rama informed his mother of the King's latest order. "This I have heard," she replied. "May you live a long life. Be a wise ruler. Conquer your enemies while protecting your subjects and relatives. You've satisfied your father and made me happy."

Rama then left his mother and stepmother and proceeded to his apartment. Vasishtha went to Rama's house as commanded by the King. He greeted him at the door, and Vasishtha initiated Rama with appropriate mantras during his pre-coronation fast.

As Vasishtha returned to the King, he noticed groups of people on the royal path, cheerfully discussing the upcoming great festival. Vasishtha made his way past the masses to the King's residence with difficulty. The King was glad to learn that the fast had begun and that everything was ready for the ceremony.

The city was in a frenzy of anticipation. Every house, every street, men, women, and children saw the coronation as a big and fortunate occasion in their own life, and they eagerly awaited it.

Rama and Sita concentrated on Narayana for a long time in their house, fed the sacrificial fire with ghee, sipped what remained of it reverently, and slept on grass strewn on the floor.

They were roused from their slumber by music early in the morning and prepared to proceed to the palace and await the auspicious call.

But the summons that arrived were completely different.

CHAPTER IX: KAIKEYI SUCCUMBS

QUEEN Kaikeyi had a female companion and confidential servant, as was customary in royal houses. Manthara, a hunchback, was her name. She claimed extraordinary intimacy with the Queen despite being a distant relative.

Manthara happened to climb up to the terrace of the women's apartments and stood observing the town below on the day Dasaratha called the Assembly and decided to anoint Rama as Yuvaraaja. She noticed that the streets were lavishly decorated and showered with water. Flags soared from the roofs of the houses. People went around in masses, immersed in joyous chatter, wearing new garments and sparkling diamonds, covered with sandal paste and decorated in flowers. Musical instruments were heard playing in the temples.

Manthara couldn't comprehend why all of this was happening because she didn't know what the King had decided. She imagined there was some sort of celebration going on.

Manthara approached a servant and inquired: "Why are you dressed in this silk gown? What's going on in the city? Kausalya appears to be giving gifts to Brahmanas. She is a frugal lady who would not be doing this for free. There are joyous sights and sounds all around. Do you understand what's going on?"

"Why, do you not know that our Ramachandra is going to be anointed Yuvaraaja tomorrow morning?" the young servant girl replied, joyfully dancing.

This was news! Manthara was overcome by an outburst of rage. She hobbled downstairs quickly. She walked right inside Kaikeyi's room. Kaikeyi was dozing off on her bed.

"Come on, foolish woman! A river of misery is on its way to drown and devour you! You have been betrayed and ruined. Your sun is going down. Is it time to sleep, foolish girl?"

Fearing that some disaster had befallen Manthara, Kaikeyi softly inquired: "What is bothering you? Why are you so agitated?"

And then the astute Manthara began: "Destruction has befallen both you and me, my dear. Dasaratha has made Rama Yuvaraaja the true king of this land. What more reason do I need to be sad? How can I remain careless when you are bereaved? I've dashed over to you. You were raised in a royal family. You married into the royal family. All is now lost, sadly.

"You, like the dumb lady you are, have been duped. Your husband tricked you with flattering phrases. As anyone can see, it's an intricate plot. He got Bharata out of the way by sending him to his uncle's faraway location, and he's taking advantage of his absence by hastily crowning Rama. It will all be over by tomorrow. And you sit in bed, doing nothing, while you and everyone who depends on you are destroyed."

So Manthara continued to speak. Kaikeyi's ears picked up on the words without really paying attention to them. Like the rest of the royal household, her thoughts were now consumed by the ecstatic anticipation of Rama's coronation, for she, like everyone else, loved and admired Rama. "You have brought me wonderful news, Manthara," she said. "Is Rama going to be crowned tomorrow? What greater joy can there be for me? Please accept this. Please contact me if you require anything more." Kaikeyi then removed the necklace from her neck and handed it to Manthara. It was a royal custom to reward the bearer of any major good news with a lavish gift.

This only added to Manthara's sadness. She threw the necklace aside and said: "Oh, you dumb woman. Everything is lost, and you blindly chuckle with delight. How can you be blind to your impending misfortune? Rama's mother, your opponent, has plotted to make him King. And you leap with delight. What would happen to Bharata if Rama took over? Wouldn't Rama fear Bharata and regard him as a dangerous foe? Rama understands human nature. He understands that keeping Bharata alive would pose a perpetual danger to his power and that he must be killed. Is it possible to kill a cobra out of fear? There is no longer any protection for Bharata's life." Kaikeyi pondered over all of this: "Why should Manthara be afraid? Is she unfamiliar with Rama? Isn't he dharma manifested in human form?"

She stated, "Manthara, have you not witnessed and rejoiced in Rama's honesty, integrity, and humility? He is the elder prince and inherits the throne. Bharata will get it after him one day. What's the problem with this? Bharata will rule for a hundred years after Rama. Do not shed any tears. You know how sweet Rama is to me. He loves me more than he loves his mother. It is not proper for you to be afraid of Rama."

"Alas!" exclaimed Manthara. "Why are you so stupid? What chance does Bharata have once Rama is crowned king? Do you not understand the succession rule? When Rama ascends to the throne, all royal prospects for Bharata and his line are over. After Rama, Rama's son will be king, and after him, that son's son will be king, and so on. The eldest son succeeds the eldest son. A younger brother has no chance, no matter how good or manly he is. You have no idea, my dear. Rama will not abandon Bharata once he is anointed. Bharata's life will be in jeopardy. If you want Bharata to live, tell him to stay away, as an exile from home, since if he returns, he will die.

"And Kausalya is not one of your friends. She holds a vendetta against you since you are the King's favourite and have frequently let her down. And now she's out for vengeance on you. When a competing wife's rage finds an opportunity, it becomes a blazing fire. You may argue that if Rama is king, Bharata is effectively dead. As a result, think carefully. Bharata must be crowned in some way. Rama should be expelled from the kingdom."

Fear had invaded the Queen's heart. Manthara was victorious. Kaikeyi's face reddened, and her breath grew warm. She clutched to Manthara for comfort and safety, helpless.

Dasaratha had ordered the coronation to take place without waiting for Bharata's return to the capital, fearing that a delay would bring unexpected complications. Manthara used the same dread and rush to encourage Kaikeyi to go the wrong way. "Consider this, my Queen. What's the rush? Why is your husband rushing through the ceremony while your son is not present? Isn't it to deprive him of his right? Isn't the motivation obvious? The King pretends to be in love with you. But this is just his hypocritical cunning."

So tempted, Kaikeyi considered Manthara's advice. Kaikeyi, like every other lady, was frail. She possessed good taste and culture, as well as a sharp brain. But she knew very little about the world. She was easily duped and could not anticipate the full ramifications of her actions.

Kaikeyi, who had considered Rama to be her son, became entangled in Manthara's arguments and rendered impotent. "I am terrified," she admitted impatiently. "Tell me what you think we should do. Is it my duty to serve Kausalya? Never. Bharata has to be crowned. You are entirely correct. Rama must also be sent to the wilderness. But how are we going to get all of this done? Please tell me. You are astute and know your way about the world." She clutched Manthara.

"Very nicely," Manthara said. "I'll tell you. Do not be irritable. Do you recall how your husband Dasaratha battled against Sambara in the south many years ago? And weren't you with him when he went to help Indra? Indra requested Dasaratha's assistance since Sambara of Vaijayanti was too powerful for him. Wasn't Dasaratha injured in combat and lost consciousness? Then you skillfully drove his chariot off the battlefield, tenderly removed the arrows from his body, revived him, and saved his life. Have you forgotten everything?

"And what did he say to you after that? 'Ask me for two boons,' he said gratefully. I'll give you whatever you want.' Then you said, 'I'll ask for my boons later.' 'I don't want anything right now.' 'You will have your two gifts whenever you want them,' he vowed. You told me all of this a long time ago. You could have forgotten about it, but I haven't. The time has come for him to keep his pledge. Demand that he crown Bharata rather than Rama. This is the first of two gifts he has promised. Request that Rama is sent to the wilderness for fourteen years as the second gift. Do not be afraid or think it is evil to demand this. Rama's influence on the people will only be relaxed and vanish over time if he is thrown into the forest, and your son's position will be secure.

"Go lie down in the sulking room right now. Wear an old saree and stretch yourself on the floor instead of your expensive gown and diamonds. Do not address the King as he enters the chamber. Don't even bother looking at him. I'm sure he can't bear your anguish. You will then have complete control over him. He will present numerous choices. None of them are acceptable. Insist on the two benefits. Maintain your composure. The King, bound by his pledge, will eventually come around. I know how much he adores you. Your wish will not be granted unless Rama is sent to the jungle. Rama must be expelled. Only then can the position you obtain for Bharata be genuine and long-lasting. Keep this in mind."

Kaikeyi's face lit up with hope as she listened to this exhortation. "What a mind you have, Manthara," Kaikeyi said. "You protected me from disaster." And she leaped around in delight. Manthara insisted on sending Rama to the jungle again and again. "Do not postpone. This must be done all at once. Keep in mind what I've said. Everything is dependent on your resolve. If you do not surrender, you will win."

Kaikeyi assured Manthara of her hardness and entered the sulking room right away, taking off her jewels and scattering them on the floor, changing her clothes, and stretching herself on the floor. Then, in a weak voice, she added: "Manthara, you will personally deliver the news to my father Kekaya. You will tell him one of two things: Bharata is about to be crowned or Kaikeyi is dead. Manthara, my dear, Manthara!"

In her rage, Kaikeyi believed Dasaratha had been truly cruel to her. This immoral concept had been lodged in her head, and her entire nature had been altered. The idea that she would live as a slave and that Bharata's life was in danger had gripped her. She set aside her sense of guilt and sin for the first time in her life, hardening her heart. Kaikeyi unbraided her hair and sprawled on the floor, heaving large sighs, perspiring, and her eyes closed, like a bird shot down by a hunter. Flowers and sparkling jewels that had once graced her body lay scattered in the dark room like stars in the midnight sky.

Dasaratha sought the chambers of his favourite consort after dismissing the Assembly and issuing orders for the proper celebration of the coronation ritual. He had decided on Rama's coronation after getting the approval of all those who were entitled to be consulted, and he felt glad and free as if he had laid down a huge load. Thus, he went into Kaikeyi's chamber to deliver the wonderful news and spend time talking with her. The abode of the junior queen was a wonderful palace with lovely gardens and tanks, birds playing in the water, peacocks dancing with tails stretched out, and trees resplendent with vivid blooms. It appeared unusually gorgeous that night in Dasaratha's cheerful attitude. Thus, the old King smiled as he entered Kaikeyi's home.

The incense pots and refreshments were where they should have been, but he didn't see the Queen, whom he was delighted to meet. Kaikeyi was the one with whom he sought blissful respite from all state responsibilities because she never interfered in public issues and always waited for him at the entry and welcomed him with a warm embrace. But she was nowhere to be found today. He went around looking for her in all of her favourite places, thinking she was playing a fun game of hide and seek. He was unable to locate her. Nothing like this had ever happened before! He inquired of a maidservant as to where the Queen was. The girl answered, folding her hands in reverence: "The Queen is enraged, Lord. She has entered the inner chamber."

The shocked King walked into the chamber. And he saw something that both shocked and disturbed him - she lay on the naked floor, in draggled garments and unkempt hair, as if in grave torment. She didn't appear to be able to look at him when he walked in. The dear guileless King, entirely unaware of having caused any offence, behaved with the doting tenderness of an old husband, reclining himself beside her on the floor, caressed her hair, and tried to soothe her with loving words and caresses: "What has happened to you? Are you sick? Do you feel any discomfort? Do I not have the top doctors in the country? I'll send them right away. They are capable of curing any disease."

Kaikeyi sighed heavily but remained silent.

The King continued: "Was there any discourteous behaviour in the palace? Inform me, and I will punish him. Did anybody wrong you, or was there anything you desired that I didn't provide you? Please tell me. You are aware of my full power; I may give and take as I like. I can do whatever I want to anyone and wherever I want. Ask me anything, and I'll do it right away."

Kaikeyi stood up. The King was overjoyed. And she started: "Nobody slighted or disrespected me. But there is something you can do, and it is something you must do for my sake. Please give me your word that you will fulfil my wish. Then I'll tell you about it." The unsuspecting old man was overjoyed when he heard this. He did not doubt that he could fulfil her requests, whatever they were, and so he boldly and joyfully said: "So, Kaikeyi, tell me what you want. It will be completed. I swear to you. I swear it on you, the dearest among women, and on Rama, the dearest to me among men! I swear in the name of Rama that I will do everything you want, I promise." Kaikeyi was overjoyed when the King swore in the name of Rama. She was now certain she had won, for the King would never betray a commitment accompanied by that cherished name.

Dasaratha stared at her with earnest, joyful eyes. She recognised her man and proceeded confidently: "Do you remember, King, how I drove your chariot in the night, brought you out of the battlefield, removed the arrows from your body, and comforted and revived you when you were ready to die on the battlefield? Didn't you say something when you awoke from your faint?

"'You have restored to me the life that my enemies had robbed from me,' you said. 'I will offer you any two gifts you desire.' Then I said, 'I don't want anything right now.' It's enough for me right now that you're alive. I'll request my gifts afterward.' Do you recall this?" The King responded: "Yes, I do recall this. Request your two prizes. You will have them right away."

Kaikeyi stated, “Remember, you pledged. You have committed. You have sworn in Rama’s name. Your commitment has been witnessed by the gods and the five elements. I’ll express my desires. With the coronation preparations underway, crown my son Bharata. This is my first wish. The second boon I request is that you send your son Rama to the Dandaka forest for fourteen years. Remember your serious promise that you will not breach. Your great dynasty’s good repute is in your hands.”

CHAPTER X:
WIFE OR DEMON?

DASARATHA was astounded. When his thoughts returned to normal, he questioned the veracity of what had occurred. He closed his eyes and fell unconscious, unable to bear the jumbled anguish of shapeless terrors. After a long period, he regained consciousness and shouted out, eyes fixed on his tormentor and heated with hopeless rage, "O evil ogress! Destruction of my dynasty! What harm has Rama caused you? Has he not considered you to be his mother? I mistook you for a lady. I now see you are a deadly serpent brought from afar and kept in my bosom solely to sting me to death!" Kaikeyi was unaffected and said nothing.

"On what excuse can I expel Rama, whom everyone loves and praises?" the King continued. I could lose Kausalya and still live. I might lose the pure-hearted Sumitra and still live. But if I lose Rama, I will be unable to live. Remove this sinful notion from your head. 'Two dear sons I have,' you've remarked many times. 'And Rama, the eldest, is the dearest to me? So why do you desire such terrible boons? No way, no how could you possibly mean this. You're just putting me to the test to see if I love your son Bharata. Do not, by committing a grievous sin, destroy our illustrious dynasty of Kings." Kaikeyi didn't say anything, but her eyes burned with disdainful rage.

"Until this day, you have done nothing to cause me sadness, never spoken an unworthy word," the King added. "Who has now corrupted you? I can't believe you had this wicked way of thinking. Rama has treated and served you so well! How could you forget all of this? What blunder has he made? The entire world adores him for his wonderful and admirable features. How did you, among so many others, come to despise him? How can I, as his parent, tell him, "Son, go to the forest?" This will never happen. Ask for anything else in this kingdom, anything else, and I will give it to you. I beseech you, with folded hands, please not send me to Yama. "Redeem me from sin!"

Pitiless Kaikeyi whispered terrible words to the Monarch as he struggled in a sea of grief: "King, if having pledged the boons you regret it and would be forsworn, what kind of king would you be, and what right would you have to speak of Satya and dharma? How can you stand up against other kings? All monarchs will avoid you as a disgrace to the monarchy! And the common people would mock their rulers, saying, 'Kings violate pledges even to their queens. Expect kings to break their promises.' Do not break your sincere promise. If you do not provide me the presents you promised on oath, I will drink poison and die tonight. You may anoint and install Rama, but I will die before your eyes, O promise-breaker. This is unquestionable. And I swear it in Bharata's name. It will be fine if you keep your pledge and send Rama to the jungle. Otherwise, I'll take my own life." Kaikeyi came to a halt with this forceful declaration. Dasaratha remained silent, staring at his pitiful wife. Was this beautiful creation Kaikeyi or a demon? The King then shook and toppled down, like a massive tree felled by a forester's axe, and lay stretched asleep on the floor in pathetic wreckage.

After regaining his composure, he said quietly, "Kaikeyi, who has twisted your mind to see me dead and our species destroyed? Do you believe Bharata will agree to be king after banishing Rama to the forest? He'll never do it, and you know it. Can I bear telling Rama to go to the forest? You can easily say, 'Send Rama away to the wilderness,' but will Kausalya or I survive his departure? And have you considered Janaka's daughter? Wouldn't it kill her to learn that Rama is leaving for the Dandaka forest?

"If I instruct Rama to go to the jungle, he will gladly obey and go there. Myself, followed by Kausalya and Sumitra, will perish. How will you enjoy the kingdom that has been secured for you, O sinful, ignorant woman? And will Bharata go along with your plans? He will not execute my obsequies if he agrees. Kill your husband and become a widow to enjoy the kingdom with your son, O shameless woman, my life's enemy. What a shame that my Bharata has this monster for a mother! No way could I ever accomplish this. Kaikeyi, I come to you and beg you. Please feel sorry for me!"

The King writhed and rolled on the ground in anguish. "You have yourself bragged that you are a truth speaker," Kaikeyi replied firmly, no matter how humbly he begged. "But now, after swearing before the gods that you have granted a favour, you try to back out of your vow. If you violate your word, I will very certainly murder myself, which will not add much to the grandeur of your dynasty, of which you are so proud!"

After a while, the old King let go of his emotions once more and begged: "Pity me, Kaikeyi. Forget the nasty words I said in rage. In the name of the love you bore me, I beg you. You are free to take the kingdom from me. It's all yours. And you can offer it to Rama with your own hands, ensuring that the coronation takes place. The Raaja Sabha has determined, and I have informed the elders and Rama, that his coronation will be held tomorrow. This announcement must not be made untrue. Please feel sorry for me. Give Rama your entire kingdom. Rama should be crowned according to my wishes, the wishes of the people, the wishes of the elders, and the wishes of Bharata. Do this, my love, this is my life." The King clung to Kaikeyi's feet, murmuring this.

But she replied, "When you're done with this nonsense, make sure you don't break your word and force me to keep mine, or I'll kill myself. It is pointless for you to strive to avoid."

"With proper rituals and in the sight of the sacred fire, I grasped your hand and called you wife," the King stated. I renounce you and the son you bore right now. The night has passed; dawn is approaching, and the morning will witness not

Rama's coronation, but my cremation."

"You're prattling vainly," Kaikeyi cut him off. Send for Rama right away. Allow him to come here. Tell him that the kingdom belongs to Bharata and that he should go to the jungle. Keep your word. "Do not squander your time."

"Very well," Dasaratha moaned. "Let me finally look Rama in the eyes. My demise is approaching. Allow Rama to enter. Please allow me to see his face before I die. This old fool is powerless because he is bound by dharma."

CHAPTER XI:

BEHOLD A WONDER!

DASARATHA was in excruciating pain, torn between natural compassion on one hand and the moral need to fulfil a vow on the other. He had hoped that Kaikeyi would relent and that the conflict of obligations would be resolved somehow. But now he knew that this was not going to happen. He still had one glimmer of hope: "Rama is not bound by any of my vows or pledges. He may violate my pledge and stand on his rights, as strong as he is in people's affection and his unmatched prowess, but I cannot see him doing so, for my smallest request has always been sacrosanct to him. However, if he did so, it would save the situation."

The old King consoled himself with such false hopes in his perplexity and misery, forgetting that Rama would never conceive of breaking his father's word and that filial duty was a fundamental tenet of his existence. However, the false hopes did not last long. He realised he had no choice but to keep his pledge to his nasty wife and delegated all decision-making to Kaikeyi.

The sun came up. The appointed time for the coronation was coming. The procession of Vasishtha and his students bearing golden jars containing holy river waters was approaching the palace. The main street was decked and bustling with excited men and women. They were overjoyed to see Vasishtha and his students marching to the palace with the holy waters and installation paraphernalia. The people yelled loud and happy acclamations as they watched the honey, curds, clarified butter, sacred grass, flowers, elephants, horses, and chariots, the white umbrella, the bull, the horse, and the tiger-skin seat move to the accompaniment of music from various instruments.

When Vasishtha saw Sumantra approaching the palace gate, he whispered to him, "Pray, go in immediately and inform the King that the people are waiting and all preparations are complete."

Sumantra approached the King's bed-chamber and delivered Vasishtha's message while chanting the morning hymn. "Oh King," he murmured, "wake up to the hymn of your charioteer. May all the gods be kind to you. The elders, generals, and chief citizens await your arrival. The night goddess has withdrawn. The day's work is ready for you to order. Be glad to rise, O King of Kings. Holy Vasishtha and his troops are on the lookout." The King was mute with pain at the time, but Kaikeyi courageously responded for him and told Sumantra: "The King stayed awake all night discussing Rama's coronation. So he's dozing off now. Go right away and bring Rama."

Kaikeyi dispatched Sumantra to find Rama and deliver the King's decree. Dasaratha had consented, but he lacked the strength to carry out her obligations. So, Kaikeyi decided to do everything herself.

Sumantra visited Rama's palace. Sita and Rama were preparing for the coronation. Sumantra then informed Rama that the King and Queen Kaikeyi required his presence. Rama quickly obeyed.

The unexpected delay, as well as the weird goings and comings, garnered questions, but no one dared to raise them. The men involved hoped that everything would work out and went about their business.

The streets were brightly decked, and the crowd became larger and eager. The big hour was nearing, but weird and ominous happenings were taking place in the Queen's chamber.

Sumantra led Rama to Kaikeyi's palace, navigating the crowd with difficulty. Rama walked into the Queen's apartment. As he crossed the threshold, he was astounded to see his father in agony on the bare floor. The King had been stricken down with deep grief. His face looked like a wilting paarijaata blossom in the sun.

He touched his father's feet and paid Kaikeyi the same filial adoration.

Dasaratha spoke the word Rama in hushed tones and came to a halt. He couldn't say anything else. He couldn't bear looking Rama in the eyes.

Rama was bewildered and terrified by the sight of his father, who lay there unable to speak, engulfed in some enormous suffering that even he couldn't fathom. He addressed Kaikeyi, saying: "This is very unusual, Mother. My father would always speak gently to me, no matter how upset he was. Have I offended him in any way without realising it? Is he suffering from a sudden illness? Please tell me what occurred."

Kaikeyi took the opportunity and declared: "Nobody irritates the King. Nothing is wrong with his health. But he has something on his mind that he is hesitant to share with you. That's it. He is hesitant to speak anything to you for fear of upsetting you. Once upon a time, he offered, and I accepted, the gift of two boons because he was delighted with me. The King now, like an uneducated person, regrets his actions. Isn't it unseemly for a King to make a promise and then break it? You can fulfil his promise, but he is afraid to tell you about it and is considering breaking it. You will give him the strength to act righteously if you assure him that he does not need to be concerned about your attitude and that he must follow his word at all costs. You must provide him with the assistance he requires. I'll tell you what it is, but only after you swear to assist the King fulfil his vow."

Rama, heartbroken at the prospect of causing his father any pain, said to Kaikeyi: "Is it true, Mother, that I am the source of all this trouble? I do not deserve for you to have any reservations about me. If my father wants me to leap into the flames, I will do so without hesitation. If he orders me to swallow poison, I will do so without hesitation. You are aware of this. You are well aware that at his command, I would drown in the sea. I give you my solemn vow, mother, that I will keep the King's commitment to you, and I will never violate my word." Kaikeyi rejoiced as Rama said these words, knowing she had triumphed. The King, for his part, was despondent, realising that all avenues of escape were now closed.

The pitiful Kaikeyi then offered these dreadful words: "Rama, your words are commendable. What higher duty does a son have than to assist in the fulfilment of his father's word? Now I'll tell you about your father's pledge to me. When your father was injured during the battle with Sambara, I rescued and revived him. In appreciation for being rescued by me while critically injured, your father bestowed upon me two boons to be claimed and described whenever I like. I have now claimed and specified them. They are that Bharata is anointed Yuvaraaja and that you be banished to the Dandaka forest now to live in exile for fourteen years. You have firmly promised to carry out his promise to me, and it is now your responsibility to keep your word. That is another situation if you find proper behaviour as difficult as your father did. Otherwise, pay attention to what I say. It is now up to you to resign the installation and go into exile with matted locks and hermit weeds, leaving the preparations set for Bharata's installation."

The King writhed in misery as she spoke these wicked words, but Rama heard her unaffected. Kaikeyi witnessed a miracle. Rama's expression was devoid of any hint of disappointment or regret. The Prince smiled and said: "Is that all, mother? The King's vow must undoubtedly be kept. My hair will be twisted, I will wear the bark, and I will walk to the forest today. I'm not bothered in the least. Would I refuse to give Bharata anything? I would joyfully give him my everything even if no one asked. And how can I resist a moment when my father orders it? What bothers me a little is that my father had doubts about my willingness. Aren't I, his son, obligated to do his bidding? What greater honour or joy can I seek than to keep his word? My only complaint is that he did not send for me straight away and give me his command. I have no regrets about going to the forest today. Send quick messengers to bring Bharata home."

As the ghee was poured into the Prince's face, it blazed like a sacrificial fire exploding into flame. Kaikeyi was overjoyed at her apparent accomplishment. Greed had led her astray. It kept her from fully comprehending her son Bharata's intellect.

Dasaratha lay in agony, caged in on all sides like a captive elephant. Kaikeyi urged Rama, telling him, "Do not wait for the King to speak and prolong the situation."

Rama responded by saying: "Mother, it appears that you do not know me well. No pleasure is more important to me than keeping my father's promise. Let Bharata bear the weight of kingship and care for our elderly father. It will bring me the most joy."

Dasaratha, who had been silent until now but was listening carefully, moaned aloud. Rama rushed out of the chamber, kissing his father's and Kaikeyi's feet.

Outside, Lakshmana was standing. He knew what had happened, and his eyes were ablaze with rage as he pursued Rama. Rama noticed the vessels holding the sanctified water for the coronation on the way. He walked around them with reverence. With calm majesty, he walked away from the crowds, leaving behind the white umbrella and other royal emblems. The Prince, who had defeated desire, went to Queen Kausalya's house to inform her of the news and to seek her blessing before going to the wilderness.

CHAPTER XII:
STORM AND CALM

RAMA went to the palace of Queen Kausalya. Many people had gathered there to watch the coronation. The Queen, dressed in white silk, stood before the sacrificial fire, invoking blessings on her son.

As soon as Rama walked in, she embraced him and led him to a special high seat, believing him to be the Yuvaraaja.

"Mother, this seat is now too high for me," Rama said. "As a hermit, I should sit on the grass on the floor. I have some sad news to share with you. Please pay attention and bestow your blessings on me." And he explained succinctly what had occurred: "The King desires to bestow the throne on Bharata. His order is for me to spend fourteen years in the Dandaka forest. I have to depart today, mother, and I've come to ask for your blessing."

When Kausalya heard this, she collapsed to the ground like a plantain tree that had been suddenly cut down. Rama and Lakshmana carefully lifted her. "Is my heart built of stone or iron that I still live?" she clung to Rama.

The Queen's sadness was too much for Lakshmana to bear. He yelled angrily: "This ancient King has inflicted on Rama a fate reserved for the most heinous evil-doers. Rama, what vice or crime have you committed? How can a king listen to a woman while breaking the law? Even your adversaries, O! Rama, learn to adore you when they see you, but your father sends you to the forest. Look here, brother, let us all throw out this King and take over the kingdom for ourselves. Who would dare to resist us? Anyone who dares will meet their end. Only permit me, and I'll do this on my own. I must carry out my responsibilities. Mother, you will now see the power of my arm, as well as yours, brother."

Lakshmana's comments brought some comfort to Kausalya, but the bizarre talk of deposing the King and capturing the throne terrified her. She stated: "Consider what Lakshmana says, Rama. Don't go into the woods. How can I stay here alone amid enemies if you leave? I will accompany you."

Rama had listened in silence to Lakshmana's outburst, knowing that it was best to let pent-up rage find a release in words. He then turned to face Kausalya and said: "Let there be no talk of anyone accompanying me to the jungle, Mother. You must remain here, serving the King and sharing his grief in his old age. How can the crowned Queen of an Emperor stroll the forest with me like a widow? This is not possible.

"It is my responsibility to keep my father's word. If I fail in my essential job, no amount of wealth or power will bring me satisfaction or a good name. Your suggestions, Lakshmana, are completely incorrect. I am aware of your immense might, and I am confident that you will overcome and destroy all opponents and secure the kingdom for me. I am also aware of your feelings for me. But the manner you want to utilise it is unworthy of the dynasty to which we belong. Our biggest responsibility is to keep our father's word. If we fail in it, no other accomplishment can be used to compensate for the deed."

Rama attempted to calm both his mother and brother, but Lakshmana's rage was uncontrollable. Perhaps it could have been if he had been the victim rather than Rama. However, Rama was the victim of this heinous injustice. As a result, Lakshmana writhed in anguish like a wounded cobra. Rama separated him, made him sit down, and tried to calm him: "Lakshmana, aren't you, my other self, my soul in a different body? Take my advice. You are brave and strong. Control your rage and sadness on my behalf.

"Consider our father's health. Our hearts should go out to him in sympathy, for he is bereaved. Whatever the reason, he made a promise, and if he broke it, he would be committing a heinous sin that would tarnish and obliterate all of his great and glorious deeds. He gave us the life we have, and we owe him peace of mind. So far, we have never given him a reason to be sad or dissatisfied. We have now become the source of immense anxiety in his thoughts about what would happen to him in the other world. We can easily get rid of him. Are we going to add to his problems by doing this? As a result, my thoughts have shifted away from the coronation and onto the trek to the forest."

"My only desire right now is to get to the jungle and witness Bharata crowned. This would suit me the finest. Mother Kaikeyi will become suspicious if I delay. As a result, I should go to the forest today and bring her calm. Our father will be relieved of the anxiety of breaking a promise and assured of my eager and glad acceptance of his demand. We should also not be furious at Mother Kaikeyi. Has she not been nice to us throughout the years? That she suddenly has this thought is undoubtedly the product of fate. We should not hold that against her. Even the most persistent sages have deviated abruptly from their path. "How can Mother Kaikeyi seek to defy fate?"

"Let us vow to turn this grief into joy. That would demonstrate our nobility and bravery, Lakshmana. I will walk to the forest with the blessings of my mothers and elders. Brother, do not be depressed by thoughts of dominion or fortune; life in the forest will be my greatest joy."

This explanation temporarily calmed Lakshmana. But his rage quickly resurfaced. He stated: "So there you have it. This is fate's doing. I admit that our stepmother's unexpected folly was the result of fate. And I'm not mad at her. But, on that basis, are we to stand still and do nothing? After announcing your coronation to the town and country with a drum beat, the deceitful King invokes some old-forgotten boon and orders you to travel to the wilderness. Is it manly to call this fate and quietly obey it? I am not a wimp who will succumb to fate. Today you will witness the force of a hero versus fate. I will exile all who conspired to exile you to the forest. You can go to the forest later if you want to change things up. It will be appropriate when you have reigned as king for many years and have passed the throne to your sons. That was our forefathers' way. If anyone now disputes your kingship, I will annihilate him. I'm waiting for your orders. Give me the command and put my skills to the test."

Rama softly calmed Lakshmana's fury, which had erupted into a conflagration. "We must obey our parents as long as they are alive," Rama added. "I could never imagine disobeying my father. It is our primary responsibility to do his bidding and enable him to keep his promise. What fun is it to be crowned king after disrespecting our parents and murdering Bharata, the personification of dharma?"

And he brushed Lakshmana's tears away with his palm. Lakshmana became calm when Rama accomplished this. Because Rama's passionate hands might do wonders.

CHAPTERS XIII: SITA'S RESOLVE

RAMA had left Sita to visit the King in response to Sumantra's message, and she expected him to return in a chariot with the royal parasol, accompanied by a large retinue. But now she saw Rama return alone and unsupervised, with no royal insignia. And she noticed a determined look on his face. Rama was contemplating how he would break the news to his beloved that his father had ordered him to go to the forest as he approached.

"Something bothers my lord's mind," Sita reflected. "What's the matter?" she inquired. "Why do you have such an odd appearance?"

Rama related the narrative briefly before adding, "Princess, my darling, I can well imagine your anguish at having to leave me and stay here. Janaka's daughter does not require my assistance with her responsibilities. Consider the King's and the three Queens - your mothers' - comfort. You should not expect any better treatment than the other princesses in the palace. Respect Bharata, who will be the ruler, and avoid offending his sentiments. I am confident that your affection for me will not diminish during your absence. After fourteen years, I will return to the forest. Do not disregard traditional rites and ceremonies until then. In her grief, Mother Kausalya will require your undivided attention. Bharata and Shatrughna are two of my favourite characters. You will regard them as brothers. Conduct yourself per your royal lineage and your temperament. Today I had to go to the forest. Maintain a steady and quiet mind."

When Sita heard this unexpected speech, her love for Rama revealed itself as the rage that he should even consider parting with him and living in comfort in the palace while he remained a lonely wanderer in a pathless wilderness.

"You delivered an excellent speech, O Knower of Dharma. It seems bizarre to me that a wife is different from her husband, that his responsibility is not hers, and that she has no right to participate in it. It will never be acceptable to me. I believe that your fortunes are mine, and if Rama is required to go to the forest, the command extends to Sita, who is a part of him. My father and mother have taught me dharma. What you say contradicts everything they've taught me. My only option is to accompany you everywhere you go. There is no place for debate here. Don't believe I can't handle woodland life. I'll eat fruit and roots like you, and I'll keep up with you while we travel.

"I've long desired to accompany you to the woods and revel in the sight of big mountains and rivers. I don't care about Heaven itself while I'm not with you. If you abandon me, I will undoubtedly perish. I beg you to take me with you. Do not abandon me now."

Her statement began in rage and ended in sobs. Rama emphasised to Sita that life in the jungle was not as easy as she had imagined, and he went on to discuss the obstacles and risks, again emphasising that she should not consider accompanying him. Tears welled up in Sita's eyes. "Tigers, lions, bears, and snakes will not approach me. When they see you, they will flee from us. I am not terrified in the least, and on the other hand, you may be assured that life will leave my body if you leave me here and go. I beg you, do not separate me from you, for separation is crueller than death."

Rama allowed himself to be persuaded, partly because his love was as great as hers and every impassioned word she spoke found ready lodgment in his heart, and partly because he was confident of his capacity to protect her. Sita was assigned to follow Rama to the forest.

She sent for the destitute, gave away everything she owned, and readied herself for life in the jungle. Lakshmana also resolved to accompany his brother and serve him in the forest, and Rama had no choice but to accept. The three proceeded to say their goodbyes to the old King.

Crowds of people watched from the streets and balconies. Men and ladies watched Rama and Lakshmana and the princess walking like the poorest in the kingdom through the windows and terraces of houses.

"What kind of King is this that sends such a noble prince to the forest?" the people exclaimed, filled with enormous anguish and outrage. "And there walks Sita, a princess who should command the royal chariot. Can she withstand the heat and wetness of the forest? This is terrifying!"

"We'll also go to the forest. Let us take our belongings and flee to the wilderness with these princes. Our Ayodhya will be the forest where Rama lives. Let these houses, infested with snakes and rats, be abandoned from now on. Allow Kaikeyi to rule over the Ayodhya ruins. The forest's wild monsters and vultures will come to stay. This will turn into a forest, and the forest will turn into Ayodhya."

Rama overheard others speaking in this manner but paid little attention. Rama noticed Sumantra seated sorrowfully aside in a corner at the entrance to Kaikeyi's palace. "The three of us have come to see the King," Rama said softly. "Sumantra, please notify Father of our presence and beg his blessing."

Sumantra stepped in to inform the King of their arrival. What a scene he encountered there! The King lay prostrate on the floor, his grandeur gone, his face reduced and deformed with pain. "The Prince waits at the gate and seeks audience to accept your blessings before he starts for the Dandaka jungle," he added, his palms clenched together. Sumantra was told by the King to let the Prince in.

Rama approached from afar and bowed before the King. The King quickly rose and rushed with outstretched arms to embrace Rama, but he collapsed in a swoon before reaching his son. Rama and Lakshmana delicately lifted him and placed him on the couch. "My Lord," Rama began, "we have come to seek your permission to travel to the forest." Despite my best efforts, Sita and Lakshmana have decided to accompany me. Please accept our benedictions and farewell."

"Rama, I am bound by the boons that I have granted to Kaikeyi," Dasaratha remarked. "But you are not so restricted. Why don't you ignore me and capture the kingdom by force?"

"I have no ambition for kingdom or power, father," Rama remarked. "May you reign for another thousand years. My heart is now set on visiting the forest, and I am eager to begin after receiving your blessing. I will return and pay my respects after fourteen years."

It was now evident that the King's flimsy hope had to be abandoned. "My boy! Bring honour to our kingly line. Go, but return unscathed. Hold on to dharma. You are unwavering in your resolve. Your will is firm and unwavering. But don't leave today. Spend the night with me here. Allow me to fill my eyes with your image. I pledged to Kaikeyi without understanding what was in her thoughts as if I were handling a live coal deceptively wrapped in ash. I'm suddenly helpless and entangled in her web. And you say, 'I will keep my father's vow. I'm going to leave the kingdom and go to the jungle.' Where on earth can one find a son like you? I swear to you, I did not plan to do such a terrible thing."

The King murmured pityingly. It was Dasharatha's wish to die with Rama's respect even in his final moments. "Father, send for Bharata right away and keep the promise you made to mother Kaikeyi." Do not be bothered by the thought that you are wronging me; I had no desire for the throne and do not consider being denied it a deprivation. Unaffected by grief, crown Bharata and bestow your blessings on him.

"My only wish is to keep the promise you made.

I'm going to spend my time blissfully in the woods.

Where else but in the woods can one find beauty and joy? You are my God, Father. I believe that God has sent me to the jungle. You will see me again when the fourteen years are up.

"What does it benefit me to stay here another night and go tomorrow? Time is made up of a series of tomorrows, and no two days are alike. Postponing inevitable sorrows does not turn them into joys."

"Well, then, send for the commanders and order them to prepare the chariots, elephants, horses, and foot soldiers to accompany Rama to the forest," the King said to Sumantra. "Along with the troops, send all the supplies Rama needs to dwell among the Rishis of the forest. Let there be no want of men, money, or goods."

Kaikeyi's face flushed with rage as he spoke. "A good and generous king definitely!" she sneered at the King, her voice trembling with scorn. "You will give Bharata this kingdom after squeezing out all the good it contains as if mockingly offering an empty tankard to a thirsty man! What joy or glory can my son derive from ruling a desolate state?"

Dasaratha sighed helplessly, amazed at the brutality that could stab a man who was already crushed under an unbearable burden. Rama put an end to all debates by declaring that he would not consent to take paraphernalia that was incompatible with woodland living. "What use have I, Honoured Lord, who am leaving for the forest to live on what sylvan nature supplies, for an army or the sparkling equipage of a royal pageant?" he asked. "Father, I have happily abandoned my claim to the kingdom in favour of Bharata and his mother, along with all the responsibilities that come with it. For my fourteen years of forest living, I only need bark clothing like Rishis wear and simple forest necessities like spades and baskets."

Rama had barely finished speaking when the unashamed Kaikeyi hurriedly produced the woodland clothing she had kept ready and handed it to him. Rama dressed in bark right then and there. Dasaratha saw all of this in hopeless misery as Lakshmana changed into bark attire. Kaikeyi then brought Sita a bark garment as well. She accepted it, perplexed because she had never worn such clothing before and had no idea how to change into them.

Sita approached Rama, who was radiant with divine effulgence, and asked hesitantly, "Pray do tell me, how does one put this thing on?" The ladies-in-waiting sobbed aloud as Rama wrapped the bark dress around Sita's silk and tied a knot over her shoulder, and Dasaratha fell into a swoon.

When he recovered consciousness, he scoffed at Kaikeyi, who merely smirked scornfully. She was undoubtedly not to blame for Sita's visit to the forest. The princess went to the forest with her spouse for her happiness and would not be deterred.

Rama stated as he walked away, "Father, I leave behind my mother Kausalya, blameless and tender-hearted, bereft of her son in her old age. This unexpected fate is as painful to her as death, yet she agrees to live only for your sake, to share your grief and soothe you. Be gentle to her when I'm gone, and when I return after my lengthy exile in the hope of placing my head on her shoulders, don't tell me she died of sadness."

Rama spoke in this manner, unable to endure the thought of his mother's anguish. Dasaratha couldn't bear the sight of Rama leaving, so he covered his face with his hands.

CHAPTER XIV: TO THE FOREST

THE stricken King remained prostrated in mute despair when Rama left his father's presence with these words, and it took some time before he could even think. "Sumantra, get ready the chariot and transport my boys and Janaki to the kingdom's frontier," the King stated later, his thoughts clearer.

Lakshmana touched his mother Sumitra's feet and said the sole word "Mother." " Your love for your brother has filled your mother's heart with pride and joy," she remarked as she embraced him and kissed his head. It is your responsibility, youngster, to protect and serve Rama. In the wilderness, always keep an eye on Rama. Your elder brother serves as both preceptor and king to you. This is our race's dharma. Lakshmana, take my blessing. Go in joy, my beloved son, and God bless you."

Sita enthusiastically climbed into the chariot. Kausalya had prepared a bundle of personal requirements for her. The chariot was loaded with the two brothers' shields, bows and arrows, and other weapons, as well as pickaxes and baskets. Rama and Lakshmana rode up in the chariot. Sumantra propelled it ahead.

"Go slow, go slow," the spectators chanted to Sumantra, the charioteer. "Faster, faster," Rama said to the charioteer. Sumantra managed to get the chariot out of the clutches of the bereaved town, where, in addition to the loud sorrow of the crowded streets, the houses were packed with bereaved women and children.

The King emerged from Kaikeyi's apartment and gazed out the window at the leaving chariot. He stood there for a long time, staring at the cloud of dust as if he saw Rama's adored shape in it. He collapsed, moaning, as soon as this was out of sight. Kausalya and Kaikeyi sat on each side of the table. "Do not touch me," Dasaratha said to Kaikeyi. "I despise seeing you, sinful woman! Everything between you and me has come to an end. I renounce you right now."

"If Bharata agrees to your plans and takes the kingdom," he stated again, "he does not need to conduct my obsequies, and even if he does, my departed soul will reject his offering of waters."

"How will Rama survive in the forest? Will he sleep on the ground with nothing but a stone or a log for a pillow? Will he eat fruits and vegetables?", the monarch continued to weep helplessly.

Rama's chariot was followed by a large crowd of city dwellers. They attempted to halt the chariot by yelling, "Do not go to the forest! Go back to the city."

"Citizens of Ayodhya, I know the love you bear for me," Rama said as he stopped the chariot and addressed them. "You will best demonstrate it by transferring money to my dear brother Bharata on my behalf. Nothing else will make me happier. Bharata is good and noble, possesses all royal traits, and is completely deserving of affection. He is strong enough to protect you. He is your king, and you owe him your love and loyalty. I'm heading to the jungle to keep my father's promise, and the King has named Bharata Yuvaraja. Both you and I must obey the King's orders. You should go back and try to ease my father's grief at losing me."

Rama spoke to them in a kind tone. But they loved him even more because of it and refused to be consoled. Looking at the chariot, several Brahmanas, elderly in years and great in virtue, grieved and exclaimed, "Why, O horses, do you carry our Rama into the forest? We've heard that horses have excellent hearing. Listen to us, and return our Rama." Rama came to a halt as he heard the ancient Brahmanas' yearning words. The three descended from it and began walking forward.

The common people, leading citizens, wise elders, penitent men, and even birds on wings tried to stop Rama from going to the forest. Tamasa River appeared to be conspiring with them, as it flowed across his path. The chariot came to a halt on the riverbank. Sumantra unyoked and watered the horses before releasing them to graze.

"Lakshmana, this is the first night of our jungle life," Rama stated. "Let us spend it beside this holy river's bank. As you and I both know, there is no suffering in the forest. Look at how the birds, animals, and even the trees appear to sympathise with humans. The only anguish comes from remembering our parents' grief in Ayodhya, but I am comforted by Bharata's dignity and goodness. He will undoubtedly show genuine affection to our parents. Sumantra, go take care of the horses." Then, at the river, Rama offered evening prayers and said, "Let us fast on this first night of our jungle life, Lakshmana. Your being at my side relieves me of any anxiety." Lakshmana put some grass on the ground for Rama and Sita to sleep on, but he stayed up all night talking with Sumantra.

Long before morning, Rama awoke and told Sumantra, "The folks who have followed us are fast asleep, exhausted by their long journey. I am sincerely moved by their affection, yet I cannot let their love compel me to return. Let us, therefore, proceed while they are still sleeping."

The horses were hitched, and the chariot crossed the river gently. Standing on the southern bank, Rama said to Sumantra, "If you take the chariot to the other shore, where the people are sleeping, and drive it for a short way towards Ayodhya, and then bring it back here, we can continue our journey before they wake up. They will observe the chariot track heading towards the city and, believing that we have come home, may return themselves. Unless you do this, the throng will continue to pursue us."

Sumantra accomplished this, and when the chariot returned, the three got back into it and drove south.

CHAPTER XV:
ALONE BY THEMSELVES

THE residents who had slept on the Tamasa's bank awoke in the morning and glanced about. They were taken aback to discover that Rama and the chariot had vanished. They tracked the chariot wheels but were unhappy to discover that it had become lost on the major road to the capital.

They went back to their homes and found delight in mocking Kaikeyi. The city was devoid of beauty and shrouded in melancholy without Rama.

Sumantra and the princes had ventured far into the forest after crossing the Tamasa before morning. When they reached the kingdom's southern limit, Rama stopped the chariot and, looking north towards Ayodhya, bowed his head in prayer, saying: "Oh, city of jewels! O Ikshvaakus's ancient capital! Will I live to see my father, mother, and you once I do my penance in the forest? Please grant me that utmost bliss."

The chariot arrived at the Ganga's bank. They continued along the bank, savouring the river's splendour. "We'll spend the night here," Rama declared after discovering a site of unparalleled loveliness. They rested under a tree after untying the horses. Guha, the region's chief, came forward with his retinue to greet Rama and Lakshmana, having learned of their arrival via his men.

He had boundless affection for the royal family and Rama. He was a man of tremendous status and power as the leader of the tribes that lived on the banks of the Ganga. Even though Guha was still some distance away, Rama and Lakshmana rose to greet him. Guha greeted them with a warm embrace, saying: "Consider this country to be yours. This place belongs to you just as much as Ayodhya. Who could hope to have a guest like you? That is my fortunate fortune."

Guha had planned a grandiose celebration. He stated, "In my domain, I feel completely at ease and content. You are welcome to spend the entire fourteen years with us here. I tell you that you will not be lacking in anything. It will be a pleasure and privilege for me to look after you. Accept my invitation to stay with me."

Rama embraced Guha once again and whispered, " "I know how much you care for me, brother. Your request is as good as the welcome you have received. My vows bind me, and I must refuse anything else. I've come to live in the forest, not to live as a chieftain's guest. These are my father's favourite horses. Please feed them properly. We'll make do with minimal meals and sleep for the night."

They spent the night under the tree. Guha and Lakshmana remained awake, talking with Sumantra.

Guha told Lakshmana: "Do go and relax, brother. There is a bed prepared for you. My men will keep a close eye on things. Nobody dares to do anything in the forest that is unfamiliar to me. Do not be concerned about Rama. Get some rest."

Lakshmana responded, saying: "Guha, how can I sleep? Sita, daughter of the great Janaka and daughter-in-law of the great Dasaratha, is sleeping on the naked ground here. Purushottama, the great conqueror of the three planets, is sprawled down on the grass. How can I sleep with someone watching me?

"I'm curious how Ayodhya is handling it. Wailing must be audible in the queens' apartments. I even doubt mother Kausalya and my mother are still alive. My father did find the strength to tell Rama, 'Go to the forest,' but I doubt he has enough power left to survive Rama's real departure. And if he has died, our mothers have also given up their life. In any case, our father and mothers are unlikely to be alive to greet us when we return to Ayodhya after our term in the forest." Lakshmana sobbed as he talked. Guha was overcome with emotion. The entire night was spent in such depressing talk.

Rama instructed Lakshmana early the next morning: "Now we must cross the river. Request Guha to prepare a boat large enough to traverse this wide river." Guha directed his troops to complete the task and notified Rama.

Sumantra bowed low and approached Rama, seeking his further instructions. Rama recognised Sumantra's unspoken sadness and placed his hand on Sumantra's shoulders, saying: "Sumantra, hurry back to Ayodhya and stand at the King's side. It is now your responsibility to look after him."

Sumantra screamed, "O Rama! Rectitude, learning, and culture appear to be worthless. You, your brother, and Vaidehi (Sita) will dwell in the jungle. What will become of us? How would we fare under Kaikeyi's rule?" He was now sobbing like a child.

Rama responded, wiping Sumantra's tears away: "There has never been a more honourable friend in our family than you. It will be your responsibility to console my father. His heart is flooded with anguish. Whatever his orders are, carry them out faithfully. Do not question if he wants something for himself or to please Kaikeyi. Avoid causing him any mental anguish. Don't be concerned about us.

"You should convey this on my behalf to my elderly father, who is experiencing grief he has never known before. Clasp his feet like you've seen me do, and assure him that none of us, not I, Lakshmana, or Sita, are hurt or sad for being sent away from Ayodhya. We look forward to fourteen years of forest life, flying on joyous wings, and then returning to his feet for blessings. Give our love to my mother Kausalya and inform her that we are safe with her blessings, and send a similar word to my stepmothers, especially mother Kaikeyi, lest she assumes we parted in anger. Tell the Mahaaraaja that it is my sincere wish that he hurry with the installation of Bharata so that he might be a comfort to him while we are away."

Sumantra, unable to contain his sadness, exclaimed, "How am I to return, and with what words can I comfort? How shall I drive this chariot that sits lonesome without you?" he wept as he glanced at the empty chariot.

Rama comforted and encouraged Sumantra once again, urging him to be patient and sending him home. As a way of comforting Sumantra, the brothers had their hair matted with banyan milk. They assisted Sita into the boat before entering it themselves. Guha ordered the rowers to row it across. The boatmen sped them across the river.

They made it to the other side of the Ganga. For the first time, the three stood alone, unaccompanied by pals!

"Lakshmana, you are now my single-armed guard," Rama explained. "You'll be the first to depart. Sita will follow suit. And I'll walk beside you both. We must get Sita as far away from the harsh conditions of jungle life as possible. There will be no one to keep us company or provide us with entertainment in the future."

Rama's mind wandered to his mother Kausalya. "Shouldn't you go back to Ayodhya and look after mother Kausalya and Sumitra Devi, Lakshmana?" he asked. "I'll find a way to make my woodland stay work."

"Forgive me, brother; I am not returning to Ayodhya," Lakshmana said. Rama had no other expectations.

While Rama was consumed by thoughts of the moms who had been abandoned, Lakshmana ministered to him with loving words of courage and hope.

They slept under a banyan tree that night and left early the next morning for Bharadwaaja's ashrama, which they arrived at nightfall. After partaking of the sage's hospitality, they begged him to inform them where they could spend the years quietly in the forest and, on his suggestion, agreed to leave the next day for Chitrakoota.

CHAPTER XVI: CHITRAKOOTA

THE next morning, they paid their respects to the Maharishi before departing towards Chitrakoota hill. The muni treated them as if they were his children and sent them on their way after indicating the path they should travel through the forest. The three carefully followed his geographical instructions and eventually came upon the Kaalindi River. They built a raft out of logs, bamboo, and jungle creepers, and Lakshmana prepared a seat for Sita out of twigs and leaves for her to sit on. Sita saluted the river goddess and prayed that Rama would fulfil his vow and the three would be able to travel home safely.

They arrived at a large banyan tree described by Bharadwaaja after traversing a few more creeks. And under this tree, Sita prayed once again: "Grant, O holy tree, that my husband may complete his pledge and that I may meet the queens Kausalya and Sumitra once more."

They spent the night resting on the side of a river. Rama awoke Lakshmana the next morning and said: "The birds are singing to the rising light. It's time to get started." They returned to the way specified by Bharadwaaja after doing their ablutions and prayers. Summer had arrived, and the trees and plants were ablaze with multi-colored blossoms.

Rama would occasionally point out the beauty of the forest to Sita, stating as they walked: "How lovely is the woodland that has not been tainted by human intervention! Take a look at those beehives! Look at how the ground is completely covered in fallen flowers! Pay attention to the birds! How sweetly they sing to one another and live in happiness! It would be a wonderful life if we could always enjoy such sights and sounds."

Then they noticed Chitrakoota hill from a distance. They were overjoyed and began walking quickly towards it. "How lovely this area is!" said Rama. "The jungle around here has delicious edible roots and fruits. The water is very clear and delicious. Rishis live in ashramas in this forest, and we may live contentedly in their holy company."

They then proceeded to construct an ashrama for themselves. Lakshmana was a skilled craftsman. He quickly built a sturdy cabin that was both weatherproof and cosy and convenient. He finished the cabin made of mud all by himself, but with windows and doors built entirely of bamboo and jungle material.

In the cottage, alongside the picturesque Chitrakoota hill, on the bank of the river Malyavati, three young people lived carefree, completing their daily devotional ritual. They forgot they were in exile and enjoyed themselves.

CHAPTER XVII:
A MOTHER'S GRIEF

SUMANTRA and Guha stood there for as long as they could, staring at the three figures. When they vanished from view, they were overcome with grief and returned to Guha's village. Sumantra eventually returned to Ayodhya.

As the charioteer approached the city, he discovered it to be lonely and devoid of the normal cheery bustle of city life. As soon as he reached the city through the fortress gate, his chariot was encircled by a multitude enthusiastically asking: "Where did you abandon Rama? How did he seem when you left him?"

"Dear Ayodhya, Rama, and Lakshmana have crossed the Ganga," Sumantra said. They entered the jungle on foot, ordering me to come home."

A huge cry of sadness emerged from the crowd, as many hated themselves and blamed the disaster on their crimes. "Look at the chariot that departed with the princes and Sita and has returned empty," women cried on both sides of the streets as the chariot passed.

Sumantra drove forward, ashamed of himself, shielding his face with the end of his upper garment. He alighted from the chariot in front of Dasaratha's palace. Sumantra entered the Queen's apartment with increasing sadness and perplexity. He viewed the King more dead than alive there. He spoke in quiet tones of Rama's message to the King, who listened in heartbroken silence.

Then, unable to contain her rage, Kausalya approached the King: "Your minister has returned from the wilderness, having left my child to carry out your command. Why are you remaining silent? Giving Kaikeyi boons was simple and enjoyable. Why are you embarrassed about it now? Did you not realise this would be the outcome of your actions? You have kept your word. That may make you pleased. But nobody can share my anguish? I must bear it all."

Her grief and love for Rama blinded her to her husband's physical and mental state. Instead of bringing him relief, she exacerbated it.

Sumantra made every effort to pacify Kausalya. But she kept saying: "Take me and leave me in the care of Rama. Young Sita is with him as they face the difficulties of the wilderness. This pain is unbearable for me. Allow me to accompany Sita to Dandaka."

Sumantra responded: "Be brave, Queen. Get rid of this sorrow. Rama enjoys himself even more in the jungle than he did in Ayodhya. He has no sorrow. Lakshmana delights in the greatest duty of serving his brother. Sita, in the jungle as well as in the palace, lives for Rama with every breath and feels no fear or sadness. She lives there with unfettered grace, like a forest deer, spending the golden hours with Rama by her side. Every sight and sound brings her joy, and this is the topic of her conversation with Rama and Lakshmana. Everything I say is true. They are carrying out their sacred duty and teaching the rest of the world a lesson. They are keeping the King's word. Their life will be remembered and praised for the rest of their time. So why should we mourn for them?"

Kausalya would be temporarily consoled by such discussion. But she'd soon break down and wail, "Alas, alas, Rama, my child." Her anguish seemed to be heightened as she watched Sumantra return, abandoning Rama in the jungle.

Dasaratha remembered something that had happened a long time ago, which compounded his heart's anguish. The King addressed Kausalya, saying: "Is it still you, my dear? The consequences of one's actions can never be avoided. I am presently bearing the consequences of a major sin I committed in the past. In their ignorance, mankind might commit great sins for the sake of fleeting pleasure. Then, when the time comes, the cost must be paid.

"When I was younger, I was hunting in the woods, hoping for a wild beast to come to the stream to quench its thirst. I heard a gurgling sound like an elephant drinking there. I fired an arrow in the direction of the sound, which struck the object. I immediately heard a human cry out in pain. I approached the source of the sound, horrified, and discovered a young ascetic laying on the ground. He was filling his pitcher, and the water gushing into it was causing the noise. The dying youngster informed me that his elderly and blind parents were not far away. He'd looked after them, carrying them on his back. He was lamenting the fact that there was no one to look after them while he was gone. After then, the young ascetic took his last. When the boy's parents learned of the catastrophe, they died, cursing me, the one who had slain their son, with a similar fate. My old crime is now killing me. What that old father declared in agonising pain has now come true, as food forbidden by physicians and naively consumed by a sick man kills him. I've consigned my innocent boy to the forest, and now, unable to stand the pain, I've entered Yama's domain.

"I don't see you, Kausalya. My vision is gone. Death is rapidly approaching. Bring yourself closer and let me feel you. It's all over. Yama's messengers have summoned me. Will Rama show up? Will I get to meet him before I die? Oh, I'm going to die. My light is going out because the oil has run out! Kausalya, Kausalya! Sumitra, Sumitra!"

His life dwindled slowly, and that night, unnoticed by everyone, the King breathed his last. Because the King had fainted and recovered so frequently, his death went unnoticed by Kausalya and Sumitra. They, too, were exhausted by grief and waiting and fell asleep in a corner of the apartment. The musicians and singers, whose job it was to rouse the King from his slumber, arrived at his bed-chamber at dawn and played instruments and sang hymns. However, there was no evidence of the King waking up. The royal servants who catered to the King's morning necessities waited for a long time, puzzled as to why he slept so late. Then they dared to enter the flat and discovered him dead.

The word quickly spread, filling the palace with sadness. The mighty Dasaratha's widows wept like orphaned children, embracing one another in continuous mourning.

Kausalya clung to the King's body, sobbing: "I'll accompany the King to Yama's dwelling. How am I supposed to survive without my son and my husband?"

The palace elders and officers were able to separate her from the dead King and carry her away. They then talked about the funeral ceremonies. They couldn't be done right away since Rama and Lakshmana had gone to the wilderness, and Bharata and Shatrughna were far away at their uncle's house. It was decided to send for Bharata and keep the body in oil till he arrived.

CHAPTER XVIII: BHARATA ARRIVES

THUS, the great monarch's remains were maintained in limbo until Bharata arrived. Ayodhya, the City of Splendour, has fallen into darkness and mourning. Crowds of women gathered here and there to mock Kaikeyi. Men's hearts were filled with fear. The Crown Prince had disappeared into the jungle. Bharata was also far away. Anarchy was a threat.

After a hard night, the pastors, officials, and elders gathered in the hall the next morning. With Sumantra and the other ministers, Maarkandeya, Vaamadeva, Kaashyapa, Kaatyaayana, Gautama, Jaabaali, and other scholarly men bowed before Vasishtha and said, "Sir, the night we have passed feels like a century. The King is no longer alive. Rama and Lakshmana are lost in the woods. Bharata and Shatrughna are staying at their grandfather's house in Kekaya. Someone must be requested to take on the role of the ruler right away. A land without a monarch will perish. Order will go, the son will not obey the father, and the wife will not obey the husband. Thieves and robbers will roam at their leisure. People will not be able to trust one another. Agriculture and trade cannot thrive. The wells of generosity will run dry. Festivals and services will no longer be held at temples. Culture will fade and eventually vanish. There will be no sense of security. Cruelty and sorrow will proliferate and devastate the land. A ruler is required for good to flourish and for evil to be suppressed. It appears that huge darkness has engulfed the area. Let us immediately acquire a king."

"Start immediately," Vasishtha urged the messengers. "Follow the signs to Kekaya. Make sure you don't exhibit any signs of sadness on your face or in your behaviour. Bharata should not be aware that the King has died. Simply inform him that the family preceptor and ministers require his immediate presence in Ayodhya, and bring him along as quickly as possible. Tell him nothing about Rama and Sita going to the wilderness, or about the King dying of sadness. To avoid any suspicion, bring the traditional presents of jewels and precious clothing for the King of Kekaya."

The messengers were soon provided with provisions and equipment for the lengthy journey, as well as gifts of honour. They sped past rivers and forests, uphill and down dale, till they arrived in Kekaya, somewhere west of current Punjab, and found themselves in Raajagriha, its capital, where the Ikshvaaku princes were residing in the palace of their maternal uncle.

The presence of the messengers was announced to the King of Kekaya and his son Yudhaajit the next morning. They treated the envoys with respect. They paid their respects to the King and the princes before turning to Bharata and saying, "The priests and ministers extend you their blessings and request that you return to Ayodhya immediately. Your presence is urgently required. Please take these robes and jewels to be offered as presents from the palace of Ayodhya to your uncle and the King."

As a result, the prince parted ways with his uncle and grandfather to return home, and preparations were made for his departure. The ancient king and Yudhaajit gathered unique and costly items from their realm to give to King Dasaratha and Prince Rama of Ayodhya as gifts. Bharata and Shatrughna mounted their chariots and led a large procession to Ayodhya. They travelled quickly, oblivious to exhaustion, and arrived in Ayodhya on the ninth day through forced marches.

Bharata's mind was filled with dread as he reached the city. Nothing felt the same, and the air was heavy with tragedy. "Why does the city have such an odd appearance?" he inquired of the charioteer. "I don't see the typical groups of people entering and exiting the city's gardens; one used to see young men and women with bright, cheery expressions. But they all seem depressed now."

The Victory Gate welcomed Bharata's chariot into the city. The streets, residences, and temples were devoid of ornamentation. People's faces appeared drawn and starved. "How come the musical instruments are silent?" he inquired. "How come the citizens aren't dressed out with flowers and sandal paste? I am unable to suppress my anxiety."

Inauspicious omens could be found everywhere. Bharata surmised that some tremendous disaster had befallen the city, which was why he had been summoned so quickly. He walked into Dasaratha's palace. The King was nowhere to be found. His anxiety rose.

He then proceeded to Kaikeyi's palace. She jumped off her golden couch to greet her son after a lengthy separation. He knelt and stroked her feet. She kissed his head and bestowed maternal blessings on him. "Did you have a pleasant journey?" she inquired. "How are your uncle and grandfather doing? Tell me everything about your journey."

"The voyage took seven days," he replied. "Kekaya's household is happy and healthy. Grandfather and uncle offer their love to you. They have sent you valuable gifts, but they will arrive later. I arrived early. The envoys rushed me, stressing that there was urgent work that requires my presence there. What's the big deal? I went to the King's palace to express my gratitude. He wasn't there, and his couch is also unoccupied here. Maybe he's with one of my elderly mothers. I have to go see him and pay my respects."

When Bharata said this, oblivious to what had happened, the stupid queen, intoxicated with a new sense of power, replied, "My child, your father received his full share of the blessings of this life. His celebrity was enormous. He carried out all of the traditional sacrifices. He was a haven for the good. He has now joined the gods in the heavenly world."

Bharata collapsed, his long arms splayed out on the ground when he heard this.

As he stood up, he grieved like a destitute orphan at the sight of his father's vacant bed. The great hero threw his god-like frame to the ground and sobbed uncontrollably.

"Arise, O King," Kaikeyi exclaimed, looking at her son, who lay on the ground like a large tree felled by the axe. "Take a seat. It is not proper for a monarch to cry and roll on the ground in this manner. Your acceptance will bring you honour and glory. You must uphold the dharma and make sacrifices in the manner of your royal forefathers. Stand up, son, strong of limb and fearless of heart."

Bharata's thinking was pristine and immaculate. He didn't see anything Kaikeyi had put into her charm!

"When I went to my uncle's house, I had hoped that Rama's installation as Yuvaraaja would come off soon and that when I returned, I would watch the huge celebration rituals," he added. "How different things have turned out! I will no longer see my father's face. What caused his death? How did he contract the illness? And I wasn't there at his side while he was unwell! It was handed to Rama to care for him in his final hours. What a sweetheart the King was to me! And it was not given to me to assist him in his time of need. But, mum, where has Rama gone? He is now both my father and my preceptor. I need to see him right away and kiss his feet. He is now my only source of solace. What was the final message my father sent to me? I want his exact words."

Kaikeyi's response had to be consistent with both the truth and her plans. Her culture and desire were pulling her in opposing directions. She discovered words that showed that the King did not consider Bharata in his final moments. She also wanted to get him ready for the remainder of the news. "Your father breathed his final cry, 'Ha, Rama, Ha, Lakshmana, Ha, Janaki,' she continued. "It is not given to me to live to see Rama, Lakshmana, and Sita return. Those who will see their homecoming will be overjoyed."

Bharata deduced from this that Rama and Lakshmana were also away from the King's side. As his anguish grew, he asked Kaikeyi, "Where were they? What pulled them away from our father's side in his final moments?"

To appease him, Kaikeyi said, "My son, Rama, dressed in ascetic robes and went to the Dandaka forest with Lakshmana and Sita."

Bharata's awe had reached new heights. "I comprehend nothing of what you're saying," he inquired. "What sin did Rama do that required such atonement? Did he rob any Brahmana or commit bodily harm to anyone? Why was he compelled to visit the forest? Who imposed this penance on him?"

Kaikeyi, shocked by her stillness by the torrent of inquiries, spoke up, foolishly expecting the best. "Rama did not do any crime. He did not rob or injure anyone. When I saw that preparations were being made to place him as Crown Prince and Regent, I approached the King on your behalf and gained the fulfilment of two boons he had long granted to me. I requested that the kingdom be given to you and that Rama be exiled to the jungle. The King accepted, bound by his previous commitment. So Sita and Lakshmana have joined Rama in the forest. Your father died of grief, unable to take this separation. Do not waste your time now lamenting in vain. Consider what you should do immediately. Your responsibility is to accept the responsibilities of kingship. All of this was done for your benefit, and you should embrace the fruit of my actions in the spirit in which they were done. The city and kingdom have come to you without your asking or striving for them. Perform your father's obsequies following the advice of Vasishtha and other scholarly men, and then prepare for the coronation. You belong to the Kshatriya caste. Your father's empire has been passed on to you. Attend to what has been assigned to you as your responsibility."

CHAPTER XIX: INTRIGUE WASTED

Now Bharata knew everything and saw the magnitude of his mother's wrongdoing. He couldn't contain himself since he was so overwhelmed by grief and so close. His grief erupted at the notion of what she had done and the eternal infamy she had received, and he threw vicious words at her.

"What have you done?" he demanded. "Did you ever hope to force me to accept the throne? Is it likely that I would want power if I didn't have such a father and a brother? You beg me to take their place and rule the land after killing the King and banishing Rama. This is like pouring gasoline on the inferno that is my sadness. How terrible that my father picked you as his wife! Kausalya and Sumitra would likewise perish as a result of their anguish. Oh, how could you bear doing this to Rama, who was so committed to you? Kausalya, your revered mother, treated you as if you were her blood sister. How could you even consider scheming against her adored son? Did you realise how much I adored Rama? Greed obliterated your comprehension. How else could you have made such rash plans for my happiness? Rama and Lakshmana were trusted by even the great King. How could you think I could rule the kingdom in their absence? Your wish will never be granted with my assistance. I no longer consider you to be my mother. How could you possibly consider breaking with tradition and crowning your younger son? Wouldn't the rest of the world hate us for the rest of our lives? The universal law of monarchs and our family heritage cannot be broken. I will not grant your wish. I will go to the forest and bring Rama back, place the crown on his head, and exult in the fact that I am his loyal servant."

"Banish Rama indeed!" said Bharata, raising his voice again. "You, cruel women, who have abandoned the path of dharma, should be exiled. You may assume that I am dead because I would rather be dead than be the son of a murderess! Your husband's murderer!

"I will do the obsequies, go to the jungle, and fall at Rama's feet, bringing him back to his realm. Then, to purge me of the guilt and disgrace you have brought upon me, I will live as an ascetic in the Dandaka forest. I'm going to Rama right away to clear my conscience by restoring the kingdom to him."

Finding no solace in angry words and hot tears flowing from his eyes, he felt he could no longer endure the sight of his mother and raced to Kausalya's apartment, hoping to find a better place to express his grief.

As a result, Kaikeyi's air castle went up in flames. She cried herself to sleep on the floor.

The announcement of Bharata's arrival quickly travelled throughout the palace. Kausalya, who was still grieving, was relieved and told Sumitra, "Come, let us go and meet Bharata." They had only walked a few feet when they noticed Bharata himself running madly towards them, pleading for compassion.

When Kausalya heard about Bharata's arrival, her initial assumption was that he had hurried back to claim the fortune that had come to him. Hadn't Vasishtha, the elders and ministers, resolved to send for Bharata so that he may perform his father's obsequies and be anointed king? As a result, seeing Bharata, Kausalya, her heart broken by the loss of her husband and son, murmured, "Bharata, the kingship is waiting, secured for your sake by Kaikeyi. You have nothing to worry about from us. Take everything, and may you be happy. I only want one favour from you: let me join your father on the funeral pyre."

These words stung Bharata's ears like venom. He collapsed at her feet, clinging to them. Bharata collapsed in a faint, unable to withstand Kausalya's piteous words and unable to speak. After some time, he got up and asked, "Mother, why do you torture me, who is innocent? You know I was far away and had no idea what was going on here. Do you have any idea how much I adore Rama? Would I ever do something like that to him? May all the world's sins descend on me if I had even the slightest inkling of the evil simmering here! I have absolutely nothing to do with it. I have no desire to reap the benefits."

He raised his hands and recounted all of the heinous offences that could be committed, as well as the consequences that would befall him if he was involved in the conspiracy. He could only declare his innocence repeatedly. He had no desire for the kingdom, wealth, or power, and it was a horrible torture to him that Kausalya thought him capable of greed for things at the expense of his brother. He could never accept the crown that belonged to his adored brother.

His intense sincerity persuaded Kausalya that her suspicions were unjust, and her heart went out to him. She gently lifted him from the ground, placed his head on her lap, and caressed him as if he were Rama himself.

"My dear son, watching the sorrow pouring in your innocent heart doubles my grief. What are we going to do, child? We are the puppets of fate. May you be rewarded for your compassion in this world and the next!"

Kausalya did not believe Bharata was aware of the plot, but she was afraid he would condone it and succumb to the lure of its consequences. She was now certain that Bharata's heart was fully stain-free. Although her son had gone to the forest, she was relieved that another son had come to her in his place.

The dead King's obsequies were suitably performed. Vasishtha and other wise men and elders offered Bharata and Shatrughna deep shaastric solace. Fourteen days following the King's death, the ministers convened the Assembly and addressed Bharata as follows: "The King has passed to the world above. Rama and Lakshmana are lost in the woods. There is no longer a ruler in the kingdom. You are correct in assuming the rule at our request. The coronation preparations have been completed. Citizens and ministers are waiting for your approval. This is your ancestors' rightfully descended kingdom. It is for you to be anointed and to rule over us righteously."

"I do not feel it proper that you should ask me to accept the kingdom in this manner," Bharata remarked to the assembled elders, his hands folded around the items brought for the coronation. "The throne is traditionally held by the eldest son of our House. With all due respect, I have decided to go to the jungle with Lakshmana and bring Rama back to Ayodhya to be crowned. Please prepare the soldiers and resources for the journey. "I have made the decisive and irreversible decision not to take the crown."

The entire assembly was filled with joy as they listened to the prince's speech. They applauded Bharata's idea.

The army and a large retinue had been assembled to follow the prince to the woodland. An army of workmen rushed forward with their tools to prepare the road. Men who knew their way around the forest, pioneers who could dig wells and canals, raft and boat builders, carpenters, and engineers all worked tirelessly to reclaim Rama. Culverts were built, trees were removed, and a wide road was quickly laid for the prince and his entourage.

While preparations for Bharata's travel to the jungle were being made, Vasishtha and the other ministers formally summoned the Assembly once more. They did not give up hope of seeing Bharata crowned. They dispatched messengers to Bharata's palace, inviting him to the Hall. They approached him with music on several instruments. All of this bothered him.

He halted the musicians, returned the messengers, and informed Shatrughna, "Why should they continue to harass me when I have declined the kingdom? This is due to our mother's curiosity. My father has gone to Heaven, leaving me to face the brunt of this on my own. The land requires a ruler; without one, it floats aimlessly like a rudderless and derelict ship. We need to bring Rama back as soon as possible."

The Assembly waited for the innocent prince with bated breath. As the full moon rose in the sky, he entered the Hall. He sat down and bowed before the elders.

"This kingdom has been granted to you by your father and brother Rama; accept it and defend us according to ancient custom," Vasishtha replied.

Bharata's heart belonged to Rama. His eyes welled up with tears. Amid the royal Assembly, the young prince wept aloud and spoke words of respectful rebuke to the preceptors: "How can you ask one of my race and upbringing to take what belongs to another far nobler and more worthy than I? Can anyone imagine such heinousness? Rama owns this kingdom, including me and everything else in it. He is the eldest son, the noblest among us, and a dharma follower. He is the legitimate king. Standing here, I pay my respects to Rama, who is present in the jungle. He, not I, is the King."

When Bharata said this, the Assembly fell into tears of joy.

"If I am unable to persuade King Rama to agree, I will remain there conducting penance," Bharata continued. "It is your responsibility, O Elders, to employ all available ways to bring Rama back. I will do all in my power to bring Rama back to Ayodhya and make him King."

He then told Sumantra, who was standing nearby, to hurry up with the preparations for the trip to the jungle. The city celebrated in anticipation of Rama's return because everyone believed that nothing could withstand the might of Bharata's devoted love.

CHAPTER XX:
BHARATA SUSPECTED

GUHA, the hunter-king, noticed a strange noise on the opposite bank of the Ganga while gazing across the river. There was a large army encamped there. "Who is this, and why has he come here with a great army, evidently to cross the river?" he asked his kinsmen standing by his side. "According to the flag, it is Kaikeyi's son Bharata and his army. Yes, I see the flag flying from the chariot's top, and I recognise the tree painted on it. That is the King of Ayodhya's flag. Isn't Bharata, Rama's adversary, the current King of Ayodhya? He appears to have chased Rama to slay him after securing the kingdom unfairly through his mother Kaikeyi. Gather our warriors, kin, and friends. Allow them to prepare on this bank. Fill all of the boats with armed troops ready for a fight. Let us see what happens. If the newcomers are friendly to Rama, we will assist them in crossing the river and coming over to this side. If their goal is hostile, however, we will prevent them from crossing the Ganga."

So, after making all the necessary arrangements, Guha took some gifts, boarded a boat, and set off to meet Bharata.

At the same moment, Sumantra was telling Bharata at the other bank, "Look! Guha, the hunter-king and Rama's faithful friend, has arrived with his people to greet us. He is the region's ruler. He and his relatives are well-versed in every nook and cranny of this woodland. They could tell us where Rama was and lead us there safely and quickly."

Meanwhile, Guha crossed the creek and approached Bharata, bowing and saying, "Though your unexpected presence has taken us by surprise, all that is mine here you may treat as your own and command me. It is an honour for me to be able to welcome and entertain you and your army."

"It is exceedingly kind of you, O friend of my brother, to extend hospitality to such a huge army," Bharata said. "I'd like to go to Bharadwaaja's hermitage. We don't know how to get there, and we also need to cross this massive river."

Guha bowed before him and said graciously, "My lord, my slaves, and I are ready to accompany you and function as guides. But please excuse me for voicing a scepticism that comes to mind when I observe the size of your army. Surely you have no ill will toward Rama?"

"Alas, what greater dishonour can come to me than this, that men who adore Rama should fear and accuse me?" Bharata remarked, pained by these words and speaking from a heart as bright and pure as the June sky. "Have no doubts, Guha. Rama is now my father, having taken the place of my deceased father. I've come to ask him to return to Ayodhya. I swear, I have no other intention."

Guha was overjoyed to observe Bharata's passionate love for Rama as well as his anguish over what had happened. "My Lord, who in the world can equal such sacrifice?" he replied. "Who else but you would turn down such undeserved money and power? Your radiance will last forever."

The hunter-king provided everything Bharata's army required. The hosts and guests retired for the evening.

The meeting with Guha only added to Bharata's grief. He sighed and rolled sleeplessly on the ground, saying, "Alas, that it should come to this." His entire body burned with memories of the infamy that had settled over him, his father's murder, and his separation from Rama. Guha comforted him and attempted to calm him.

"What meals did Rama eat while he was here?" Bharat inquired. "Where did he take his seat? What did he sleep in? What exactly did he say? What exactly did he do?"

Guha patiently answered each question and pointed to the spot where he had slept. "Where did Lakshmana sleep?" he was asked. "How can I sleep when Rama and Sita are sprawled out on the naked earth?" he answered. And he cried and stayed on guard the entire night, bow in hand.

Bharata's sadness became unbearable as he imagined this scene. He pointed to the sobbing queens the location where Rama and Sita had slept that night.

"My Lord, they fasted that night," Guha said when asked what Rama ate. "Lakshmana brought some water, which Rama drank before passing it back to Lakshmana. The meal I brought was not consumed. They matted their hair and walked into the jungle the next morning.

"You slept on the grass for my sake, Rama. I've seen the location and still live there. On top of everything, they want me to wear a crown!" Bharata wept uncontrollably.

Then he told himself, "I'm going to bring Rama back and place him on the throne. If he wants his commitment to be honoured, I will take his place in the forest for fourteen years. He will agree to this agreement because it is only fair." As a result, he calmed down.

Guha arrived early the next morning and, after polite introductions, declared that he had a fleet of several boats ready. All of the luggage and the entire army were loaded onto boats. The heavy vessels made their way over the great river. The ferry crossing made a joyful commotion as if it were a large carnival.

The people did not notice Bharata's sadness because they had assumed, even before Bharata set off, that Rama would undoubtedly return. They marched forward, glad that Rama would soon be proclaimed king and that their previous sufferings would fade like a horrible dream.

They soon arrived at Bharadwaaja's ashrama. Bharata and his entourage proceeded to Bharadawaaja ashrama. When they arrived at the Prayaaga wood, they noticed a magnificent grove with a cottage in the midst. After learning that this was Bharadwaaja's ashrama, Bharata left his retinue behind and walked towards it with humility, escorted only by Vasishtha and a few other seniors. A bit later on, he left even the ministers behind, and he and Vasishtha proceeded forth alone.

When Bharadwaaja noticed Vasishtha, he rose from his seat and went to greet the distinguished visitor, ordering his students to bring the customary water for the guests' feet.

Bharata saluted Bharadwaaja with humility. When he discovered who he was, the rishi treated him with respect befitting a king and inquired about his well-being. He carefully avoided mentioning Dasaratha's tragic fate.

After asking the typical personal inquiries, Bharadwaaja asked Bharata, "Why did you forsake your kingly duties and come over here? Should you leave Ayodhya? Listening to his young wife, Dasaratha ordered Rama to reside in the jungle for fourteen years, and the Prince departed the city with his brother and Sita. Do you believe that the path for your rule is still unclear, and have you come to finish what Dasaratha started to be doubly certain?"

Bharata sobbed when he heard these remarks. He was speechless as tears streamed down his cheeks. "Do you have any doubts about me, master?" he inquired. "Do not hold me responsible for what my mother did in my absence without my knowledge or consent. I've come to convince Rama to return to Ayodhya and be crowned King. And I intend to be his humble slave for the rest of my life. I've come to ask you where Rama lives so that I might go and persuade him to return home."

"Bharata, I know your true nature," Bharadwaaja stated. "You are a descendant of Raghu. I questioned you to elicit a disclosure of your affection and loyalty, so establishing and spreading your glory. Do not weep. The Prince lives on Chitrakoota hill. Stay with us today. You and your ministers will go there tomorrow. You will please me by accepting hospitality in the ashrama for a day."

"My Lord, your wishes and words of devotion are a feast," Bharata remarked. "What else is needed?"

Bharadwaaja laughed when he saw Bharata was unwilling to burden a poor ascetic with the task of feeding an army. "I am compelled to entertain you in a manner worthy of your rank and goodness," he remarked. "Why have you abandoned your army and retinue?"

"I followed the rule that one should not approach a rishi's house with a retinue," Bharata said. "A large crowd is following me. It would cause you a lot of trouble if they all came here."

"Nothing of the sort," the rishi said. "Instruct everyone to come up."

So Bharata directed.

Bharadwaaja walked to the sacrificial fire and sipped water three times before calling on Viswakarma, Maya, Yama, Varuna, Kubera, Agni, and other celestial entities to prepare a sumptuous feast for Bharata and his companions.

Then a miracle occurred. The feast prepared at Bharadwaaja's ashrama was similar to the one Vasishtha had given Vishvamitra in the past. The only difference was that there was no argument or bustle here. Everyone had plenty of space. Sandal paste, flowers, food and drink, and exquisite entertainers' music and dancing were all offered. Bharadwaaja's banquet was more lavish than that of emulous monarchs. Dwellings, vehicles, and servants appeared out of nowhere. The visitors became absorbed in the feast. In their ecstasy of current happiness, the warriors in Bharata's army screamed to one another, "We shall not go to the Dandaka jungle. We are not going back to Ayodhya. We'll be here forever." The guests ate thoroughly and promptly fell asleep.

The next morning, Bharadwaaja told Bharata, "The river Mandakini runs two and a half yojanas from here. An uninhabited woodland grows along its banks, with Chitrakoota hill to the south. Your brothers and Sita live in a cabin on the hill's slope." And he went into great detail about how they should proceed.

Bharata and his vast retinue followed Bharadwaaja's instructions and entered the forest. They noticed the Chitrakoota hill from a distance, and as they proceeded enthusiastically, a column of smoke revealed the location of the Prince's home, and cheers erupted from the gathering. Bharata advanced, leaving his followers behind, followed alone by Sumantra and Vasishtha.

CHAPTER XXI: THE BROTHERS MEET

LIFE in the woodland hut at Chitrakoota went on rather pleasantly while Bharata was thus engaged. Rama had everything he needed with Lakshmana and Sita by his side. The splendour of the mountain scenery and forest, as well as the charming voices and play of the birds, delighted his heart. He had forgotten the anguish of his banishment from family and city.

As a result of being free of grief, he made Sita happy. Descending the slope, they would occasionally visit the Mandakini River and spend time there. Rama would point out the sand hillocks. "Take a look at the swans frolicking among the lotuses. The stream is just as gorgeous as you, darling. The fords where animals gather to drink are a brilliant red with new earth. Even the river in Kubera's domain cannot compare to this. We are quite fortunate to be far from the congested metropolis here in the forest. No rishis or pure spirits are bathing as we see here every day. This is Ayodhya for us. Our subjects are the birds and beasts. Our Sarayu is the Mandaakini.

"I'm very pleased and content with you and Lakshmana by my side. It's nice to see the animals drinking from the stream without fear! Why should I think of kingship or power as I swim in the river, eat fruits and roots, go through the forest, and climb the hills?"

Rama was therefore having a good time with Sita and Lakshmana.

One day, as they sat in complete serenity on the slope of the hill, they noticed a cloud of dust rising in the sky that appeared to be heading toward them. They immediately heard a large crowd making a loud ruckus. Rama noticed the terrified forest animals stampeding hither and thither. It appeared as if an army had entered the jungle.

"Can you hear what's going on?" Rama told Lakshmana, "'The elephants, bison, and deer are running wild. What could it possibly be? Is it possible that a monarch has come here to hunt? Is it a tiger or another frightening wild beast that has come rummaging? Just look around and tell me."

Lakshmana climbed a large tree and took in the view. He noticed a vast army approaching from the north, equipped with chariots, elephants, horses, and footmen. He sent a warning to Rama: "Pay attention, brother. A massive army is approaching, flags flying and in perfect formation. Let us exercise caution. Extinguish the fire. Take Sita into the cave for her protection. Let us put on our armour and prepare for combat."

Rama stated: "Don't be in such a rush. Look at the chariot's flag again and tell me which king is leading his army here."

Lakshmana was enraged as he looked. "It's Bharata, my brother. He is pursuing us here, I can see the tree on our flag blowing in the breeze, not satisfied with obtaining the kingdom. He has come to kill us, but he will not escape with my life today. What sin is there in killing this dharma destroyer? Killing someone who comes to slaughter us is certainly not a sin. The wooded paths will soon be covered in blood. Bharata, like a tree uprooted by an elephant, would be toppled to the ground by me. This army will be destroyed. We'll feed the fat to the forest's beasts."

Lakshmana was beyond himself with wrath as he spoke.

Rama then calmed him down. "If you want to, you can destroy the seven worlds. You can easily slay Bharata and his army, but there is something you need to remember before you begin. What good would winning the kingdom do us if we disobey and disgrace our father and murdered our brother? Why do we covet money and kingdom, and for whom? Who would wish to gain a kingdom through deception? And what joy is there in a kingdom that you can't share with the people you care about? I swear to you, I will never consider wealth and power that you, Bharata, and Shatrughna, cannot share with me.

"I know why Bharata is here now, and I'll tell you why. He understands the path of dharma. He is on his way to offer me the kingdom. If he had been at Ayodhya instead of his uncle's distant region, he could have dissuaded Kaikeyi and spared our father the immense anguish that has befallen him. I'm sure he's on his way back to the city right now. You are wicked to think poorly of Bharata and to talk so harshly of him."

Lakshmana shrunk inside himself in humiliation when he heard this.

"Perhaps our father, King," Lakshmana speculated. "is personally paying us a visit."

After hearing Rama, he was convinced that his dread was unwarranted. He wondered why the army was going and assumed Dasaratha was on his way to see them in the jungle, and a large retinue followed the King.

Rama encouraged Lakshmana by saying: "Yes, as you say, it could be. Thinking that living in the wilderness was difficult, the King may have arrived to take us, particularly Sita, back to the city. But we don't see the King's massive white parasol. But, in any event, you should remain cool."

By Rama, Lakshmana stood respectfully with folded hands.

Stopping the army at a safe distance, Bharata dispatched a few men to investigate and report on the source of the smoke. They brought word that this was the exact location specified by Bharadwaaja and that the cottage was most likely Rama's forest dwelling.

Bharata began with Shatrughna, Vasishtha, and Sumantra. As they progressed, they noticed signs that the ashrama was inhabited. There was a route that led to the river, and the trees on each side of it were blazed, as if to make it simple to find in the dusk. They eventually arrived at a hut thatched with leaves, near which were stacks of faggots and deer and wild buffalo dung stacked for winter usage. On the walls of the hut were enormous bows and quivers full of lethal arrows, swords that appeared to exude victory, and other weapons of unparalleled brilliance. Bharata's heart swelled as he saw all these sure indicators of his brothers' presence in the hermitage. Bharata entered and beheld the altar with its blazing fire and Rama himself seated beside it with matted locks, magnificent, though in deerskin and bark, a monarch of the earth, with his mighty arms, breadth of chest, and a countenance meant to command love and obedience. Sita and Lakshmana were with him.

He'd been thinking about the infamy that had accumulated in his head the entire time, wondering what to say and do when he faced Rama. But when he saw Rama, he forgot all of this in the enormous love that surged within him, drowning out all other thoughts and anxieties. He jumped ahead to where Rama was sitting. He couldn't say anything other than "Brother," and he sobbed at his feet. Sumantra and Guha had joined him by this point.

Rama beheld Bharata lying on the ground, hands joined in submission, with matted locks and bark clothing. His frame had grown slender from mourning and fasting, and he was browned from fatigue and exposure. Rama hugged him and kissed him on the cheek, saying: "Why did you leave our father's side and come into the forest, darling brother? And why have you become so frail?"

Bharata was rendered speechless. Rama asked him the formal questions that members of the royal family asked each other after a long absence.

After a little pause, Bharata recovered his strength and responded. "Why are you questioning me about the kingdom, brother, as if I were its ruler? How could I call myself king or rule over the land when you are the rightful king? I have to be of service to you. The burden of the kingdom should be carried by the eldest son. This is the rule of law and custom. Come to Ayodhya with me, wear the crown, and bestow your grace on our family and people. When you left Ayodhya for the jungle and before I returned from Kekaya, the King committed suicide, killed by the pain of being separated from you. Do not succumb to grief. Perform our father's obsequies. He sacrificed his life for you. His spirit will be satisfied solely by the obsequies you perform." Bharata regained his balance and spoke.

Rama collapsed like a tree felled by an axe when he learned that his father had died. Bharata didn't need to repeat all of his apologies and explanations to Kausalya, Guha, and Bharadwaaja in front of Rama. Where was the need for explanations when Rama saw that bereaved body and that torn face? Bharata, whose sole goal was to return Rama to Ayodhya, spoke solely of this and nothing else.

The princes proceeded to the river with Sita and Sumantra and offered libations for the tranquillity of the King's departed soul. The princes returned to the cottage after other traditional formalities. They clutched one other's hands and cried aloud to soothe their grief.

CHAPTER XXII: BHARATA BECOMES RAMA'S DEPUTY

When the soldiers learned that the four princes and three queens had been reunited, a chorus of excitement erupted, and everyone rushed forward to witness the wonderful spectacle. They were confident that Rama would return to Ayodhya, and the people joyfully embraced one another.

Vasishtha, the sage, led the three queens to the hut. They passed by the Mandaakini River on their journey. Kausalya and Sumitra wailed as he showed them the location where the princes took water every day for their use. Kausalya stated: "Every day, Sumitra, your son brings water to the ashrama from this pool in the river. Lakshmana is willing to joyfully perform even the most mundane chore for his sibling. He doesn't mind carrying the water jug on his regal shoulder."

They arrived at the cottage. They saw the princes, their faces clouded with grief, seated beneath a thatched roof. The royal mothers collapsed to the floor, unable to take the sight.

Kausalya massaged Ramawith her flower-soft hands as she raised him up, sorrowful and delighted. She hugged Sita and said: "Do you dwell in this cottage in the bush, Janaka's daughter? O, dust-covered golden vision! My heart melts when I see you."

Rama reverently caressed Vasishtha's feet, who appeared to be another Brihaspati, the preceptor of the gods, who had come down to earth, and then sat by his mother. Bharata sat respectfully apart from Rama. The elders surrounded them, waiting for Bharata to say something and Rama's reaction.

"Bharata, why have you abandoned your kingly duties to come here with deer skin and matted hair?" Rama inquired. Bharata tried to speak numerous times but couldn't get past the phrase 'Brother.' Then, with great effort, he gathered himself together and said: "Our father's soul flew to heaven after sending you to the forest, unable to withstand the anguish. My mother's only benefit from her terrible plot has been that she has become a sinner, a widow, and is in tremendous grief. She is despised by the world and goes through misery on Earth. Only you have the ability to save us. By agreeing to be crowned, you can undo all the harm that has been done. We have come to beg you for this, and we are all waiting for your response. This alone will put an end to our grief and restore our race's dharma. The land is forlorn and defenceless without a legitimate king. You must return to make it happy and secure. Dispel our darkness when the full moon rises. The ministers here and I prostrate ourselves at your feet and implore you. O, brother, do not refuse!"

With tears in his eyes, the mighty Bharata clung to Ramachandra's feet and said thus.

Rama picked him up from the ground and embraced him, saying: "Brother, we were born into a noble family and raised with proper manners. Neither you nor I can make a mistake. Do not be sad or say anything negative about your mum. It is not appropriate for us to blame her. Our father had every right to tell us what to do, even to deport us, just as he had every right to arrange a coronation. It is our responsibility to honour our father and mother. How could I defy or question their authority? Was it my responsibility to resist my father's instruction to go to the forest?

"He gave you kingship and gave me life in the jungle. What right do we have to change or reject his plans? It is far from inappropriate for you to govern the land. And I, too, will fulfil our father's final instruction by spending fourteen years in the Dandaka forest. Can I be comfortable with having the entire globe but failing to fulfil our father's wish?"

Bharata continually begged and pleaded with Rama. Rama realised that Bharata was upset because injustice had been done to him and that he was attempting to remove the stain.

"You are not to blame," he said. "Do not believe that all of this happened for your benefit. Everything is determined by fate. Give up your anguish. Return to Ayodhya and take control of the kingdom. Let us individually carry out the responsibilities assigned to us by the father we love and honour."

The people who saw the speech and observed the Prince's determination were overwhelmed with both delight and grief. Bharata's affection and purity made them proud and happy.

Rama informed Bharata of his final decision. "I can't possibly break my father's word. You will delight me if you do not keep attempting to persuade me. Shatrughna is here to assist you in ruling, just as Lakshmana is here to assist me in my woodland existence. I have all I need with Lakshmana by my side. Let us four, brother, carry out our father's wishes."

Vasishtha then made the following case for Rama's homecoming: "Overall, I believe you should return to Ayodhya and accept the kingdom. Of course, your father's command must be taken into account and reconciled with this step. You immediately and unhesitatingly obeyed that command, but now a new situation has arisen. Bharata has sought refuge at your feet in his helplessness, fearing infamy. We all know how much you adore him. You never refuse anyone who comes to you for assistance. How can you now deny it to Bharata? Isn't it your life's mission to assist people who seek refuge at your feet?"

Rama, on the other hand, showed no indications of giving up. Bharata then turned to Sumantra and stated, "My brother has no sympathy for me. Please make a bed of darbha grass for me. I will take the vow of fasting until death."

Sumantra paused and gazed at Rama. Then Bharata went and spread the grass and sat on it.

"This is not right, my brother," Rama stated emphatically. "Rise. Go to Ayodhya and complete your responsibilities. Do not go against Kshatriya dharma."

Bharata stood up and, as a last resort, addressed the people who had joined him - a representative gathering of soldiers and Ayodhya citizens: "O, inhabitants of Ayodhya! Why are you standing there mutely watching? Do you want Rama to leave? So why are you remaining silent?"

People responded as follows: "Rama will not deviate from the truth. He will honour his father's commitment. He is not going back to Ayodhya. What is the point of pressuring him any further?"

According to Bharata: "Here, I am as guiltless as Rama and a suitable replacement for him. If the King's pledge be kept, let me stay in the jungle in lieu of Rama. Allow him to take my position and govern in Ayodhya."

Rama chuckled and stated, "This exchange technique is inapplicable here. This is not a barter. It is true that occasionally one person does the obligations of another when the latter is too weak or unable of doing so. But how does it fit in on this particular occasion? Can any of you declare that I have no capacity for life in the forest, but only Bharata does?"

The intelligent Vasishtha then devised a solution to the problem of righteousness vs. righteousness over which should be more right. "O, Bharata, rule the kingdom as Rama's deputy and under his authority. The vow would be kept and you would not be held accountable."

Rama sat Bharata on his lap and said, "Consider the kingdom to be my gift to you, brother. Accept it and rule it according to our father's wishes."

According to Bharata: "You are both my father and my God, brother. My dharma is your wish. Please hand over your sandals. Your token will reign in Ayodhya until you return. And for fourteen years I will remain outside the city, performing the King's duties in your place, paying reverent homage to your sandals. You will return and claim the throne at the conclusion of that term."

"So be it," Rama replied.

He put his feet in the sandals and handed them to Bharata, who prostrated himself on the ground and accepted them before placing them on his head.

Bharata and his entourage returned to Ayodhya. They met the sage Bharadwaaja on the way and told him what had happened. He wished Bharata well, saying: "Your virtue will be remembered for all time. Are you not a son of the solar race? As water falls downwards, the virtue of your family runs its inevitable course in you. Dasaratha, your father, is overjoyed. He is not dead, but lives on in you forever."

They crossed the Ganga and reached Ayodhya. Bharata saw the city as desolate without the King and Rama. It appeared to be surrounded by the darkness of a moonless night. He had entered the city in fatigue, shapeless fear, and suspense when he returned from Kekaya, but today he entered it fully aware of the tragedy. He reflected on the past, considered the present, and wept all over again. He entered the meeting hall and stated "My grief is immense. But I'll put up with it. I'll stay in Nandigama and complete the tasks I promised Rama. Make all necessary preparations."

This was done and he solemnly stated before the assembly, "This kingdom is Rama's. For the time being, he has asked me to be in charge. In my brother's place, I have installed his sandals. Deriving my authority from them, I shall conduct my duties as king."

Accordingly, Bharata stayed in Nandigama and with the support of ministers ruled the kingdom as a holy duty until Rama should return after finishing his forest life. Rama took his penance in the forest for fourteen years and all the time Bharata also did his penance at Nandigama near Ayodhya.

CHAPTER XXIII: VIRADHA'S END

NOT far from Chitrakoota was a Rakshasa outpost called Janasthaana, which was directed by a legendary warrior named Khara, who was Ravana's brother, and from this station, fierce Rakshasas ranged the forest, harassing the rishis in their solitary ashramas. They made life so dangerous that the rishis abandoned their hermitages in the Chitrakoota region, despite Rama's best efforts to persuade them otherwise.

Rama was dissatisfied in Chitrakoota after Bharata's departure. The sad drooping form of his widowed mother and his beloved brother's tearful face were ever before his mind's eye, and now that the rishis' departure had deprived him of even their companionship, the lonely hut was so full of sad memories that he made up his mind to seek another resting place in the Dandaka forest.

So they left Chitrakoota and went to the hermitage of Atri, a rishi who understood the land, to seek his opinion on where they should settle. They were warmly welcomed, and Sita gained the heart of Atri's wife, the saintly Anasooya, who, pleased at discovering in her a perfect personification of wifely qualities, blessed her and bestowed her with magnificent robes and auspicious cosmetics that highlighted the charms of lovely young wives.

Anasooya was the epitome of pure womanhood, and her gifts enhanced Sita's beauty and inner power. "My Lord, the Prince loves me with the affection of a mother and a father, and I am very blessed," she remarked as she accepted the gifts.

They then inquired about the route and resumed their trek.

Rama, Sita, and Lakshmana arrived at a location where numerous rishis dwelt while walking through the enormous Dandaka forest. They realised it was a holy men's colony as soon as they saw the sacrificial supplies, bark clothes, and deer skins stretched out to dry.

The scenery was breathtaking. Birds and animals wandered around fearlessly, thanks to their affectionate acquaintance with their human neighbours. The trees were laden with ripe fruits. The lovely sound of Vedic chanting could be heard.

As they got closer, they noticed the rishis' bright faces. Rama was welcomed. "You are our defender, King," they exclaimed. "Whether we are in town or in the wilderness, you are our king," they said, giving the newcomers everything they needed and a place to lay.

The three left the rishis the next morning and returned to the forest, which was now denser than previously and home to tigers and other wild animals. They moved gently and carefully.

Suddenly, a massive figure that resembled a broken chunk of a hill charged at them, emitting a blood-curdling screech. It was a man-eating raakshasa with a thunderous roar. He was hideous, and the tiger-skin he wore was stained with blood, with gobbets of dead beasts' flesh attached to it. Three lions' bodies and an elephant's head were impaled and strung in a row on the enormous spear, which he brandished menacingly at them.

The raakshasa raised his weapon, roared horribly, and leapt forward, lifting Sita and shouting at the princes, "Who are you, little fellows? How dare you enter this forest? You look young but wear matted locks and bark garments. You have disguised yourselves as ascetics; yet you carry bows and arrows, and go about with this woman by your side. Whom are you trying to cheat? Are you not ashamed of yourselves? You are besmirching the good name of the rishis by your conduct, you hypocrites! Know that I am Viraadha himself. The flesh of rishis is my daily food. I shall have this lovely damsel for my wife, do you understand? I shall now drink your blood, you villains!"

Sita shook in his grip, terrified. Rama lost his customary composure and exclaimed: "This is intolerable, Lakshmana; Kaikeyi must have known when she sent us to the jungle!"

Rama was perplexed and unsure how to approach the Rakshasa, but Lakshmana, hissing like an angry snake, said: "Rama, you are as strong as Indra, and you should not be depressed with me by your side. Look at what my bow and arrow are capable of. The planet is about to consume this monster's blood. My rage, which was denied an outlet at Ayodhya, I will now direct against this creature, shattering him as Indra shattered the winged mountains of old. I'm going to attack and kill this beast."

Viraadha screamed once more: "What is your name? Tell me right away."

Rama's thinking had cleared, and his face sparkled with courage as he stated calmly, "We are princes of the Ikshvaaku race. We have settled in the woods. Could you please tell us who you are? "

The Rakshasa said, "So you're Dasaratha's sons, aren't you? Jaya is the name of my father. And I'm known as Viraadha among raakshasas. What can you, you insignificant kshatriyas with weapons, do to me? Brahma has granted me a gift that no weapon may harm me. If you want to preserve your life, leave this girl here and flee."

"It is time for you to go to Yama," Rama said, bending his bow and shooting a sharp arrow at the monster, which pierced his body and emerged red with blood, glistening like fire, and fell on the earth beyond. But the raakshasa was not killed. Enraged by the pain, he placed Sita on the ground and, lifting his spear and opening his mouth wide, rushed towards Rama and Lakshmana.

Rama and Lakshmana, seated one on each shoulder, wrenched off his arms and threw them down, then attacked him with their hands and feet. They couldn't kill him because of Brahma's boon, but the agony of his wounds was so great that he howled with it. Unfortunately for him, he had asked for immunity from slaughter, but not from pain.

The brothers dropped the weary beast to the ground, and Rama rested his foot on his neck to keep him from rising.

The contact of Rama's feet lifted the mist that had cloaked his comprehension due to the curse incurred in a past birth, and in the sudden light of recall he clasped his hands and humbly exclaimed, "Lord, your feet have touched me, and my eyes have been opened. I've figured out who you are. I am cursed, but you can save me. I was born a Gandharva, not a Rakshasa. The boon I obtained hinders my release. If you could murder me, I would revert to my natural form and go to heaven."

Rama and Lakshmana shattered him with no weapons and buried him in a pit excavated in the dirt, and the raakshasa returned to the domain of the Gandharvas.

The Princes then returned to the spot where Sita was afraid and told her everything that had happened.

They came to Sarabhanga's ashrama, where Indra was talking to the rishi with other gods. When Rama arrived, he cut his conversation short and left, and Rama, with his brother and wife, approached the rishi and humbly worshipped him.

According to the ancient ascetic: "I have been waiting for you. It's time for me to depart this body, but I wanted to visit you first. As a result, I've been waiting. Now that my goal has been realised, I pass on all the benefits of my penances to you."

Rama responded: "Shouldn't I, my Lord, gain my own merit? How can I get what you've earned? I've given up everything to live in the forest. Please advise me on the finest place for me to live in the forest and send me on my way with your blessing."

The rishi knew the secret of Rama's avatar and advised him, "Learn from the sage Suteekshna where you should reside in the forest."

When the rishis of that forest learned of Viraadha's death, they flocked to Rama and surrounded him, saying, "It is our good fortune, O King." "that you have chosen to live in this area Following that, we will conduct our penance without interference from raakshasas. Look at all those bones all over the place. They are the corpses of ascetics who were slain and devoured by raakshasas. The rishis on the banks of the Pampa and Mandaakini rivers live in perpetual fear of these man-eating creatures.

"The King's duty, which he may not fail without sin, is to defend his subjects; just as homeowners pay taxes, a portion of the merit of our penances goes to the King's advantage."

Rama responded: "I am compelled to execute your command, O great ones; I gave up royalty and came to the forest in response to my father's will; and if in carrying out my duty as a son, I may also serve you and accomplish some good, I will count myself double blessed.

"I'll stay in the forest and slay the raakshasas, freeing you from your troubles. Get rid of your apprehension."

Rama's promise of assistance brought relief and joy to the rishis. Rama, Lakshmana, and Sita then proceeded towards Suteekshna's ashrama, where they came to a large hill surrounded by a dense forest, which they entered, where they saw bark garments drying in the sun and later came across the old rishi himself.

The Prince saluted him and said: "O holy sage, my name is Rama. I've come to have your blessing. I beseech your favour."

The sage stood up and hugged him "Welcome, dharma defender. Your presence brightens my ashrama. It's yours now. I knew you'd come here when I heard you'd left Ayodhya for Chitrakoota, and I've lived in anticipation of meeting you ever since. Otherwise, I would have given up this body long ago.

"I now pass on the virtue I have earned to you; take it for yourself, your brother, and the princess." The sage's face shone with the brightness of a long holy life.

"O sage, I must gain merit by my own good deeds, which I still want to achieve with your blessing. I wish to reside in the forest, and the sage Sarabhanga directed me here to receive your blessing and seek your advice on where I could build a home for the rest of my stay in the forest."

"You may dwell in this ashrama. There are many rishis living around. The forest is full of fruit and roots. But bad creatures are abroad tormenting the rishis and impeding their penance. The sages are unable to tolerate this difficulty. But the place is good," the rishi remarked seriously.

The Prince realised what the sage was saying. "Holy sage! I shall murder these evil-doers. My bow is strong, and my arrows are piercing. It is not suitable that we reside in this ashrama. It may disturb your penance. We shall find a place for ourselves in the neighbourhood. Permit us to do so."

They spent the night as guests in the sage's ashrama. The next morning, the three rose and washed in the cool, scented water, kindled the sacrificial fire, did their ritual, and touched the sage's feet.

"By your grace, we had a pleasant night; we want to see the other rishis in the region and obtain their blessings; it is best to go before the sun gets too hot; please give us permission to depart."

"Visit the good rishis in the Dandaka forest. They have all gone through great austerities and obtained divine powers. The forest is indeed beautiful, with deer and birds and lotus-filled tanks, and the hills with cascades and peacocks. Lakshmana, go now with your brother and Sita. Come to this ashrama whenever you feel like it," the sage said to the princes.

The three walked around the sage as is customary and then left him. Sita handed them their swords, arrows, and quivers, and the princes set out, brighter than before thanks to the great sage's blessings.

CHAPTER XXIV: TEN YEARS PASS

THE Aranya Kaanda begins now. The princes were charged with annihilating the raakshasas who were wreaking havoc on the ashramas and tormenting the rishis who lived in the Dandaka forest. Sita's heart was filled with fear, like a shadow cast by impending events.

"Why should you and Lakshmana, who are going to be simple ascetics in the forest," Sita questioned of her beloved husband, "carry on this responsibility of protection? You've come to fulfil a commitment made by the late King. The ruler who is now governing is responsible for protecting the rishis. It is not your responsibility, as a penitent, to safeguard rishis. Killing anyone, save in self-defence, is against the vows of monastic life. But you have rashly pledged the rishis protection. I'm curious where this will take us."

Thus Sita argued softly and affectionately as they travelled from Sage Suteekshna's ashrama to another ashrama in the Dandaka jungle.

"Bear with me, my lord, for appearing to counsel you," she added. "Out of my infinite love for you, I speak as a weak woman. You understand what dharma is. Men, however, are believed to be pushed by desire into three types of sin: deception, lust, and violence. Falsehood is unfathomable in someone who has renounced a kingdom for the sake of truth and is now in the forest. And, as for lust, I'm sure you won't allow the thought of another lady to enter your head. But I am terrified of the third type of sin. Should we murder someone who does not assault us? Why should we kill everyone who leaves us alone, whether it's a raakshasa or not?

"You seemed rushed to deliver your word to the rishis. The duty of a Kshatriya is undoubtedly to destroy the wicked, but can that obligation still attach to you after you have forsaken the benefits that come with it and chosen the life of a recluse in the forest? The obligations of kingship are associated with the actual status. You are now an ascetic, plain and simple, dressed in bark clothing and with matted hair. Of course, you are the expert. I'm only urging you to think carefully before doing anything."

Rama's feelings for Sita grew stronger as a result of her reservations. "Indeed, my dear," he responded, "you speak like Janaka's daughter. But, Sita, have you not stated that the weapons carried by Kshatriyas are for the protection of others? How could a Kshatriya remain silent when helpless people are persecuted? When we arrived, the sages bemoaned their plight and begged us to defend them. They couldn't bear the cruelty of the raakshasas, who devoured them and destroyed the hermitages. Didn't they show us a huge pile of bones to indicate what had happened? 'You are the king's son,' they informed him. 'Our troubles will now come to an end as the sun rises.' 'You are our only hope.' Could we princes hear their heartfelt plea and refuse to assist them? Everyone, not just the king, must do his or her duties as a Kshatriya. Of course, you're concerned about my safety. Even if what you say is correct, I have given my word and cannot back out. They responded, 'You are our refuge,' and I promised to protect them. A pledge made in this manner cannot be retracted. What I have spoken cannot now be undone. You and I must walk the path of dharma together. How can we disagree?" They walked along the forest trail, talking as they went.

Rama, Lakshmana, and Sita lived quietly among the rishis for ten years. There were a number of ashramas in the immense Dandaka forest where the rishis practised their austerities and lived their lives of abnegation. As welcome and pleasant visitors, the princes stayed a month in one ashrama, three months in another, and possibly a year in a third.

When the end of their woodland life was approaching after ten years, Rama desired to see the sage Agastya who resided in the south. The sage, like Vishvamitra, was well-known across the three worlds. If all the wisdom and spiritual virtue between the Himalayas and the Vindhyas were placed on one scale and Agastya sat on the other, the southern scale would fall by his weight.

Rama first went to Agastya's younger brother's ashrama to gain his blessings before approaching Agastya himself. Rama continued south, nearing Agastya's house, and noted the brightness of the entire countryside, the birds and animals playing freely, and Brahmanas gathering flowers for prayer.

He instructed Lakshmana to go ahead and proclaim him to the sage. "Ramachandra, son of Dasaratha, has come with his brother and wife to seek the great sage's blessings," Lakshmana met one of the sage's pupils and sent word via him.

Agastya greeted the princes with open arms. "I heard you had come to live in Chitrakoota, and I was looking forward to your visit," he explained. "Your exile is coming to an end. Stay here in peace for the rest of it. This location is free of the fear of raakshasas."

"I am delighted to receive your benediction, and I thank you for your warm welcome," Rama replied. "But I pledged to guard the rishis of Dandaka, and now that I have your blessing, I must return to that forest."

And Agastya responded, "What you say is correct." The Sage then gave Rama the bow fashioned by Viswakarma for Vishnu, as well as an unlimited quiver and a sword. He blessed him, saying, "Rama, destroy the raakshasas with these weapons that Vishnu gave me long ago."

Agastya recommended that the prince spend the remainder of his exile at Panchavati. "May God bless you, O, Prince," Agastya exclaimed, "and take good care of Sita, who joyfully submits to hardships to which she was not born or accustomed for the love of you." Women are by nature enamoured of comfort and opposed to adversity, but Sita has none of these flaws. Ramachandra, wherever you go, with Lakshmana and Sita by your side, the place will be filled with beauty. But Panchavati is a lovely place, and Sita will be happy to dwell there, safe in your arms. There is an abundance of fruit and roots. Continue to stay on the Godaavari's bank. Your exile period is coming to an end. You will soon fulfil your father's wish. Dasaratha, like Yayaati, is served by his eldest son."

CHAPTER XXV: THE SHURPANAKHA EPISODE

FOLLOWING Agastya's instructions, the Princes and Sita travelled to Panchavati. On the way, they came across a massive person perched on a large tree. They mistook it for a Rakshasa.

"Who are you?" Rama demanded angrily. The vulture, on the other hand, responded with gentleness and affection: "My darling, I am your father's ancient friend." Jataayu was the brother of Sampaati, the son of Aruna the dawn god, who was also the brother of Garuda, Vishnu's magnificent Eagle-vehicle. "When you leave Sita alone and go hunting in the wilderness, I will care for her safety," he said. The prince was happy and gratefully accepted the offer of the bird. They then continued their voyage.

Rama was awestruck by the grandeur of Panchavati and thanked Agastya in his thoughts for recommending the location to them. He said to Lakshmana: "We can construct an ashrama and dwell for as long as we choose. Those hills are close but not too close. Look at those deer herds. Everything is lovely: the trees with their blooms and delightfully singing birds, the river, and the pristine sand. Choose a suitable location for us and construct a cottage." Lakshmana did as he was instructed and built an ashrama. Rama complimented Lakshmana's craftsmanship because of its expertise and speed. Rama and Sita lived peacefully in an ashrama in Panchavati, lovingly tended by Lakshmana.

One early winter morning, the three went to the Godaavari as usual for a bath, to offer their morning prayers, and to draw water for the day's necessities. They walked together, talking about how lovely the season was. Lakshmana considered Bharata and how he would be preoccupied with the month's ceremonies. He stated: "Bharata is entitled to live in ease, but he has chosen to live in difficulty because we live in adversity in the jungle. My heart is breaking for him. Even in this bitter cold, poor Bharata must eat sparingly and sleep on the bare floor. What a blessing it is to have such a noble brother! He leads an austere life for our sake, being pure in mind, speech, and conduct and foregoing all pleasures. He is identical to our wonderful father and diametrically opposed to his mother. How could such a terrible woman as Kaikeyi bear such a good son?"

Rama interrupted him and said, "Talk all you want about Bharata and our father, but stop condemning mother Kaikeyi. Everything you say about Bharata is true, and my thoughts today are with him in love. How long before we see him again? When are we going to experience that pleasure, Lakshmana? When will we four brothers be able to live together again? Bharata's beautiful words are still ringing in my ears." On that early winter morning, they bathed in the Godaavari, thinking longingly of home and Bharata.

Rama awoke transfigured like Lord Shiva and returned to the ashrama with Lakshmana after offering oblations to their ancestors and prayers to the sun. After their morning responsibilities were over, they sat passing the time by reminiscing about the good old days and telling stories from the past.

While they were reliving the past in beautiful companionship, a Rakshasa woman appeared and spotted them. She was Ravana's sister, Shurpanakha, and she was wandering the jungle with the idle musings of a well-fed but ill-taught adolescent. She was hideously ugly, but she possessed the magical ability to transform into any attractive shape at pleasure. When she witnessed Rama's god-like magnificence, she was overcome with uncontrolled longing for him. She pondered, "He'd be disgusted by my own form. I'll adjust my appearance before approaching him." She transformed into a lovely young lady and appeared before him like the full moon. Her slim figure looked like a golden creeper climbing Heaven's Kalpaka tree. Her fawn-coloured eyes complemented her gorgeous lips and teeth. Her walk was like that of a peacock. Her anklets made a melody as she approached. Rama looked up and saw this ravishingly beautiful creature. She stooped down and placed her hand on his foot. She then stepped back a little, modestly covering her eyes.

Rama greeted her as though she were a tourist from a foreign land and inquired: "Which is your position? What is your given name? Who are your relatives?"

She replied: "I am the granddaughter of Brahma's grandson. Kubera is my younger brother. Another is Ravana, Kailash's conqueror. My name is Kaamavalli, and I am a maiden."

"And what is your reason for coming here?"

"It is improper for a lady to express her inner turmoil. But I believe I should say something. My heart has been invaded by the God of Love. You have the ability and responsibility to save me."

She took a breather. Rama remained deafeningly silent. She continued.

"You may marry me using Gandharva customs. You are aware that it is permissible for lovers to meet in this manner. Once we are linked in this way, not only will we be happy, but you and my brother, the great Ravana, will become friends. You're alone in the woods, and the Rakshasas will molest you. Even if you don't provoke them, they'll bother you since you're dressed as an ascetic. If you marry me, you will be safe from all of this. Not only that, but my powerful personnel will be ready to assist you in any manner they can. Consider this carefully." As a result, she argued for her desire to be fulfilled, claiming authority and appealing to Rama's self-interest as well.

Rama laughed, exposing his sparkling whites. Sita was approaching them via the bushes and creepers, disguised as another creeper. Shurpanakha noticed her beauty and admired it. Shurpanakha, enraged by lust and unaware of who she was, told Rama: "This young woman is a Raakshasi in human form. She has come to trick you. Be cautious of her. This isn't her true shape. She is a Raakshasi who consumes raw meat. Get rid of her. I'm not interested in her." Rama laughed once more. "You are wise indeed," he responded. "You've discovered the truth about her."

Meanwhile, Sita had arrived and was standing by Rama. Shurpanakha couldn't figure out why Rama was laughing. She'd completely lost her mind in her passion. SShe hissed: "Why are you approaching my hero, Raakshasi? Get out of here." Sita, perplexed and terrified, clung to the prince's shoulder, becoming a lightning flash embracing a rain-bearing cloud.

She became outraged at the sight of Sita. "This pitiful little insect stands between you and me. Look. I'm going to end her right now. I can't survive without you. You and I will live happily ever after once I have moved her out of the way." After saying this, she made a menacing motion toward Sita.

Rama realised the situation had gone too far and said: "Please stop, dear woman, lest my brother hears you. When he becomes furious, he loses his cool. I recommend that you return the way you came as soon as possible." Rama brought Sita with him into the hermitage after saying this.

The Raakshasi spent the night someplace, somehow, the fire of her need unquenched. She had this notion in the morning: "If I don't get this man, I'll die. He will never come near me as long as this woman is with him. I need to find a way to kidnap her and hide her somewhere so that I can win his affection." She returned to the ashrama, her mind made up.

Sita was alone in the ashrama because Rama had gone to the river for his morning ablutions and prayer. Shurpanakha saw this as her opportunity to abduct her. She was unaware that Lakshmana was nearby in the woods. She dashed over to Sita. Lakshmana yelled and jumped on the Raakshasi. He kicked her and drew his sword while clutching her hair.

When attacked, Shurpanakha reverted to her original form and attacked Lakshmana. Lakshmana quickly seized her, mutilated her nose and ear, and drove her away. Shurpanakha, humiliated and mutilated, wailed loudly and vanished into the jungle.

She pushed herself onto the ground in front of Khara, who was sitting in state with his colleagues, bleeding and enraged. She yelled angrily as she told the story of her wrongs. The ridicule and mutilation she had experienced were an affront to the Rakshasa race that only blood could wash away.

She stated: "Take a look at me. Rama and Lakshmana did this, and they are still alive and well in your kingdom. And you're doing nothing."

Khara sprang to her feet and stated: "What is this, my beloved sister? Nothing makes sense to me. Calm down and tell me what happened. Who dared to do this to you, and where is he in this forest? Who is he who wishes to be eaten by birds and vultures? Who is that fool? Tell me, and he'll die right away. The ground yearns for his blood. Stand up and tell me exactly what occurred."

"Two gorgeous young men," Shurpanakha claimed, "had entered the jungle while dressed as ascetics and accompanied by a girl. They claim to be Dasaratha's sons. These two, using the girl as a reason, attacked me and brutally injured me. I'm thirsting for these bastards' blood. Kill them first. Everything else can be postponed."

Khara directed his generals and commanded them: "Go right away, slaughter these individuals, and bring their lifeless bodies back. Bring the woman with you. Do not postpone."

Fourteen generals were dispatched to do his bidding.

CHAPTER XXVI: KHARA AND HIS ARMY LIQUIDATED

SHURPANAKHA returned to Rama's ashrama, accompanied by the fourteen generals of Khara, determined to avenge herself and suck the blood of the princes. "Look, there stand the men who insulted and maimed me," she said to her bodyguard, pointing to the two young men. "Kill them right away." Rama immediately saw the situation and urged Lakshmana, "Take care of Sita for a moment while I deal with those fellows." He took up his bow after saying this.

Following the rules of war, Rama introduced himself to Khara's generals and said, "Tell us why you've come here. Know that we are here in the jungle at the request of the rishis to destroy their foes. Leave us alone if you want to escape with your life." But the Rakshasas desired battle, not peace. And thus the fight began. Rama's arrows annihilated the Rakshasa generals in record time.

Shurpanakha returned to Khara, crying loudly. He couldn't believe the annihilation of the formidable squad he had dispatched. With gentle words, he attempted to calm his upset sister. "I have sent unconquerable warriors, each one like Yama. They must have completed their mission by now. Why do you cry? Why should you moan when I'm here?"

"True, you sent your fourteen warriors with me," Shurpanakha murmured, wiping her tears away. "But the fourteen are now dead, stiff and cold, slaughtered by Rama, whose weaponry defies description. If you have a sense of pride, fight Rama and save the Rakshasa race right away. If you do not, our people will be annihilated. These young men who have joined your satrapy are intended to annihilate your race unless you meet and eliminate them first." These words, spoken aloud in front of all his courtiers by his sister, pierced Khara's heart.

"Why are you so afraid of a mere human being? Hold your breath for a moment, and you'll have his blood to drink." Khara rose as he said this.

"Don't go alone!" she exclaimed. "Bring your troops along."

Khara gave the appropriate orders. Dooshana led a massive army that was fully armed into battle. Khara rode gracefully on a chariot behind the army. Rama and Lakshmana readied for battle after hearing the chaotic sounds of the approaching army. "Do you see the signs?" Rama asked Lakshmana. "The Rakshasas of Janasthaana are undoubtedly heading here to die! I see the brightness of the victory that awaits us in your face. Arm yourself and accompany Sita to a cave on the hill to look for her. I will confront and annihilate the Rakshasa hordes. Go all at once. I don't need anyone's assistance." Rama put on his armour and strung his bow while he said this.

Lakshmana followed Rama's advice and led Sita to a mountain cave.

Rama stood in front of the advancing Rakshasa soldiers, bow in hand, his face glowing like Rudra's when he bent Pinaaka, his huge bow. The Rakshasas marched forward in a triumphant procession, drums and horns and the clanging panoply of war filling the quarters with tumult and sending the inhabitants of the forest stampeding in all directions. Rakshasa hordes surrounded Rama like vast black clouds disrupting the sun.

The fight began. A continual stream of lethal arrows rushed from Rama's bow, and the Rakshasa ranks wilted and fell like moths before a raging fire.

Dooshana was now standing in front of Rama. Rama drew his bow and shot his shafts in all directions at once. Arrows burst out from the location where Rama stood, spread out in all directions, and brought down warriors, chariots, elephants, and horses at the speed of light. The shafts pierced the Rakshasas' bodies and emerged, covered in their blood and glowing like fire. The army had been destroyed, and Rama had come to a halt. Dooshana returned with another massive army. For a while, he appeared unstoppable. But Rama's arrows eventually took out his chariot, drivers, and horses. He leapt down and towards Rama. Rama's arrows, on the other hand, cut his arms from his trunk, and he died on the ground like a massive elephant. Other Rakshasas rushed against Rama when they saw Dooshana fall and were killed by the arrows that shot from his bow.

The entire Khara army was exterminated in this manner. It had roared like an ocean and now lay motionless, a tangle of corpses and severed limbs, derelict weapons, and broken chariots. Khara and Trisiras were the only survivors. As Khara approached Rama, Trisiras stopped him, stating, "I shall go first and murder Rama. You might meet him when I fail to accomplish this."

Rakshasa, riding in his chariot, assaulted Rama with his arrows. Rama fired arrows that hissed like poisonous serpents at them. Trisiras collapsed, spitting blood. His supporters bolted like deer. When Khara saw this, he yelled "Hold" to the fugitives and directed his chariot at Rama. His self-assurance had faded, yet he battled valiantly. The two warriors' shafts blanketed the sky. Khara rode his chariot like Yama, shooting his torrent of arrows. Rama leaned on his bow for a split second. During that time, Rama's armour was pierced by Khara's arrows, revealing the Prince's body to be as bright as the sun. Rama used Vishnu's bow to bring down Khara's chariot and cut his bow in half. Khara then approached Rama with his mace.

Rama shouted, "You have been a terror and a plague to mankind! Body strength offers no protection to an evildoer. You have harassed and murdered rishis performing penance in the wilderness. You will now receive the punishment you deserve for your sins. The ghosts of the rishis whose flesh you ate are now watching over you from their aerial chariots. I've come to the Dandaka jungle to annihilate the evil Rakshasas. My arrows will puncture the flesh of all your relatives."

Khara shouted, "Human worm! Dasaratha's son! You are pleased with yourself because you have killed a few common Rakshasas. A hero does not brag like you do. Only a Kshatriya who has been exiled by his people can boast like this. You've demonstrated your ability to boast. Let us test whether you can fight now! I'm standing here, mace in hand, ready to kill you. The evening is approaching. Expect to lose your life. I've come to avenge the deaths of my followers, whom you have slaughtered." Having said this, he twirled his mace and flung it towards Rama. Rama's arrows broke the mace into splinters that dropped harmlessly to the ground.

"Rakshasa, have you finished speaking? You will die now. This forest will be protected in the future, and the rishis will live in peace," Rama remarked. Even as Rama was speaking, Khara yanked a massive tree from its roots and tossed it towards Rama, but Rama split it with his arrows. Fearing more delay, he hurled lethal darts at Khara. Rakshasa lunged at Rama, intending to close with him, but the latter avoided contact by moving back, and killed him with a shaft that clove his chest.

The Devas rejoiced as flowers fell from heaven, proclaiming, "Rama has killed the evil Rakshasa. Men will be able to live in peace in the Dandaka forest in the future. Rama destroyed Khara, Dooshana, Trisiras, and their entire army in less than an hour. He is, indeed, a hero."

Sita and Lakshmana came back from the cave. Lakshmana embraced Rama and was overjoyed that he had fulfilled the rishis' pledge of protection on his own.

CHAPTER XXVII: THE PATH OF RUIN

"ALMOST all of our people who occupied Janasthaana are dead, and Janasthaana is now an empty ruin," said Akampana, one of the few Rakshasas who survived the great slaughter at Panchavati. "I was the only one who made it out alive."

Ravana was filled with rage. "Who destroyed my lovely Janasthaana?" he yelled angrily. "Who was it, Yama, Agni, or Vishnu? I'm going to kill the god of death. I will destroy both the god of fire and the sun. I will strangle and suffocate the wind god. Tell me, who destroyed Janasthaana and slaughtered my men, oblivious to the fact that I am here to avenge them? Speak up right away."

It was always problematic to bring bad news to tyrants. "I shall speak if you grant me shelter," Akampana murmured, terrified by the king's fury. "Rama, son of Dasaratha, a young warrior, lion-like in furious ferocity, a hero who has already gained fame among mankind, fought with Khara and Dooshana at Panchavati and annihilated them," he explained. "What are you talking about?" exclaimed the Rakshasa monarch, hissing like a cobra. "What caused this to happen? Did Indra and the divine hosts descend to earth to fight with Rama?"

"No such thing happened, great king," Akampana replied. "Rama stood alone against our entire army and its commanders and destroyed them all, including Khara and Dooshana. Rama's deadly arrows, which resembled five-headed serpents, followed and destroyed the Rakshasas wherever they went." And he went on to explain Rama's ability and speed with his weapons in detail. And so Ravana learned that Dasaratha's son, Rama, was at Panchavati with his younger brother Lakshmana, and that he had done it all alone, without even his brother's assistance, and that no gods had come to their rescue.

"Well, I don't understand this," Ravana said, "but I'll start right now. I will return and exterminate these little worms of men." And he got up.

"Hear me, great king, before you go," Akampana continued, emphasising Rama's power and courage once more.

"Pay attention. Nobody can defeat Rama by fighting him. When I say 'no one,' I mean it. Evenyou can't do it. I dare to tell you the truth because you have pledged to protect me. There is only one way to get him. His wife is present. Her beauty is unparalleled on the planet. Rama will die if he is separated from her; that is how strong his love for her is. Consider how you can accomplish this. Do not even consider fighting him."

The Rakshasa's yearning was sparked when he learned about Sita's attractiveness. He began to believe that defeating Khara and his hosts was a lucky event that provided him with the opportunity to gain one more beautiful queen and wife. "I shall go tomorrow morning," he answered, grateful for Akampana's advice. "I believe your strategy is sound."

Ravana took off in his mule-yoked flying chariot, which sparkled like the moon among the clouds as it soared through the skies. He went right to Maareecha's house. Maareecha greeted his king and inquired as to what pressing need had brought him there. "Hear me, Maareecha," Ravana replied. "You are the only one who can assist me. Janasthaana was annihilated, as was the entire army I had stationed there. Rama, Dasaratha's son, is responsible for all of this. To avenge myself, I intend to kidnap his wife. I need your advice and assistance in this matter."

Maareecha, whose experience with Rama's power had scorched his soul, was terrified and tried to persuade Ravana to abandon his crazy venture. "What kind of scheme is this? Some enemy out to destroy you, but posing as your friend, has given you this plan to kidnap Sita. Whoever offered you this advice hopes the Rakshasa race has a happy ending. Don't you have a nice family and loving wives? Return to them, and enjoy your life and wealth. Wanting Rama's wife is a road to shame, humiliation, and the annihilation of the Rakshasa race."

Ten-headed Ravana returned to Lanka since Maareecha's advice seemed sound to him. Ravana must have then remembered the omission in his string of boons. He had gained immunity to all beings' attacks save men. Rama's shafts had defeated and killed the entire army, including Khara, Trisiras, Dooshana, and other great warriors. Ravana took Maareecha's advice after considering everything.

Ravana sat on his throne, surrounded by his counsellors. Majesty radiated on his face like a ghee-fed sacrifice flame, and his powerful frame bore the scars of numerous victories over gods, asuras, and others. He was unrivalled in torturing Devas, destroying sacrifices, and stealing women. The hosts of Devas and Asuras were terrified of him. He terrified all creatures. The ruler of Lanka knew no master or rival and feared neither God nor sin, enjoying prosperity and various pleasures and being free of the fear of death.

His shape was terrifying, with ten heads, big eyes, and massive limbs, but it also bore the hallmarks of the monarchy. As he sat on his throne, gorgeously adorned and bejewelled, surrounded by his ministers in the middle of the splendour of the despoiled world, his sister Shurpanakha appeared before him, bleeding and mangled, a shape of anguish and grief and disgrace. While everyone stared at her in startled stillness, her agony burst forth in searing words. "What a fool you are, engrossed in sensuous pleasures and arrogantly assured in your dominion, that you are not aware of the grave peril that threatens your existence right outside your door! Do you not know that your brothers, Khara, Dooshana, and Trisiras, as well as your valiant army of fourteen thousand strong Rakshasas, were slain by Rama, a mere mortal and that your outpost at Janasthaana was destroyed? I saw a single warrior stand high in the brilliant panoply of war one moment, and the next, they lay dead stained by that man's arrows, strewing the ground like ripe crops ravaged by a dreadful hail storm; and you see me, your sister, disgraced, mutilated, and heartbroken! Have you no plans for retribution, you hero, brother, and king?"

Ravana, hurt by her disrespect and moved by her anguish and sadness, remarked, "Be confident you will have vengeance. But who is this Rama? What kind of a man is he? What exactly are his weapons? What is he looking for in Dandaka Forest? And how did you come to be so mutilated?"

She described the brothers and Sita, focusing on the brothers' virile attractiveness and powers, most likely to arouse the Raakshas' envious jealousy, and waxing poetic over Sita's exceptional beauty. "I'm at a loss for words to describe her perfection. I've never seen such sublime beauty in anything produced. I'll also explain why this heinous crime was committed against me. When I saw this Sita, I felt that no one deserved her and that she was deserving of sharing your bed, therefore I tried to take her away for you out of love. Lakshmana, who was nearby, stopped it and, jumping on me, mutilated and degraded me in this way. All of this has been done for your sake. If you want to avenge this insult and safeguard the race's honour, get up and go right away.

"Aside from retaliation for the insult I've received, find yourself a woman worthy of you. The ghosts of the warriors who died at Dandaka would be delighted if you captured her and disgraced Rama. I, too, will feel that some restitution has been made for the disrespect done to me. You can easily seize Sita and claim her as your own. And are you able to ignore the insult to your race? Khara and Dooshana are both dead in Janasthaana for daring to resist Rama. Consider all of this and do what is right. Save, Lord, save our race's honour."

Ravana dissolved the council and retreated to muse alone after hearing his sister's words and her appreciation of Sita's beauty. He had to think again and again because of what Maareecha had told him. He weighed the pros and disadvantages and, after making a decision, ordered that a chariot be kept ready in secret.

His golden chariot, driven by mules with demon faces, was ready. He rode it across the sea, land, and towns. He arrived at Maareecha's ashrama and encountered Maareecha, an ascetic with matted hair and bark clothing. When Maareecha saw his king and kinsman, he exclaimed, "Why have you come all this way a second time and unannounced?"

Ravana, a skilled orator, said, "I am in serious danger, and only you can save me. Do you know how my brothers ruled Janasthaana under my orders, and how they and their troops faced no opposition all these years? But now Rama has slaughtered them and their entire army. The rishis now live fearlessly in the Dandaka forest, free of Rakshasas.

"This Rama is a useless prince who has been exiled by his father, most likely for some wrongdoing. He's been traversing the wilderness by himself with his wife, Sita. This man, clothed as an ascetic but enjoying all pleasures, proud of his might, has disfigured my sister's face and degraded our race for no other reason. My sister had come to me and cried about her anguish and embarrassment. Would I still be a king if I did nothing with all of this? To exact my revenge, I plan to kidnap Rama's wife from the Dandaka forest. I owe it to my race to shame and punish this Rama. And I need your assistance with this. I'm not afraid, with you by my side. Nobody on Earth can match your bravery, strength, skill, or magical abilities. That is why I've come to see you.

"You should transform yourself into a golden deer with silver spots, casting a spell on all eyes. Romp in front of Sita near Rama's ashrama in that shape. She will insist on Rama and Lakshmana pursuing and capturing you for her, as is typical of women. I'll easily carry her off if they're so engrossed and she's left alone. Sita is a stunning woman. Rama will surely languish in sorrow and lose his manly spirit if he loses such a bride. It will therefore be simple to assassinate him and avenge ourselves."

Maareecha locked his gaze on Ravana. His face turned pale, and his mouth felt parched. Ravana's scheme terrified him. Maareecha predicted what would happen based on his knowledge of Rama's abilities and his own wisdom gained through penance. Ravana's sinister plan had little chance of success, he knew. It was evident to him that fate had a rope around Ravana's neck, bringing him to his doom. He had spoken of the Rakshasas' honour, the duties of kingship, and the insult to Shurpanakha, but he was really motivated by a lusty desire to possess Sita. All this Maareecha saw.

CHAPTER XXVIII: THE GOLDEN STAG

Maareecha told Ravana, "I've heard everything you've spoken, my king, and I'm overcome with grief. Your spies did not tell you the whole story regarding Rama. Do not be misled by what others have told you about this Rama. He is not a renegade or a criminal, but a devoted son who is in the wilderness to keep his father's promise. Far from being a coward or a weakling, he is a powerful warrior without an equal in weapons. Don't make him your unyielding foe, bringing disaster to your people and kingdom. On your account, the Rakshasa race and Lanka itself shall be obliterated. Who gave you this awful advice that would lead you, your kingdom, and your species to peril and destruction? Who warned you he was a lover of pleasure and deception? Rama is the personification of dharma. He puts his power and courage to good use in the service of dharma. Rama is the first mortal man, just as Indra is the first among the gods.

"How could you look longingly at Sita? Will Sita ever surrender to you? Take her away from Rama! Rama can never be defeated in battle. Do not turn a deaf ear to my words, O Rakshasa Ruler. Do you recall how, boasting of my prowess, I once disrupted the rites and sacrifice of the sage Vishvamitra? Rama was a boy back then, and I came up against him. What do you believe happened? He shot an arrow that killed Subaahu instantly, and with another, he swept me off my feet and threw me into the sea. Rama has grown into a man, enormously stronger and more skilled in battle!

"Do not provoke his rage. Don't think about Sita and bring down destruction on your rich and lovely city, as well as certain death on yourself. I see the disaster that awaits you if you persist in your misguided project, O Ravana. I see Lanka in flames, her streets covered with bodies, and her widows and orphans weeping aloud. If you are unhappy with Rama, confront him and meet your end like a hero. Do not take a deceptive route and draw me along with you. Do not encourage Yama to race on your land!"

Thus, Maareecha argued fervently for Ravana's good, but he was neither pleased nor convinced. How could decent advice persuade a lustful victim? Ravana, like a sick man who refuses medicine, refused to listen to Maareecha's advice.

"If I were a king," Ravana remarked, "and I want to know if something should or should not be done, it is up to his counsel to weigh the benefits and drawbacks, but I have not come to you for such advice. I am King, and I have come to inform you that I have made the decision to do this. You disregard your responsibilities and dare to tell me that what I am considering is incorrect. You should do what I tell you to do, which isn't much. Transform yourself into a bizarre and attractive stag and appear in front of Sita to catch her eye. Sita will dispatch Rama to pursue and apprehend you. You should draw Rama away from you and mimic Rama's voice and call for aid. Sita will decide that Rama is in danger and will force Lakshmana to go to his aid. When she is alone, I will transport her to Lanka. You will be free to do whatever you want once you have completed this task for me. But understand that if you do not assist me right now, your life will be forfeited."

Maareecha pondered within himself. "Ravana, who is already in the grip of doom, will not listen to advice. He is being drawn to Yama by sinful desire. Rama killing me is preferable to Ravana killing me. At the very least, I would give up my life to an adversary."

As a result, he consented to the plan.

He stated: "I've given you sound counsel, but you won't take it. If I carry out your wishes, I am certain to die, but not more certain than that you will also die, not long after with everything you own. Someone who envies you has set you on this path because some of our enemies aim for our downfall. I'd rather be slain by an adversary I admire than by you. Let us go to Dandaka together."

Ravana rejoiced and embraced Maareecha, saying, "Now you are my dear old Maareecha again."

The two ascended the chariot and began their journey towards the Dandaka jungle. They soared above cities, mountains, rivers, and nations. When they arrived at Dandaka, they discovered Rama's ashrama in a banana garden. They landed at a distance, and Ravana took Maareecha's hand in his and told him to execute his role according to their plan, pointing to the ashrama.

Maareecha instantly changed into a magnificent deer. Every component of the animal was different in colour and wonderful in appearance. It enchanted the beholder's eye like a rainbow in the sky. It was like a living stream of pearls cascading over a lovely golden body.

The magical deer roamed here and there, now resting for a bit and then resuming its exquisite gambols. It would stoop and nibble on the grass on the ground, then raise its head to devour the fragile leaves of plants. Sita, who was collecting flowers in the forest at the time, gazed in awe at the stag's wonderful beauty. The deer, too, glanced back at her and darted in front of her, adding a new dimension to the environment.

"Come take a look! Come take a look!" Sita called out, anxious for Rama and Lakshmana to witness the magnificent stag.

"Come swiftly, come quickly!" she exclaimed. Rama and Lakshmana emerged from the home, stunned by the gorgeous creature's beauty.

Lakshmana became suspicious. It appeared to him to be a Rakshasa disguised as a deer. Both Rama and Lakshmana had heard about Maareecha and how, in the appearance of a deer, he would frequently deceive and destroy anyone who came to hunt deer in the forest.

Lakshmana warily said, "This is no ordinary creature. This is a Rakshasa technique."

However, Sita pleaded with Ram: "Please capture this deer for me. We'll raise it as a pet in the ashrama. This is the most lovely creature I've ever seen. Please catch it for me."

Sita noticed that Lakshmana didn't seem to like her intrusion. This just fueled her determination to urge Rama to obtain it for her. "Look, it's all gold!" she exclaimed. "Take a look now! Everything is silver! If you can't catch the monster alive, at least take it down with an arrow and give us the skin. We will never see such lovely flesh again. It would be a nice place to sit. Look. It is being phased out. Go ahead and catch it alive. Otherwise, give me at least the skin."

Rama could no longer ignore her advances. He also instructed Lakshmana to fetch him his bow and arrows. Although Lakshmana's heart was not in it, he followed.

And Rama began by saying, "But, Lakshmana, stay by Sita's side and keep a close eye on her. I'll be returning shortly, either alive or dead, with this stag. Do not be concerned. What difference does it make if this is a Rakshasa? It doesn't matter if you're a stag or a Rakshasa."

He stated once more, "Take care. Remember, Sita. Everything can happen at any time. Maintain vigilance."

Lakshmana, who was normally fast and eager to act, was suspicious on this occasion, while Rama, who was usually careful, surrendered to Sita's stupid wish and proceeded in search of the Maareecha-stag, ignoring Lakshmana's warning.

Maareecha kept Rama in sight but out of reach, drawing him further away to give Ravana plenty of time and chance. The deer would go a few feet, then come to a halt and turn to face the pursuer. Then, as though in panic, it would begin. It would vanish among the woods for a while. It would soon appear on some lofty mound, its gorgeous outline framed against a passing cloud. This continued till Maareecha brought Rama far away. The Rakshasa then realised that this game would not go forever and that his death was approaching. Rama, bored with the chase, drew his bow and fired an arrow. It slashed the stag. Maareecha reverted to his normal shape and, imitating Rama's voice, exclaimed, "Ah Sita, Ah Lakshmana!" before collapsing.

"Lakshmana was correct," Rama thought to himself. "Yes, this deer was a Rakshasa."

He considered it further, "Sita may be duped after hearing his final cry. She will most likely be overcome by terror."

He then repeated to himself, "What if Sita has irrational fears? Lakshmana is at her side."

His heart filled with pride and excitement at having a brother like Lakshmana, who was so devoted and steady. How would Rama know what was going on in the ashrama at the time, and what agonising words Lakshmana had to hear from Sita?

CHAPTER XXIX: THE GOOD BIRD JATAAYU

"Ah, Sita!" Ah, Lakshmana!" So cried Maareecha, impersonating Rama. And Sita was duped. "There, Lakshmana, do you not hear your brother's voice?" she shouted, trembling like a plantain tree in a hurricane. "Run, run to his assistance!"

Overwhelmed by terror and seeing Lakshmana unable to move, she cried out in agony to Lakshmana, "I hear my Lord's voice in despair. Go, go, go!" she exclaimed. "He is in grave danger. Did you not hear his cries for assistance? Why are you still here? Your brother is almost certainly encircled by Rakshasas and screams out for aid. Instead of rushing to his aid, you remain stationary!"

Lakshmana was well aware of the Rakshasas' cunning and remembered his brother's command. He refused to move.

Sita became enraged in her anguish of fear and doubt. She beat her breasts with both fists and said angrily, "Son of Sumitra! Have you also become a foe? Have you been a fraud all these years? Have you been with us only to see Rama die? Pretending to be his friend, were you wishing for his death to protect my future? Why else would you stand here, vile creature, and refuse to come to his aid when he calls out? Traitor! Imposter!"

Like poisoned arrows, these terrible remarks pierced Lakshmana's heart. He used his hands to cover his ears. "Vaidehi, Rama can meet and defeat any foe in the world," he said gently to Sita, who was in tears of rage. "There is no need to be concerned. Keep your cool. Nobody in the cosmos has the power to touch or harm our Rama. My mother, what you have said is unworthy of you. Rama will undoubtedly return with the body of the desired stag.

"We did not hear his voice. It's a Rakshasa's ruse. Do not be duped into grieving for nothing. My brother has assigned me to keep an eye on you. Do not request that I leave you alone and go. I can't defy my brother. You have nothing to be terrified of."

But Sita's terror escalated to a fever pitch, and she shouted the fateful words: "Taking advantage of what you call your brother's command, you stand unmoved by his cries of misery and are willing to let him perish! Oh, Rama and me, how totally you've been misleading us all these years! Do you delight, you deceitful man, that Rama is in danger? Now I understand why you followed us into the forest. Have you been manipulated by Bharata? Have you all turned against my lord? Have you all joined forces in a sinister plot? Will I ever look at you or another, having lived with Rama? When Rama passes away, I pass away with him. I am certain about it."

Sita flew into a wrath that fully engulfed Lakshmana. Like poisoned arrows, her vicious words pierced and burned into him. He clasped his hands in prayer and exclaimed, "O Mother! Greetings, Goddess! How can such words come out of your mouth? These are cruel and unjust thoughts of yours. I swear to all the gods that your suspicion is incorrect. After all, you are a woman who, like most women, is quick to judge others. I'm afraid a tremendous catastrophe is on its way for you. You couldn't have thought and spoken ill of me otherwise."

And the defenceless Lakshmana shuddered in terror of the impending disaster.

"Look here, there's lots of dry firewood," Sita replied. "I'm going to start a fire and fall into it. Or else I'll drown in the Godavari. Unless you quickly seek the assistance of Rama, I will hang myself. Will you not depart, I ask once more?

This was too much for Lakshmana. "Very well, sister," he responded, raising his hands in serious adoration. "I will obey you while disobeying my brother. I'm going to leave you alone. May you be safe and healthy! May the woodland gods keep you safe! I will carry out your instructions. I'm getting an awful feeling. I'm not sure I'll ever see you with Rama again. But I'm going!"

Before Lakshman went to look after Rama, he chanted some mantras and drew a line surrounding the boundary of the cottage. He pleaded with Sita not to cross the border, whatever may happen, and wait until he and Rama returned. The boundary was meant to protect Sita from anyone who would dare to cross it. The line would burn anyone other than Rama, Lakshman, and Sita. And he went, reluctantly, occasionally looking back and praying that Sita does not cross the Lakshman Rekha.

Lakshmana walked with a disturbed heart, burdened with rage and sadness. How could he withstand Sita's venomous words? How could he have forgotten them? The prince's heart had been severely hurt because he had given up everything to be with his brother.

Lakshmana went in the same direction as Rama. Ravana, who had been anticipating this moment, now approached Rama's ashrama. He changed into a mendicant ascetic, dressed in immaculate saffron robes, and his lips murmured lovely Vedic melodies.

Sita stood at the cottage's door, her gaze set on the forest, eagerly waiting for Rama. Ravana looked at Sita.

The desire placed in his heart by Shurpanakha took strong root and was quickly irresistible. He was more determined than ever to get his hands on Sita.

Ravana chanted the name of Shiva and came close to the hut.

Sita heard his chants and observed him.

"O divine lady, I beg of you for some alms," he said. "I have been travelling far away and would like to rest and regain my strength."

"Certainly, O Messenger of God, It would be an honour to serve you," Sita replied, "However, due to my circumstances, I cannot cross the boundary."

"What ill circumstances you talk of, O lady? I could be of service," he replied.

Sita recounted the story to him of how Rama followed the golden deer and his ailing voice that she and Lakshmana heard. And how she sent away Lakshmana, who was assigned to guard her, to look for her husband. While leaving, Lakshmana drew the boundary for her protection, and because of this, she could not serve him as requested.

Ravana heard her plight and said, "O lady, if you cannot cross the boundary, allow me to come inside and rest."

Ravana tried to cross the boundary and realised it was a powerful mantra, and he could not reach Sita unless she came to him.

Disturbed and enraged, he states, "O lady, if you do not give me alms, I will curse you and your future generations for this demeanour."

A reluctant Sita then calms him and goes inside the hut to fetch food and water. She comes out with a plateful of fruits and crosses the Lakshman Rekha.

The ascetic sat down and returned his gaze to Sita. His desire intensified. Even as a Rakshasa and a sinner, he had the instinct to capture her heart; he desired not to ravish, but to acquire Sita's ready assent and make her his wife.

The King of Lanka desired and hoped to convince Sita. He expected her to turn her back on poverty-stricken Rama in exchange for his wealth and influence. He also believed that this would be the most effective manner of defaming and punishing Rama. He anticipated Sita to act like the other women he'd met.

Seated in front of Sita's fruits and roots, the ascetic began to laud Sita's beauty in language that was far too effusive for a genuine ascetic. The guest gradually disclosed himself and described the greatness of his background and family, his power and fortune. He exalted himself before running down Rama and concluding. "Be my wife and have a lovely life in Lanka with me. Come on, let's go!"

Sita's purity gave her the strength to defy the powerful monster, whom she now saw for what he was. "Base and evil fellow! Your demise is imminent. If you want to live, leave this ashrama," she hissed.

The Rakshasa was enraged. He abandoned all pretence of camouflage and tenderness and assumed his true domineering wickedness. He grabbed her hair with one hand and picked her up and took her to the chariot that was waiting for him beyond the woods, forcing her into it and rising with her into the air.

"O my lord!" exclaimed Sita. "Where have you gone, Rama? Oh, Lakshmana, most devoted of companions, why did I drive you away with stubborn folly?"

The Rakshasa gripped her tightly and drove away in the aerial car. Sita pleaded with the trees and plants below to inform Rama of her fate.

The chariot happened to pass by while old Jataayu was half-asleep on a tree. He was startled awake by a woman's distressed cry and recognised Sita by her voice. She also spotted him and begged him to save her.

The sight of her pitiful situation ignited Jataayu's blood, and he placed himself in the path of the aerial chariot, yelling, "Hold, hold! What exactly is this?"

"The King of Lanka is forcibly dragging me away," Sita lamented, "but what can you do to stop it, my poor old friend? Fly to Rama and Lakshmana and tell them about my terrible situation!"

But Jataayu's fighting blood, the blood of generations of lordly ancestors who ruled the air and knew no fear, was on fire; he didn't care about Ravana and his might; he only saw a princess in distress; he remembered his friend Dasaratha and his promise to Rama, and he was determined that this atrocity should not happen while he was still alive to prevent it.

"Oh king, I am Jatayu, king of the eagles, a king like you," Jataayu said directly to Ravana. "Pay attention, brother king! Please refrain from this heinous conduct. How can you call yourself a king and do such a heinous crime? Isn't it a king's duty to safeguard women's honour? Sita is also a princess. I warn you that unless you leave her and go, you will perish.

"I'm old and unarmed, while you're youthful, fully equipped, and riding in a chariot.' But I can't stand by and watch you kidnap Sita. Why are you acting so cowardly behind Rama's back? If you have a complaint against him, confront him. You'd fly away from me, wouldn't you? You will not be able to flee while I am still alive! Get out of your chariot and fight if you're not a coward and a thief!"

Ravana erupted in a rage. He assaulted Jataayu. It was like a powerful wind colliding with a large rain cloud. The conflict raged above the woodland in the sky. Jataayu fought with the ferocity of a winged mountain.

Ravana hurled lethal darts at him. But the eagle intercepted them all and tore Ravana's flesh with his talons. Rakshasa, angry, launched pointed, serpent-like projectiles at the bird.

Jatayu was severely injured, but fought on unafraid, while Sita observed the unequal battle with a racing heart and tears in her eyes. Jataayu's attacks on Ravana became much more ferocious when he saw her. But his years were catching up with him, and he felt compelled to gather all of his might for a heroic endeavour to conquer. Regardless of his wounds, he charged Ravana with his wings, breaking off and throwing down his jewelled crown and robbing him of his bow. He attacked the chariot, killing the demon-faced mules and the charioteer before smashing it into a thousand pieces. Ravana collapsed to the ground, embracing Sita. The elements rejoiced at Ravana's defeat.

The valiant old bird swooped down on Ravana's back, ripping large chunks of flesh from it and attempting to twist off the arms that held Sita. But Ravana had twenty arms, and as soon as one was removed, another took its place, and Sita was kept helplessly writhing. Ravana finally released Sita and unsheathed his blade, severing the bird's wings and talons. The old bird had become helpless and had fallen to the ground, unable to move.

Sita dashed forward, embraced Jataayu, and shouted, "O my father! You have sacrificed your life for my cause. You are my Lord's second father! And now you're gone. Oh, our courageous and loving companion!"

Ravana then turned around to pick her up again. She raced helplessly here and thither, weeping. She sobbed as she clutched to the trees. "Where have you gone, Rama? Where have you gone, Lakshmana? Will you not come to my aid?" The Rakshasa finally caught up with her and ascended into the air.

Sita straining in his hands seemed like a flash of lightning across a big black cloud as the dark and massive Ravana sailed with her in the sky. The Rakshasa carrying her resembled a forest fire on a mountain. Ravana's body, illuminated by Sita, raced across the sky like a disastrous comet.

The Rakshasa thus carried Sita away. The sun faded, and the earth was plunged into darkness. Looking skyward, the earth's dumb creatures shed tears. Ravana flew away from the princess, brutally grabbing her. The petals from the flowers she was wearing at the moment tumbled down as she was taken away, and as they were strewn along the path below, they seemed to signal the scattering of Ravana's prosperity and affluence.

CHAPTER XXX: CLOSELY GUARDED

SITA screamed at Ravana, her eyes blazing with rage and grief: "Base fellow! You spoke about your fame, great ancestry, and warlike abilities, but have you acted like a brave warrior? Are you not embarrassed by yourself? What kind of warrior waits for his husband's absence to abduct his wife? What a brave act to murder the elderly bird who tried to save me! What a bold speech you gave at the ashrama! The world will undoubtedly remember and admire this wonderful hero who refuses to fight but is willing to steal! And what do you intend to gain by carrying me away? How long do you think you'll live? Rama's arrows will soon find you and take your life. Know that the moment Rama looks at you, you're dead. So, what are you gaining by cheating? You will never have me. I will die before I succumb to you, and you will not be able to escape my lord's anger, having earned his fury. Rama annihilated your army of countless Rakshasas in Janasthaana in less than an hour. Will he let you go? He'll send you to Yama soon."

Ravana, chariot-less, flew across the skies towards Lanka as Sita spoke words of scorn and warning. They passed through several mountains and rivers, and Sita noticed some people standing on a hilltop below. She removed her sash and threw the package down, wrapping up her jewels in it.

She did this in the hope that Rama would notice the ornaments she had lost and give him a hint as to where she was being transported away.

Ravana arrived in Lanka after crossing the Pampa and then the sea. He headed to his apartment with the bereaved Sita. He summoned some demon-like Raakshasis and told them to keep an eye on Sita, specifically directing them not to let anyone approach her without his consent.

"Give her everything she wants, whether it's clothes, gold, or jewels. Serve her and honour her as you would serve and honour me," he commanded.

"Anyone who utters a word that may insult her will be punished with death," he warned. "No one should consciously or unknowingly incite her rage or grief."

He contemplated what to do next after installing Sita in the inner flat. He dispatched five astute spies with the directive, "Go immediately to Janasthaana, where Khara lives. Keep an eye on Rama and let me know what he's up to. I can't sleep as long as Rama is alive. He should be slain in some way. Go on and perform your work, then come back."

Sita was imprisoned behind a citadel on a sea-girt island and had no idea where she was or how far she was from Rama. She expected her master to appear, slay Ravana, and redeem her. Despite her anguish, she was strong and stable in her mind, remembering her lord's power and prowess.

Ravana returned to Sita's presence after dispatching his soldiers to Janasthaana. He watched her overcome with emotion and sobbing. The Raakshasis were keeping a close eye on her.

He believed that once she saw his wealth and power, she would submit to him. As a result, she was made to tour throughout the magnificent palace and shown the wealth and splendour on exhibit. No king on the planet had ever possessed such wealth and pleasures.

Sita was shown a plethora of gold, diamonds, and silks, as well as intricately constructed platforms, vehicles, and towers, as well as hundreds of maid attendants and every symbol of wealth and regal authority. But her mind was elsewhere.

Ravana attempted to persuade her of the size of his army as well. But she had already formed an opinion about his abilities and had presented them to him in harsh words.

"All this you can count on and enjoy as your own," Ravana contended. "You will be my queen, more precious to me than life itself. I have many wives, but you will be the mistress of all of them. The sea surrounds this island, which is guarded by thousands of powerful troops, for hundreds of miles. What joy or honour does it bring you to be with a poor human creature exiled from his realm, a pauper wandering in the forest? You will never see Rama again; you can be confident of that. Rama is unable to approach this city. Consider the entire kingdom yours. You shall be the queen of Lanka and the bride of the Lord of Lanka, Kubera's conqueror. Let us have fun floating around the world in the Pushpaka vimana. Allow the veil of grief to lift off your face and reveal the moon of joy."

Sita's eyes welled up as Ravana continued to talk. She covered her face with the hem of her saree so her attackers wouldn't believe she was scared.

Ravana implored and pleaded with her, "Do not be shy. There's nothing wrong with accepting me, and there's nothing to be ashamed of. It is written that one should accept God's gifts. O lovely one! I bend my head at your feet and seek your forgiveness. I am your servant. I ask your forgiveness, forgetting my greatness and might. Never in my life have I bowed so low in front of anyone."

He truly believed he could persuade her and win her love.

Despite her anguish, Sita spoke up to the Rakshasa. Before addressing him, she put some grass between herself and Ravana.

Ravana, dressed in sanyasi robes and sitting in front of the fruit provided by her in Panchavati, uttered boastful comments. Sita, who was imprisoned, now spoke as though echoing their words. "You know who I am. Dasaratha was known throughout the three realms and reigned for many years as a bastion of dharma and defender of truth. My husband is Rama, his god-like son with lion-like courage. He and his brother Lakshmana will undoubtedly murder you. You have dared to make Rama your enemy since you have obtained the blessing that no god or Asura can kill you. You believe that your boon will save you. But I assure you that you will not be able to flee. You will undoubtedly die at his hands. You will meet your end the instant Rama focuses his wrath gaze on you. You stole me in his absence like a robber. But you can't get away. Your fate compelled you to do this sin because the hour of your ruin and the annihilation of your race is approaching. Do not imagine that I will submit to you out of fear or to save my life." She fell silent after saying those words.

"Is that correct?" Ravana inquired. "All right, then, I'll give you twelve months. That's fine if you agree to accept me. If you still reject me at the end of that period, my cooks will prepare meat from your body for my breakfast."

After warning Sita in this manner, he issued the following commands to the attendant Raakshasis: "You should shatter her pride and obstinacy by some means or another. Place her in the Asoka garden alone and use fear and temptation to bring her to her senses. You should educate her to submit as we tame a wild female elephant." And he stormed into his palace, furious.

Sita was taken to the Asoka garden by the Raakshasis. It was a lovely park adjacent to the women's apartments. The trees were blooming with flowers and fruits, and gorgeous birds flitted about among them. Sita was imprisoned here, encircled and guarded by hideous Raakshasis.

Despite her sadness, she had trusted that Rama and Lakshmana would find her and rescue her, that her lord would destroy Ravana and return her to a happy life with him.

She was not afraid of threats or misled by temptations since she was sustained by her faith. Sita was imprisoned in the Asoka garden for months, not just a day or two.

CHAPTER XXXI: RAMA DISCONSOLATE

When Maareecha was about to die after being struck by Rama's arrow, he reverted to his Rakshasa form and wailed aloud in a replica of Rama's voice.

Rama realised how the Rakshasa had duped them and how he had been pulled away a considerable distance by the devious Maareecha, and he was filled with fear about what it all meant. "Unfortunately, we have been duped. It would be awful if Lakshmana is also duped by this cry and abandoned Sita to rush to my aid. The Rakshasas appear to have plotted this scheme to kidnap and eat Sita. There is trepidation in my heart, and it is a harbinger of some peril nearby." Rama hurried back to the ashrama, saying this to himself. On his way, he noticed Lakshmana running toward him. "Alas, the worst I feared has happened," Rama said.

He sobbed while holding Lakshmana's hands. "Why did you abandon Sita in the wilderness, Lakshmana? You may be certain that the Rakshasas slaughtered and ate her. It was wrong of you to abandon her. I'll die if I don't see Sita in the ashrama when we return, Lakshmana. You will return to Ayodhya, the only survivor of our three, and inform them of what has occurred. How will Kausalya deal with her loss? The Rakshasas will have visited Sita by now. How could Maareecha's phoney cry fool you? My faith in you was misplaced, and I will never see Sita again."

"What else, brother, could I do?" Lakshmana said, tears in his eyes. "When Sita heard the cries, she exclaimed, 'Ah Sita! 'Oh, Lakshmana!' she exclaimed, terrified. She was trembling with terror and encouraged me to come to you right away. I told her not to be afraid and convinced her that no foe was powerful enough to harm her, but she would not listen. She accused me of turning traitor to you and of coming to the forest with treasonous intent. I was practically dead with fear after hearing those words of hers, and then she threatened to kill herself if I did not leave immediately. She maddened me with her reproachful remarks, and I hurried towards you, not knowing what else to do."

They dashed to the ashrama. On their way, many ominous omens arose. "I fear, I fear we shall never see Sita again!" Rama said as he saw them one by one.

When they arrived at the ashrama, it was, as expected, deserted. Sita was not present. The deerskin, kusa grass, and the mat laid out as a seat were all dispersed on the ground. Rama sobbed and raced back and forth in the grove around the cottage. The trees' foliage and blooms were withered. Sita was nowhere to be found.

He ran around like a lunatic. His eyes were swollen with blood. "Alas, have they eaten her up?" he screamed. "Oh, how she must have shivered in fear! I can't even think about it. Could she have gone to the river to get some water? Could she have gone out to pick flowers?"

And he began looking for her among the trees, believing she was hiding and playing a practical joke on him.

After a lengthy period of walking and lamenting in vain, he collapsed on the ground, moaning, "Ah Lakshmana! "Ah, Sita!"

"Lakshmana, Sita has vanished. The Rakshasas had kidnapped her, ripped her to shreds, and devoured her. How can I go on living? My demise is approaching. However, when my father sees me in the other world, he will ask, 'Why have you come here, my son, before obeying my command?' I've failed. I have failed in every way."

This was too much for Lakshmana to take. "It is not right, Brother, that you should cry like this," he said. "Let us look into the woodland. You know how Sita enjoys exploring tunnels and thickets. She could be bathing in the river, playing, or picking flowers. Let us try again. She's just putting us through our paces. Come on, let us look again. Don't cry."

They looked all over the area, on hills, around pools, and along the river bank. However, they were unable to locate her. "Sita is nowhere to be found, Lakshmana," Rama replied. "What should I do next?"

"How can I return to Ayodhya, Lakshmana?" He sobbed. "Won't they mock me for returning alone after permitting Rakshasas to kill and eat Sita? What shall I tell Janaka now that I've brought her to the jungle and failed to safeguard her? No, you should go to Ayodhya by yourself. Go take care of our mums. Greet Bharata for me, and tell him it was my final wish for him to continue ruling as king."

Lakshmana's efforts to console him were futile. He was convinced that the Rakshasas had kidnapped Sita, ripped her to shreds, and devoured her. He vividly imagined the anguish of her suffering and sobbed in his grief, "I must have committed awful sins. How else could such anguish have come to me? Sita, who joined me in the hope that I could protect her, has been devoured by the Rakshasas, and there is nothing I can do about it. Is there another sinner in the world like me?"

"Do not lose heart," Lakshmana said. "A determined intellect can overcome fate. Let us search the woodland more thoroughly. Instead of succumbing to unending grief, let us be manly and active." But Rama would not be consoled.

CHAPTER XXXII:
A SECOND FATHER DIES

THE two brothers scoured every mountain, forest, and riverbank, shouting Sita's name. But it was all in vain, as they didn't find a single clue. A herd of deer, on the other hand, seemed to convey to Rama and Lakshmana that they should also move in the same route. They did so, and after a while, they discovered some flowers spread along the road.

Rama immediately recognised the flowers and exclaimed, "These are the flowers I gave her. They had to have fallen out of her hair." They looked all over the area where they discovered the flowers. They spotted the marks of a Rakshasa's large feet and little footprints which they knew were Sita's.

They discovered some gold beads strewn from Sita's jewellery. "Look!" shouted Rama again. "The Rakshasa has been following her like a beast of prey to shred her precious skin!"

Then they noticed multiple chariot fragments and large clots of blood, as well as royal headgear and diamonds scattered over the ground. They were perplexed as to what these occurrences may mean.

Soon they arrived and found a huge bow broken, the flag torn and the armour destroyed. A bit later, they saw the dead bodies of a charioteer and of mules. It was evident that fierce combat had taken place there.

"Two mighty Rakshasas must have fought here," Rama sighed, "each claiming the sole right to eat Sita."

Lakshmana tried everything to calm the distracted Rama. "Even the strongest minds are unbalanced by great sorrow," he added. "Otherwise, why should you lose control? How many times, my brother, have you soothed my rage and guided me in the correct direction? However, a big loss has unsettled your mind, and it is now the younger brother's job to give bravery and counsel patience to the elder, restoring him to his natural heroism. Let us identify and deal with our adversary."

Lakshmana sought to give courage and consolation with such compassionate words, and both moved on. They hadn't gone far when they came across Jataayu, bloodied and mutilated, lying on the ground.

Rama initially mistook it for some Rakshasa disguising himself to trick them and said angrily, "Look! Look, a Rakshasa has swallowed Sita!" and ran up to him, bow in hand.

Jataayu then murmured in a faint voice, battling with death, while lifting his ruffled and gory head in severe anguish. "Do not kill me, beloved Rama, who has only a few minutes to live! Ravana has abducted the dear princess you seek, and he could only do so by first robbing me of my life!

“When I saw Sita in his flying chariot in the air, I intercepted it and engaged him in combat. I broke his bow and destroyed his chariot. I killed his charioteer. You can see the scars from my last big fight all over this location. Finally, as I was exhausted from toil and still fighting a hopeless battle - age against youth, beak and talons against sharp weapons - he severed my wings and legs, and as I fell wounded to death, he lifted Sita and flew with her into the sky in a southern direction. Despite the fact that I am dying, I have clung to life for the sake of telling you what I know. Bless me and let me die now that I’ve done this.”

Rama’s eyes welled up with tears as he listened to Jataayu’s story. He tossed his bow down and embraced the bird. The princes’ grief was limitless. They wailed and rolled on the ground. “I am the most unhappy guy alive, Lakshmana,” Rama confessed. “After giving up the throne, I came to the forest, where I lost my Sita. Now Jataayu, who was like a second father to us, gave his life for my sake.”

After a few moments, Jataayu spoke again quietly: “Do not be afraid, Rama. Sita will undoubtedly be found. Nothing bad will happen to her. You will be overjoyed to reclaim the treasure you have lost.” He spewed out blood and died with these words.

Jataayu, old and defenceless, had fought with wing and beak and talon to defend Sita from the tragedy that their carelessness had brought upon her. Bharata and Shatrughna performed their father’s obsequies in Ayodhya when he died. Because Rama and Lakshmana were in the forest, they were denied this opportunity. They considered Jataayu to be their own father and performing his obsequies provided some solace for not being by Dasaratha’s side. What other assistance or honour could they bestow on the valiant Jataayu?

“Lakshmana, get dry faggots,” Rama instructed. “I’m going to stir the fire. We did not attend our father’s obsequies. Let us do it for the sake of the eagle father, who gave his life for us.”

“O king of birds, may you experience all the bliss of the pious who perform enormous sacrifices!” the princes chanted as they poured libations into the departed spirit. “May you share in the joy of those who have given generous contributions of land! May you experience the delight of those who fight valiantly on the battlefield! May all nice people’s happiness be yours!”

CHAPTER XXXIII: LEFT EYELIDS THROB

RAMA and Lakshmana frequently lost heart in the face of the unanticipated problems that befell them one after the other. Their fortitude gave way to deep despair at times. But they were able to encourage one another and continue on their path.

Rama and Lakshmana arrived in Pampa while looking for Sita. They accepted the hospitality of the aged sanyaasini, Sabari, a disciple of Rishi Matanga, in that wonderful location.

Sabari was a forest tribe woman who served faithfully in the ashrama of the old saint Matanga. When he left this world, she wished to die as well; however, he remarked that the time had not yet come and that she should await the advent of Rama, an incarnation of Vishnu, for the bliss of his darshan. So the old and wrinkled woman lived her saintly life, faithfully looking after the ashrama as before and keeping it fragrant in preparation for the coming guest.

When the princes arrived, she displayed the fruits she had harvested and stored for them, and she narrated and demonstrated the wonders of the Matanga ashrama to them. Then, with their permission, she lit a fire and ascended to heaven. The meeting with this saintly woman and the waters of the Pampa River gave the prince mental fortitude. "Lakshmana, I'm beginning to believe we'll succeed," Rama stated. "Let us seek the woodland for Sugreeva, whose assistance we require." They travelled throughout the Pampa region. The setting was wonderful, yet the beauty of the setting and the animals, birds, trees, and creepers only added to Rama's anguish.

Lakshmana attempted to reawaken his spirit. He stated. "We shall find Sita even if she is buried in the womb of Aditi, the mother of the gods. Ravana cannot escape. It is not proper for you to be so depressed. If we lose anything valuable, we must try tirelessly to recover it. Let us not give up hope; let us forget the anguish caused by love and focus our thoughts and body to effort. Get rid of your misery, brother!" Rama was advised in this manner by his younger brother.

Sugreeva, the fleeing Vaanara prince, and his ardent disciples were disturbed with concern when they saw Rama and Lakshmana roving in the forests. Sugreeva chose this hilly location after being ousted from his kingdom by Vaali because he believed it was made inaccessible to Vaali by a rishi's curse. And now he was afraid that Vaali in disguise was pursuing him to kill him. Alternatively, he feared that Kshatriya warriors allied with Vaali were there to kill him.

Sugreeva's chief minister was Hanuman. He calmed Sugreeva, adding, "This is not Vaali, nor do they appear to be Vaali's ministers. There is no reason to be afraid. I'm going to talk to them and find out the truth." Sugreeva was pleased and said, “Go, discover the truth, and return. Use all of your abilities. I am filled with scepticism. They act as if they are looking for someone. Could it be that they are looking for me?”

Hanuman approached Rama and Lakshmana in disguise as a Brahmana. His heart was filled with confidence as he stood in front of them. He went on to uncover the truth without being discovered. But as he continued to speak, he threw caution to the wind and detailed everything about himself and the Vaanara King.

He was beside himself as a devotee in the presence of the Lord when he saw Rama and Lakshmana and complimented them. He claimed to be a Vaanara who had arrived in disguise at the request of his King. “Royal saints,” he said, “your presence here brings delight to my heart. You have an aura around you as if you were gods. The forest creatures regard you with veneration and wonder. What is your name? What nation are you from? You are clearly born to control some huge country, but you are clothed like ascetics. You carry bows and arrows along with your matted hair and bark clothes.

“Why are you so quiet? Sugreeva, the Vaanara King, is hiding here after being pushed out of his country by his brother Vaali. I am his minister, and he is bereaved. Hanuman is my name. Vaayu is my father. As my monarch directed, I disguised myself as a brahmachari and am now standing before you.”

Rama remarked to Lakshmana after hearing Hanuman’s kind remarks, “Brother, Hanuman’s statement has inspired me with confidence. I have complete faith in him. Have you noticed how beautiful his language is, as well as how accurate and rhythmic his enunciation is? He speaks with the authority of someone who has studied the Vedas and grammar. He’s an excellent messenger. He who we are looking for is also looking for us. We came here to visit Sugreeva, and he sent us this message.”

They then proceeded to converse freely with one another. Rama and Lakshmana, on the one hand, and Hanuman, on the other, told their stories, their pleasures, and sorrows, their hopes and worries. Lakshmana developed a strong attachment to Hanuman as a result of this conversation.

“My brother, born to an immense fortune, the eldest son of an emperor, has abandoned his empire and come to the jungle,” he told Hanuman. “Ravana kidnapped his wife, who meant more to him than life itself.”

“Sugreeva, too, has been persecuted by Vaali and stripped of his kingdom and wife,” Hanuman responded. “He will almost certainly regain both. My king would benefit greatly if you support him, and you will benefit from his assistance as well.”

The three then proceeded to Sugreeva. The path could only be traversed by a Vaanara. Hanuman reverted to his normal form and carried both princes on his back. Ascending the Malaya hill, Hanuman went ahead to Sugreeva and announced Rama and Lakshmana’s presence, saying, “Rama is a prince full of wisdom and morality. He is the renowned Emperor Dasaratha's eldest son. He left Ayodhya with his brother and wife to fulfil his father's pledge and came to the jungle. Ravana kidnapped Rama's wife in the jungle, taking advantage of the prince's absence. Rama has come here to ask for your assistance in finding her. The princes deserve your friendship. Friendship with such heroes would benefit you considerably as well."

Sugreeva disguised herself as a handsome guy and had a long and heartfelt conversation with the princes. "Princes, if you care for the friendship of a Vaanara, here is my hand, accept it," he continued, stretching out his hand to Rama. "Hanuman has told me everything I need to know about your virtue and excellence." Rama hugged him and gripped his hand.

Hanuman quickly gathered some faggots and lit a fire. Rama and Sugreeva swore mutual friendship while circumambulating the flames: "Let us share our pleasures and sorrows. Let our relationship be eternal," they swore.

They cut down a tree branch, and Rama and Sugreeva were sitting on it, as were Hanuman and Lakshmana, who was seated on another. Sugreeva told the narrative of his life, how he and his elder brother, the magnificent Vaali, were once dedicated to one another, and how fate had turned them into deadly adversaries through no fault of Sugreeva's.

It had happened in this manner. Maayaavi, a Rakshasa, once came to the entrance of Kishkindha, their capital, at midnight and vauntingly challenged Vaali to sudden combat in fulfilment of an ancient feud. Vaali, who never denied a fight, dashed forward, followed by Sugreeva, and the Rakshasa retreated when he saw them. They pursued him until he vanished into a large cave, the opening of which was overgrown with brushwood. Vaali commanded Sugreeva to wait at the cave's entrance for him before plunging into the darkness after the opponent.

Sugreeva waited a long time, but no Vaali appeared, and as he stood trembling, hazy yells and groans, which sounded to his horror-struck senses to be his brother's, emanated from the cave, and suddenly there spilled out of it frothy blood, which convinced him that Vaali had died in the conflict. To ensure that the victorious Rakshasa did not rush out in triumph and demolish Kishkindha, Sugreeva blocked the cave's entrance with a massive rock and returned to Kishkindha with the story of Vaali's death. The ministers and elders then convinced him to take the empty throne. Vaali sprang on them, haggard with fury and wounded, accusing him of treason and unnatural conduct towards one who was once his brother and king, drove him out with derision and forbore to slaughter just because he was regrettably his brother.

As a result of a sad event, he had been deprived of his home, crown, and everything, including his wife, and had to seek refuge in the forest with a few devoted companions. At least he was safe here because Vaali had been barred by a rishi from entering the precincts under pain of death. Sugreeva ended his story with a heartfelt plea to Rama. "I am a woodland wanderer because I am afraid of Vaali. I live here, disguising myself. Could you, will you, murder Vaali and return my kingdom and wife to me?"

"Certainly," Rama responded. "Vaali will never be able to escape. Rest assured."

CHAPTER XXXIV: HE SEES HER JEWELS

SUGREEVA then learned about the disaster that had befallen the Raghu princes at Panchavati. Sugreeva, who was deeply moved, attempted to calm Rama. "I've heard it all from Lakshmana," he said. "Ignore all doubts and anxieties. We will undoubtedly find Sita, wherever she may be. My companions and I spotted a Rakshasa rushing across the sky carrying a weeping lady. 'O Rama! O Lakshmana!' she cried. She, too, noticed us and removed her sash, wrapped her diamonds in it, and threw down the small bundle. We took it up and kept it. Check to see if the jewels are Sita's." When Rama heard this, he exclaimed, "Fetch the bundle, fetch it!"

They carried it from the cave, and Rama was overcome with anguish when he saw the sash. He removed all of the jewels from his sash and placed them one by one in front of his eyes. "They must have fallen on the soft grass and thus are undamaged," he explained. "Yama's gates are wide open to greet the Rakshasa," he muttered, his anguish giving way to wrath. "He and his people will be exterminated soon."

Sugreeva got concerned after witnessing Rama's anguish and rage. Sugreeva was concerned about the issue of priorities, even though they had vowed mutual friendship and assistance in the presence of the sacred fire.

Sugreeva's heart went out to Rama in his pain because he knew what it was like to lose a kingdom and a wife, but first things first. He considered that the first step in the venture should be to capture the resources of the Vaanara kingdom by assassinating Vaali and assuming the throne. This alone would bring Rama and himself success. But, realising Rama's state of mind, he chose to proceed with caution.

"I don't know the strength or the location of this evil Rakshasa," he replied. "Still, I swear to you that wherever Sita is, I will find her and her kidnapper. You will triumph by killing the evil Rakshasa. Do not give in to despair or anguish that weakens the spirit. I, too, have lost my wife; I have been exiled and shamed from my realm. Despite this, I manage to keep my spirits up and my melancholy under control. If I, a Vaanara, can do that, you should find it much easier. As a result, I ask you, friend, to limit your grief."

Sugreeva's remarks left an imprint on Rama's heart. He wiped his tears away and embraced Sugreeva. He overcame his weakness at the sight of Sita's gems and regained his fortitude and self-control. "I treasure your friendship, Sugreeva," he said. "I'll take your counsel. Consider when and how we should start looking for Sita. I will take up your cause and set you on the throne of Kishkindha, and I have never said a vain or dishonest word in my life and will never do so again. Tell me

exactly how I can help you. I'll do it."

Sugreeva and his ministers were ecstatic when they heard Rama's statements. They were confident that their difficulties would soon be over and Sugreeva would be crowned King of the Vaanaras once more.

CHAPTER XXXV: SUGREEVA'S DOUBTS CLEARED

SUGREEVA wanted to restore his country and family, but he didn't know how. Vaali's might was an impenetrable barrier between him and his longing. Hanuman, his minister, tried to persuade him that he would succeed with Rama's help, but Sugreeva's doubts remained. Can Rama's strength overcome Vaali's? Vaali's body was made of steel. Rama had no notion how he planned to kill him.

Sugreeva is sceptical of Rama. But he had no one else to fall back on. And he wasn't about to give up on his ambition. He made the decision to put Rama to the test. But how does one put a friend to the test without raising suspicions? How did the opportunity to judge his skills come about? Sugreeva deliberated for a long time before coming up with a plan.

"Rama, my Lord! Your comments have taken away my sadness. I am aware of your bravery. The three worlds can be destroyed with a single arrow from your bow. How can Vaali's frame compete with it?" He spoke quietly. "However, I must inform you about Vaali's strength. He can circle the four oceans in his palm and sip the water with his morning prayers. He can toss and play with a large rock as well."

Sugreeva required proof of Rama's power to give him confidence, so Lakshmana said, "How would you like Rama to demonstrate his confidence to overcome Vaali?" Sugreeva responded, "I have no reservations. I am aware of Rama's abilities, but they are now embers in ashes. I've sought sanctuary beneath him. And yet, when I recall Vaali's mighty deeds, I tremble. That is all."

After witnessing Sugreeva's faith in him and his severe fear of Vaali, Rama determined to put an end to his doubts. He drew his bowstring to his ear and fired an arrow. It pierced the sal tree Sugreeva indicated, as well as six other trees standing behind it. Before returning to Rama's quiver, the gorgeous arrow penetrated the seven trees.

When Sugreeva saw this, he was content. He was now convinced that Rama's arrow could pierce Vaali's unyielding shield. "I have now witnessed your prowess with my own eyes. Even if all the gods, led by Indra, come to confront you, your triumph is inevitable. So why bring up Vaali? I've acquired your friendship, and I'm no longer afraid or sad. Defeat Vali and save me. Let us travel to Kishkindha today." Saying this, he knelt in front of Rama.

Both Rama and Lakshmana agreed. Sugreeva agreed to arrive in Kishkindha and challenge Vaali to a single duel after they debated how to proceed. Vaali was bound to appear, and Rama would dispatch Vaali with an arrow as the brothers fought. They went on to Kishkindha. Sugreeva continued. Rama followed him and hid behind a tree deep in the jungle.

Sugreeva screamed. Vaali, shining like the morning sun, stormed out of the fortress when he heard the shout. The two brothers clashed vehemently. Rama, on the other hand, was bewildered as he stood behind a tree with his bow in hand. Rama couldn't differentiate Vaali from Sugreeva when they were battling since they were so similar in shape and appearance, equipment, and fighting style that he was afraid to shoot for fear of killing the wrong fighter.

Meanwhile, Sugreeva, who was having the worst of the fight, fought his way free from his brother's grip and fled for his life, hurt and tired, disappointed and depressed. Even this he was able to accomplish since Vaali had no intention of killing him and was prepared to give his brother a second opportunity.

Rama and Lakshmana returned to help Sugreeva. He did not raise his gaze but instead lowered it to the ground. He was furious that Rama had broken his promise and refused to help him. "You should have told me sooner if you didn't want to kill Vaali," Sugreeva added, "and knowing Vaali's strength, I would never have challenged him to a fight. Instead, you convinced me, and I'm astonished I'm still alive."

"Don't be furious, Sugreeva, but listen," Rama said. "There was a reason I couldn't release my lethal arrow. Your height and girth, pace and shouting, attire and jewellery were all similar to Vaali's. I couldn't tell you who Vaali was until the brawl started. And there I stood, perplexed and helpless. It would have been far worse if I had murdered you instead of Vaali. Do not be upset. Vaali must be challenged once more. I'm going to kill him this time."

Sugreeva was overjoyed. His spirits were back. Lakshmana's neck was bound with the creeper. Sugreeva returned to Kishkindha in better shape than ever. Rama and Lakshmana, as before, followed him.

CHAPTER XXXVI: THE SLAYING OF VAALI

THE evening was drawing near. Sugreeva shouted once more at the Kishkindha gate, challenging Vaali to a fight. Vaali, who was then contently resting, was surprised and paled with bewildered concern for a minute, but was soon overcome with wrath and jumped trampling the earth as if he would break it.

Taara, his queen, held him in her arms in a close hug, her heart full of loving fear, and sought to temper his impetuosity with gentle admonition. "Put away this wrath, my dear lord, for you have had enough fighting today. Your brother was defeated and fled for dear life, concealing himself for safety. Your brother is not such a fool as to challenge you again so soon unless he was assured of help and protection from an invincible ally. I shall tell you what I heard from Angada, who had it from our scouts who range the forests.

This counsel irritated Vaali. His mind was clouded by anger. He couldn't see reason as he was caught and tugged by the rope of death, and his resolve only became stronger. "What do you mean?" he asked. "Do not be afraid of Rama. He knows dharma; he is one brought up in the fear of sin. I may tell you I shall not kill Sugreeva - only I shall teach the arrogant fellow a lesson he will never forget and let him go. I shall humble Sugreeva and send him back and return soon with victory. Have no fear for me."

Vaali hissed his way out of the fort, leaving Taara and her companions behind, and went to meet Sugreeva. He girt his loins and jumped on him as soon as he saw him standing there, bright and fearless. Sugreeva, too, dashed forward to meet Vaali. "If you love your life," Vaali cautioned, "go away; do not fall prey to my fist!"

The battle began when Sugreeva replied aggressively. Sugreeva, enraged by past wrongs and pumped up by the certainty of Rama's assistance, maintained equal combat for a long time, but Vaali's greater power eventually won, and Sugreeva was in such obvious misery that Rama, who was waiting with a ready bow, knew he couldn't hold out much longer. Rama fired a lethal arrow at Vaali's strong chest, laying it on the string and tugging it to his ear. Vaali plummeted down, pierced by that unstoppable shaft, and lay bloodied on the ground. Nonetheless, he was stunningly beautiful, his majestic body gleaming like a cloud illuminated by the setting light. The heavenly necklace that Indra had given him flashed on his breast, guarding his life and prosperity. This diamond, Rama's dart, and the bleeding wound gilded his strong body.

Vaali looked around in bewildered amazement, having been hit and lay low when he least anticipated it from an unknown source. He saw Rama and Lakshmana approaching him, bow in hand. He accused them of ignoble perfidy in inflicting causeless death to a person engaged in conflict with another, with tears of outraged indignation and a voice feeble with nearing disintegration.

"How did you bring yourself to do this deed, Rama?" he asked, "born of a noble race and famous by your exploits? The world is full of praises for your valour and virtue. And yet, while I was absorbed in a battle with another, you came unseen and, from behind, shot a fatal arrow at me. What harm have I ever done to you? For a royal prince to kill an innocent person in this way is a grievous sin.

"Or if you needed help recovering your Sita, I could have had her back in a day. I would have killed Ravana and carried his body to your feet with a rope around his neck. I would have found Sita no matter where he had hidden her and returned her to you. I do not mourn my death. Still, your fault is severe in killing me in this devious manner," said Vaali, son of Indra, as he died.

Vaali lay in the throes of death, battered and bleeding from his many wounds from his fight with Sugreeva. He survived just long enough to see his queen and his beloved son Angada - a poor befuddled child who prostrated himself in silence at his mother's behest 'to fall at the feet of his father who was departing on a long long journey,' too startled to realise the enormity of his loss. Vaali addressed his dying words to Rama. "All is over, I will no longer blame you. My dear, dear son Angada is orphaned. You and Sugreeva should look after him. I entrust him to you. Tell Sugreeva that he should not think it was Taara who set me up against him. Ask him to treat Angada with honour and affection, as he should treat a prince. Do this for me. The warrior's Heaven is calling me!"

CHAPTER XXXVII: TAARA'S GRIEF

When word arrived that Vaali had been killed by an archer, fear gripped Kishkindha, and the Vaanaras fled in hopeless disarray. Taara, witnessing this, set aside her grief and, like a queen, inspired her husband's subjects, saying: "You fought beside the King till today! So why are you fleeing in terror now? You are not at any risk. Rama murdered Vaali to make Sugreeva king. Your lives are not in danger; you will simply have a different ruler."

When she attempted to go to where her husband was killed, the Vaanaras stopped her, saying: "We will proclaim Angada as king and secure the fortress. We will protect the town from Sugreeva and his allies. Now that my great master is dead, nothing matters," she remarked. And she confidently proceeded to where Rama and Lakshmana were standing.

When she saw her husband lying wounded to death, she couldn't hold back her tears and sobbed. "Ah, my hero!" she sobbed as she embraced the injured Vaali. "How many heroes have you slain, and now you are one of them? And you've abandoned me here!"

Vaali's son Angada arrived soon after. Sugreeva was struck with regret as he witnessed this scenario, realising that this disaster was entirely his fault. The remorse was no doubt genuine, because revenge, especially revenge on former friends, always results in bitterness and anguish, and the fleeting sense of triumph is all ashes to the taste.

Taara rolled about on the ground, lamenting: "You have embarked on a trip from which there is no return, leaving darling Angada an orphan and myself a helpless destitute. My God!"

Hanuman attempted to comfort her: "The dead find their way to heaven. Why bemoan Vaali? Angada will be crowned in due time, and we will exult. It is our responsibility to look after Angada. Let us now consider carrying out Vaali's obsequies."

"I care about nothing," Taara replied. "Sugreeva is responsible for performing the obsequies and caring for Angada. What am I supposed to do? Can a thousand Angadas replace my husband in my eyes? I'm going to Yama's house with him. That alone will make me happy."

Vaali, who had been unconscious until now, opened his eyes for the last time and remarked to Sugreeva: "Brother, we could have been friends and reigned blissfully over the kingdom, but such wisdom and happiness were not bestowed upon us. You will govern the kingdom in the future. I've given you Angada, my son, who means more to Taara and me than life itself. Be a father figure to him and take good care of him. This is the only request I have for you. And remember Taara, who was not only a faultless and loving wife but also a highly knowledgeable and foresighted adviser. In no case should you dismiss her advice. Take the necklace that Indra gave me and its secret power with you. My life has ended, and so has my resentment. May you have a wonderful life!" As a result, the benevolent Vaali bestowed blessings on his brother Sugreeva.

He gave Angada his final piece of advice: "Sugreeva is now your monarch. Be devoted to him and serve him with patience and affection." Taara lay on the ground, clinging to Vaali like a blossoming creeper enveloping a forest tree fallen by an axe.

Vaali's life had abandoned him. Taara wailed angrily. "For the last time, salute your father," she said, her voice shaken with emotion. "Oh, my dear spouse! Your beloved son has bowed before you. Will you not say anything to him? Alas! He is an orphan, and I am a widow."

Sugreeva was moved to tears by the sight of all of this. He thought to himself: "I locked the cave's entrance, leaving Vaali within, and took and enjoyed his fortune. Despite my heinous sin, he would not kill me. He drove me away and let me escape with my life. But I plotted and succeeded in killing him. There is no sinner like me in the world, and yet he gave me the kingdom to rule with his dying breath. He was, indeed, noble."

Vaali's obsequies were carried out with proper form and ceremony. Sugreeva was anointed king after the auspicious bath, and Angada was named Yuvaraaja.

CHAPTER XXXVIII: ANGER AND RECONCILIATION

THE rainy season had started. Sugreeva and his comrades had a good time at Kishkindha, while Rama and Lakshmana were tired and waited in a nearby cave. The forest paths were flooded and turned into raging streams, making them impassable. As a result, the search for Sita had to be put on hold. Rama was overcome with grief as he contemplated Sita's position; Lakshmana advised him to accept the wait till the rainy season passed. And Rama patiently held his soul.

Kishkindha mourned her Vaali for a time, and then rejoiced in Sugreeva and the survivors; Sugreeva forgot the privations of his exile and his brother's death and enjoyed his present prosperity to the fullest, and even Taara reconciled and adapted herself to changed circumstances in the interests of her son.

The royal mansion of Kishkindha was brimming with joy and wassail, and the dismal months of rain, which the Raghu brothers spent in leaden-footed wailing, raced with golden-winged delight for Sugreeva and his household. Only Hanuman was concerned. He couldn't get his mind off Rama's business. He was seeking a chance to remind the king of his promise to Rama.

Finally, the rain stopped and the sky cleared of clouds and lightning. The air was fragrant with flower perfumes and bird melodies, and joy returned to the woodland. Hanuman, who was wise and noble, approached his king. He knew that in such circumstances, even the brightest and best of men would break their vows, so he addressed the king with great politeness: "You have returned the kingdom of your forefathers and are in secure ownership and enjoyment of it. But there is still work to be done. You must keep your commitment to your pals to build your fame and power.

"One should not wait for one's friends to remind them of what was promised to them. You already know all of this without my telling you. Remembering what Rama had done for us, we must take action to keep our pledge without waiting for him to remind us. The rainy season has ended. There is no reason to delay any longer. We can no longer put off the task of finding Sita. Rama's patience is admirable, but it does not justify any further delay on our part. Didn't Rama dispatch your adversary without regard for the danger or the consequences? We must keep our pledge as soon as possible."

Maaruti (Hanuman) delivered his advice to Sugreeva in this manner. The latter accepted it and, in gratitude to Hanuman, directed Neela to mobilise the Vaanara army. "The entire world must be searched for Sita," he said. "Order the most powerful Vaanaras to come and join us right away. Those who fail will face severe punishment." Sugreeva, on the other hand, returned to private residences.

Rama and Lakshmana spent the time in their cave waiting for the rainy season to end and for Sugreeva to fulfil his promise. When the rains stopped, Rama was overcome with grief at the thought of Sita suffering at the hands of the Rakshasas. "The world is full of life and joy," Rama declared. "However, Sita is in pain somewhere. And I'm still sitting here, hoping for the favour of this ungrateful Vaanara king. This king has forgotten his vow to me, lost in his wine and revelling in the company of his women. Lakshmana! Immediately go to Kishkindha and tell this vile monarch, 'Remember! Know that the path that the killed Vaali took to his demise is still open. Do not follow him, but instead keep your vow to me. He who forgets generosity and ignores friends will face ruin. You incur Rama's wrath and seek your doom by delaying.' Go inform Sugreeva about it." Rama wanted Lakshmana to deliver to Sugreeva an angry and agitated message.

Lakshmana was prepared to go, carrying the burden of his brother's sadness and rage. Then Rama reconsidered. He was aware of Lakshmana's character and feared the consequences of his hastiness. So he called him back and pleaded, "Do not be harsh in relaying my complaint to Sugreeva. Regardless of his flaws, he is our friend. Point out his flaws, but do not be rude." Lakshmana consented, but when he approached the gates of Kishkindha, he found it difficult to suppress his rage.

The Vaanara sentry grew alert and prepared to guard the stronghold after noticing Lakshmana's harsh expression and the fact that he was fully armed. This infuriated Lakshmana even more. Some Vaanaras dashed to the inner chambers and informed Sugreeva: "Lakshmana, enraged, is rushing here bow in hand." We were powerless to stop him."

But the Vaanara monarch was drunk and surrounded by women, so he didn't notice. The sentry at the gates was told by the king's servants to stand steadfast and prevent anyone from entering. Lakshmana's rage became unrestrained. Lakshmana pushed his way inside. There he met young Angada, whose youth and misfortunes took some of the strings out of his rage. "My kid, go and tell the Vaanara monarch that Lakshmana is waiting at the palace gate to see him on behalf of his bereaved brother," he said.

Angada went to the king's apartment and told him about Lakshmana's visit. Sugreeva, on the other hand, was in no condition to comprehend. Angada noticed this and conferred with the ministers on what should be done. Hanuman and some of the other ministers carefully explained what was going on, and Sugreeva was finally awakened from his trance. "I'm not at fault, am I?" Sugreeva asked. "Why should Rama and Lakshmana be upset with me? Someone must have spread rumours about me and used them against me."

"It is my job, O king, to speak these things, and I say them," Hanuman replied. "Do not be upset with me. We have failed to keep our promise to Rama. We've forgotten about Rama's pain. It's late, but it's not too late. As a result, let us do what we need to accomplish as soon as possible. Let us seek Lakshmana's forgiveness. Let us take immediate action to fulfil our promise to Rama."

Sugreeva then agreed to receive Lakshmana.

Lakshmana marvelled at the beauty of Vaanara and the culture of Kishkindha as he entered the town. He stood outside the king's palace after passing through gorgeous streets. Hearing the sounds of merriment, dance, and song emanating from within, he realised that the Vaanaras had forgotten their vow and had become engrossed in their enjoyment. He couldn't keep his rage in check. Still, he refrained from entering the women's chamber and twanged his bowstring in a corner outside. The sound instilled terror and trembling throughout Kishkindha. Sugreeva realised the prince was upset when he heard it. He recognised the danger and directed Taara to go pacify the prince. "When a chivalrous man like Lakshmana speaks to a girl, his anger will slip from him, and it will be impossible for him to be wrathful," replied the king, perceptive even in his tipsy state.

Taara moved closer to Lakshmana. Taara was unrivalled in appearance, knowledge of the world, and speaking ability. "After enduring poverty and persecution for a long time, Sugreeva is enjoying the pleasures and affluence you have won for him," she told Lakshmana. "This delight has gone to his head, and he has lost touch with reality. I understand his mistake, but you should forgive him. I can promise you that he has never forgotten his debt or duty to you. He has already issued instructions to mobilise Vaanara warriors from all directions. They'll all be here today or tomorrow. The hunt for Sita and the struggle against Ravana will then commence. Now, come in, pray, and see the King."

Lakshmana entered the apartment, no longer enraged. Sugreeva rose from his seat and greeted Lakshmana. "Please forgive my flaws," he remarked. "I am King today thanks to Rama's friendship and assistance. How can I ever forget what I owe to Rama, the brave and good? He can defeat his opponents without my assistance. All I can do with my forces is follow him. Ravana will undoubtedly perish. The hunt for Sita will begin soon. Please accept my apologies for the delay."

Lakshmana was overjoyed. "No one can match Rama in honour and prowess," he remarked. "Come with me to Rishyamooka and comfort him in his sadness."

Sugreeva and Lakshmana rode in a carriage to Rama and satisfied him by stating the arrangements that had previously been arranged.

Rama was overjoyed. "You are a true friend," he said. "A good friend comes to one's aid naturally, much like the clouds producing rain, the sun dispelling darkness, and the moon gratifying human hearts. I am grateful for your friendship. Ravana's and his race's demise is now guaranteed."

While Rama was expressing his gratitude and excitement, vast crowds of Vaanaras headed by their separate leaders arrived and gathered. They came from faraway forests, mountains, and coastlines. The dust they created clouded the sky. Millions of monkeys and bears of various shapes and colours were present.

CHAPTER XXXIX: THE SEARCH BEGINS

"LOOK at this Vaanara army, Rama," Sugreeva added. "You have mastery of all these myriads of marvellous strength. They are willing and able to provide you with all of the services you require. Consider this vast army yours, and command it to do whatever you want."

Rama, overcome with delight, embraced Sugreeva. "First, we need to find out if Sita is alive and, if so, where she is," he stated. "Next, we need to find out where Ravana is. Then we'll get to work on what needs to be done. But it is up to you, not me or Lakshmana, to lead this army. You are their ruler. Besides, you are the most knowledgeable about what needs to be done and how to execute it. How fortunate I am to have a friend like you and a brother like Lakshmana!"

Sugreeva then issued immediate orders to his commanders to dispatch divisions of the army to the four corners of the globe to conduct a thorough search for Sita.

Sugreeva took Hanuman aside after dismissing the other leaders and informed him, "Son of Vaayu, possessing the strength and splendour of your father, you alone can succeed in this job. You have the strength, courage, and knowledge I need to take on the duty of finding Sita."

Rama, too, believed that Hanuman's efforts would be rewarded. Whatever hurdles arose, he was confident that Hanuman would find a way to overcome them. He handed Hanuman his signet ring and added, "Take this ring. I am hopeful that you will find Sita. This ring will convey her to the fact that you are my messenger. Dear Hanuman, may you reunite Sita and me!"

Sugreeva issued his army's final commands. "Sita must be found in any case; no matter where she is hidden, you can and must find her. You must return with news of her within a month." And the army spread out in four directions like ants from an anthill.

Satabali and his troops marched north. Vinata travelled east, Sushena went west, and Hanuman, Angada, and General Taara went south.

"You describe every quarter and territory of the earth like one who has seen the entire planet with his own eyes," Rama inquired of Sugreeva. "How and when did you see everything?"

"You will recall, my Lord," Sugreeva continued, "how Vaali followed me in all directions. He followed me wherever I went. I was forced to wander throughout the entire planet as a result. Thus, I got the opportunity to travel to every region of the earth. Later, I discovered the location of Rishi Matanga's ashrama. The sage's curse would cause Vaali's head to shiver if he approached that place. I knew he wouldn't come there and couldn't hurt me even if he did. So there I lay, safe."

The hordes that went north, east, and west returned a month later and reported that Sita was nowhere to be found. "We searched carefully in forests, mountains, rivers, and cities, but she was nowhere to be found. Hanuman, who had travelled south, is the lucky one. Didn't the Rakshasa carrying Sita travel south as well? And Hanuman hasn't returned yet."

When Rama heard this, he was relieved that the Vaanaras had done their best.

Hanuman and Angada entered and searched the Vindhya caves and woodlands. They then arrived in the desert, where a rishi was performing tapas. It was cursed to be barren of trees, plants, birds, and mammals. As a result, they expanded their search. They'd get tired of their pointless hunt and sit down in blank misery. Angada, Gandhamaadana, or some other leader would encourage them and force them to restart their quest at such times. Many days were spent in this manner. However, Sita was nowhere to be seen, and they feared Sugreeva's wrath.

They travelled a long distance south in their hunt.

They were passing across the desert, fainting from hunger and thirst, when they came upon a cave from which a variety of birds full of life emerged. The lovely breeze that blew from it bathed them in lotus pollen and filled them with scent. "Undoubtedly, there was water where the birds and perfume originated from," the Vaanaras decided. With hearts full of hope, the Vaanaras formed a chain with joined hands and plunged cautiously into the murky darkness of the cave. Finally, light dawned, and they saw a wonderful grove with streams of clear water and trees sagging beneath their abundance of fruit. Then they arrived in a city with streets lined with gold-set jewels and huge palaces as gorgeous as a dream. They proceeded until they came across an elderly tapasvini dressed as a recluse and seated on dark skin. The Vaanaras trembled in the presence of her celestial brightness.

It required bravery for Hanuman to approach her. "Salutations to you, Mother," he murmured, bowing low before her. "Could you please tell us who you are? We entered the dark tunnel, thirsty and exhausted, hoping to find some water. And now that we see this uninhabited golden metropolis with trees and tanks, we are concerned that it is a chimaera born of the craziness of too enormous suffering. Explain everything to us and allay our anxieties."

"How did you get into this cave?" she replied. "You'll find plenty of fruits and beverages here. Maya, the Daanavas' architect, designed this castle. Sukraachaarya taught him the art.

"Maya lived here long and blissfully until he earned the wrath of Indra, who murdered him. Later, Indra gifted this golden castle to my friend Hema. These structures and parks are hers. She is currently in the realm of the gods. But what is your reason for coming here? Why did you tire yourself out walking through the woods? First, eat, drink, and refresh yourself, and then tell me everything about yourself."

They ate, drank, refreshed themselves, and were content. Then Hanuman explained to the ascetic why they were roaming. Finally, he added that they were looking for Sita under their King's orders.

The ascetic woman's name was Swayamprabha, and she exclaimed, "Alas! You cannot leave this cave on your own. No stranger who enters it can leave with their life. But yours is a noble mission, and I must transport you out as part of my tapasya. Now close your eyes."

As a result, they closed their eyes. They found themselves on the beach all of a sudden.

When they arrived at the beach, they were surprised to see that it was the beginning of spring. "Alas!" sighed Angada. "The time limit has been exceeded. If we return to Kishkindha without knowing anything about Sita, the King will undoubtedly sentence us to death. Instead of going there and risking our lives, let us fast here and now and seek death." Angada's companions were mostly in agreement with him.

"I disagree," remarked Vaanara General Taara. "Why should we put an end to our lives? Let us return to the cave of Tapasvini Swamyamprabha and live happily ever after. There is lots of everything there. We will spend the rest of our lives carefree."

"What despicable talk is this!" Hanuman exclaimed. "What is the point of eating, drinking, and sleeping in the cave while our folks are far away in Kishkindha? Sugreeva is a noble monarch whom we should not be afraid of. And, if Sugreeva is truly unhappy with us and intends to punish us, how can this cave provide us with safety? Taara's advice is of no use to me. Let us return and tell Sugreeva everything and ask his pardon. This is the only way out."

"I disagree with Hanuman," Angada stated. "Sugreeva has no feelings for me. He's going to murder me. Remember what he did to my father? He sees me as an impediment to his and his descendants' ability to inherit Kishkindha. Breaking a pledge means nothing to him. Did he not remember his solemn promise to Rama to find and return Sita? Was it not because he was afraid of Lakshmana and his bow that he dispatched us on this search? My widowed mother has succumbed to terror and agreed to accept Sugreeva's protection. She clings to life for my sake, and if she finds out I'm dead, she'll take her own life. Alas! If I return to Kishkindha, I will die. Fasting until death is far preferable here."

He sat facing east, sprawled on the ground in the manner prescribed for the death vow. When he accepted this promise and sat in the posture of a fast till death, the other Vaanaras wept and sat facing east, resolving to fast with him and die as well.

Sampaati, the vulture King, watched this multitude of Vaanaras surrendering themselves to fate from a nearby hill. Sampaati had been famishing for a long time after losing his wings and becoming unable to move. He was suddenly ecstatic, telling himself, "So many monkeys are going to die here together. I'll have enough food for a long time without having to work hard."

Meanwhile, the Vaanaras were reminiscing, talking to one another, and wailing loudly about everything that had transpired. "Because of Kaikeyi, Dasaratha perished," they explained, "and Rama was forced to live in the wilderness. Ravana kidnapped Sita. Jataayu sacrificed his life to save Sita. Rama and Lakshmana would have arrived on the scene and recovered Sita if the gallant bird had been able to fight for a little longer. All of this happened by chance, and the result is that we are dying here. What strange ways does fate work!"

Sampaati was listening to these laments until he noticed the mention of his brother, Jataayu. Hearing his name mentioned as dead, he naturally wanted to hear the entire story.

Sampaati was rather old. He and Jataayu were the offspring of Aruna, the Dawn deity and brother of Garuda, Hari's vehicle. In their youth, Jataayu and Sampaati battled to see who could fly higher and rise higher in the sky. As they got closer to the sun, the heat grew unbearable, and Jataayu was going to perish. But Sampaati stretched his wings and shielded his brother from the sun's wrath. Sampaati's wings were burned off, but Jataayu was preserved. He was unable to fly and crashed into a hill. Since then, he has been unable to move and has remained in the same location, always hungry for a meal and just alive.

"Who has brought me the sad news of my darling brother Jataayu?" He sobbed in misery. "Oh, Vaanaras, is darling Jataayu gone? Why did Rama, King Dasaratha's son, go to the forest? What happened to his wife? Ravana murdered Jataayu? Tell me everything."

The Vaanaras had decided to end their life. The wingless, elderly vulture had hoped to make a quick meal of them. But now, things had changed. The Vaanaras rose, approached Sampaati, and gently escorted him down the slope. They then conversed and shared knowledge. Sampaati told his story. Angada told old Sampaati everything that had happened in Kishkindha and inquired how Rama could be helped. Sampaati was elderly and frail, but his eyes remained sharp. He could see things from a long distance away. He could see Sita imprisoned in Lanka and detailed the wealth of Ravana's country. He witnessed and described Sita sitting in Lanka surrounded by raakshasis.

The Vaanaras were overjoyed. "Now we know everything about Sita," they exclaimed. "There is no need for us to die; Rama's goal will be accomplished."

Sampaati's problems also ended. The boon he had gotten that if he aided

Rama, he would regain his wings came true, as baby feathers began to rise and grow on his sides even as they were talking. Sampaati now sparkled with new beauty, and he felt delight in executing Jataayu's funeral obsequies.

CHAPTER XL: SON OF VAAYU

THE Vaanaras learned from Sampaati where Sita was imprisoned in the Rakshasa realm, a hundred yojanas across the ocean. Of course, returning to Sugreeva with this second-hand information would be inappropriate. They had exceeded their time limit, and only exceptional success could rescue them from penalty. They couldn't stop looking till they saw for themselves what Sampaati had described. Only then could they complete Rama's mission.

But they had to cross the sea first.

They went to the water's edge to talk about things. "How are we going to cross the sea, enter Lanka, see Sita, and then return?" They were overcome with anxiety and fear.

Jaambavan gave Hanuman a flattering and appreciative gaze. "I believe the son of Vaayu, is the one best suited by power and talent to perform this deed," stated the old Vaanara, walking up to Hanuman and bringing him into their midst.

Addressing Hanuman in front of a swarm of gloomy Vaanaras, Jaambavan said: "Why are you sitting silent and distant, O Warrior, skilled in all areas of knowledge? Do you not outshine the rest of us in power and splendour? Why aren't you as powerful as Rama and Lakshmana? There is no one like you in the entire world. O Hanuman, when you were a child, you imagined the rising sun to be a fruit and flew towards it to pluck it. When Indra, King of the Gods, saw your effortless and fearless flight, he got anxious for the safety of the sun and hurled his thunderbolt at you. You were hit by it and fell on a mountain, breaking your right jaw. Enraged by this, your father, the Wind God, came to a halt and stood still. In the quiet, all living things became breathless and felt strangled. The gods implored Vaayu to let go of his rage and shower him with blessings. Brahma and Indra bestowed boons on you.

"There is no weapon that can kill you. Death can only come to you when you want it to. You are invincible. You are comparable to him in splendour, knowledge, and strength since you were born of Anjanaa and begotten of the Wind spirit. Despite your might, you remain moral and modest. Only you can assist us in carrying out Rama's mission. You have no trouble crossing the sea. You must save this vast army of Vaanaras stranded in a stormy sea. You should not waste your ability to cross the sea.

"Improve your stature. Recognize your true strength and leap forward. You can cross the sea in a single leap, just like Trivikrama. Do it, and our problems will be over."

Thus, the aged Jaambavan commended Hanuman, reminding him of his power and reawakening his dormant courage. Hanuman's figure immediately began to swell like the sea at high tide. Even while the Vaanaras looked on, Vaayu's son increased in size. Angada and his buddies were taken aback by the brilliance of his body.

Jaambavan had reminded Hanuman of his power, and he was now determined to complete Rama's mission. And he declared his beliefs with zeal: "May your wishes be granted. I'm sure I'll see Jaanaki when I fly through the skies and land in Lanka. I'll be back soon with wonderful news. To jump, I must press my foot firmly against the ground. This hill may be able to withstand it." He remarked this as he climbed Mahendra hill.

He stood there for a time, then poured all of his might into his foot and took a few steps. The critters on the hill couldn't take it any longer and fled.

Standing on the hill, Hanuman gazed out at the sea and focused his thoughts on Lanka. He thought to himself: "I'm going to look for Sita. I'm going to fly over the sky and cross the sea."

With this resolve, he prayed to Surya, Indra, Vaayu, Brahma, and all creation. Then, facing east, he bowed to his father Vaayu, and turned towards the south, enlarging his frame even more.

He shoved his feet against the hill and struck it with his hands. The blossoms fell from the trees and covered the hill as a result of the collision. The slope, squeezed irresistibly by the pressure of his feet, let out springs of water, similar to the furrow streaming down the elephant's cheeks. The creatures screamed in terror as they emerged from the tunnels.

Hanuman's hair stood on end, as he roared and slashed his tail on the ground. He tightened his abs, held his breath, pressed his feet down, folded his ears, and hardened his muscles. Then, with a triumphant shout, he rose into the sky and flew like Garuda at the speed of Rama's arrow. Many trees were uprooted as a result of his haste. Hanuman's arms, with their outspread fists, resembled two five-headed cobras as he flew through the sky. As he flew onward, he appeared to consume the sky. His eyes glowed like burning mountain forests. It appeared to be a massive mountain with wings flying through the sky. He gleamed like the moon travelling across the sky, hidden by clouds at times and emerging from them at others.

He flew over the ocean, approaching the coast of Lanka, which was densely forested with plantain and coconut trees. He noticed trees, mountains, forests, and river mouths on the island's shore. Hanuman witnessed Ravana's kingdom's wealth and the walled city's splendour.

"I have arrived at my destination," Hanuman thought to himself. "Now, without revealing myself to the Rakshasas, I must examine the area and discover where Sita is confined."

He shrunk down to the size of a normal monkey and landed on a hilltop in Lanka.

CHAPTER XLI: THE SEARCH IN LANKA

HANUMAN alighted and landed in Lanka, full of hope. But the euphoria of having completed the voyage was quickly replaced by sober reflection. "Although I have crossed the water, my mission has only just begun. Ravana's majestic city stands suspended in the skies atop Mount Trikoota. How beautiful, wealthy, and secure it is! How can an army cross the sea that I just did? Even if it crosses the sea and reaches this land, it cannot attack and destroy this stronghold, which is fortified by bulwarks manned by well-armed men! But first, I need to find out if Sita is still alive. When and how should I enter this heavily fortified city? If I were to find the location of Sita, I must fully search for it. If I do something carelessly now, the blunder will be irreversible, and a noble purpose will fail due to my hurry or negligence. The Rakshasas will notice if I enter the city during the day. It's best if I come in at night. To avoid suspicion, I must disguise myself in a little, inconspicuous shape." As a result, he shrank to the size of a small monkey, no larger than a cat. This would be the most convenient way to enter and search the palaces and parks of this large city.

The sun had already set. Vaanara made his way to the fortress entrance. The moon was shining brightly. Hanuman was overjoyed and grateful for this assistance in his hunt.

Even from afar, Hanuman was struck by the richness and beauty on show in Ravana's capital. Flags and festoons adorned the streets and palaces, which shone with gold and exquisite diamonds. From the water, a gentle breeze blew. Ravana's capital, like Indra's Amaravati and Kubera's Alakaapuri, had reached its pinnacle of wealth. Rama's messenger was filled with astonishment and fear about how to defeat the master of such wealth and military power.

Hanuman scaled the wall and leapt into the city. He entered the castle of Lanka with his left foot first, vowing to crush the Rakshasas. This signified a defeat for the enemy.

He walked down the royal street, which was adorned with lovely flowers. He clambered onto the mansions and went along, admiring the splendour of the city from their roofs. The Rakshasas' homes, streets, and decorations radiated unfathomable beauty. Mantras were being sung in some homes. Vedic hymns were heard in some of them. Songs commemorating Ravana's great feats and splendour were being sung in others. Soldiers and scouts might be seen everywhere. The armoured guards carried arrows, swords, cudgels, slings, lances, and other weapons. Some were attractive, some were not, and their skin tones ranged from fair to brown to black. Some characters were towering, while others were short. Thus, Hanuman observed that the population was drawn from a diverse range of climates, and the army was selected from a diverse range of nations.

He came to a large palace standing aloft in a nobility of splendour far transcending all the splendid buildings surrounding after passing through many residences and gardens filled with laughter and music. He decided that this was Ravana's palace, the central splendour of magnificent Lanka, based on the elephants, horses, and foot-soldiers in front, the high walls encircling it, the beauty of its structure, and the richness of its decorations. He walked into this palace. It was heaven on earth worthy of Ravana's unrivalled strength and grandeur in every way. He was taken aback for a moment. But then he remembered that he still hadn't located Sita. Concern over the unmet objective for which he had come replaced admiration.

He visited Ravana's innermost private room after passing through numerous mansions and was almost overcome by the elegance and wealth of its suites, which made it look like an abode of the gods. There was gold and silver everywhere, ivory, diamonds and pearls, and exquisite carpets and furniture, and he noticed the Pushpaka Vimana among them. Kubera acquired a magical vehicle from Brahma. Ravana took the vehicle from Kubera as his prize after defeating him.

Hanuman entered Ravana's chamber, which was an ocean of bliss. Countless beautiful women slept in the vast chamber, some connected arm in arm. Hanuman glanced about at all these sleeping women, one more lovely than the next and all full with joy and love, to see whether any of them may be Sita. Hanuman shook his head, cursing himself for thinking for a moment that Sita could be in that delicious paradise of joyful damsels.

Then he went somewhere else. He noticed more beds in another chamber. He saw one that was more beautiful than the others, covered in gold and jewels, and Ravana lay on it, like another Mount Meru. Even Hanuman trembled at the sight of his shape and overwhelming magnificence. He stood on one side and surveyed the sleeping figure, unable to take his gaze away from the massive form's magnificent and virile majesty; the great muscles now in repose, the symmetrical grace of limbs that made the Rakshasa King both beautiful and terrifying.

Hanuman then looked about at the women in the beds and on the rugs. Some of those who had fallen asleep while singing were still bugging their instruments.

His gaze was drawn to a figure laying on a gloriously gorgeous cot. Hanuman assumed it was Sita because of the shapeliness of her limbs and the beauty of her looks. He jumped for delight.

The next thing he knew, he was cursing himself for his folly. "Fie, fie," he thought to himself, "What an idiot I've been! Could Sita sleep so carelessly in a stranger's chamber, draped in jewels? Even thinking about it is a sin." And he was overcome with humiliation and grief over his blunder.

He had now searched Ravana's palace's interior apartments. The bedroom, dining room, bar, and music room had all been examined, but Sita was nowhere to be seen. "I've explored every nook and cranny. I even stared at everyone in the women's chambers, which is against good manners. But it was all in vain."

After saying this, he left the hall of wine and proceeded to the garden, where he looked into the small shrines and creeper arbours. But it was all in vain.

"I've seen all of Lanka," he thought, his eyes welling up with tears. "I've explored every inch of Ravana's palace. What else could I possibly do here? Is it okay for me to leave without seeing Sita? No. I'd rather die here than anywhere else. Yes, that is the only thing I can think of."

But he reminded himself, "Fie, fie on me for succumbing to such unworthy and dishonourable melancholy."

He jumped up and searched every inch of the places he had been through once more. He peered through every door and window. The Rakshasa had taken ugly ladies, beautiful humans, and Naaga maidens, but not Sita.

His heart sank once more. He had no idea what to do. He thought to himself: "If I fail in my goal and return to Kishkindha, how will I meet my friends? What happens if Rama loses all chance of reuniting with Sita? He would undoubtedly perish. What would happen to others after that?

"Was Sampaati mistaken when she said Sita was in Lanka? Or has she been murdered by the Rakshasa since Sampaati discovered her on this island? She could have been eaten by the Raakshasis. Nothing is certain, and everything is shrouded in uncertainty. So, what should I do?"

Hanuman was therefore buried in thought and tension. Just then, his gaze was drawn to something he had previously overlooked: a park adjacent to a shrine and protected by high walls. "Oh, here's a park I've never seen or searched for before. I'm sure I'll find Sita here."

As the son of Vaayu reflected on Rama with these words, hope arose inside him. The remote park was fortified with thick walls. "Sita must be here," he thought to himself. He bowed to the gods once more. He jumped up and sat on the Asoka Vana's wall, surveying the lovely park.

CHAPTER XLII: SITA IN THE ASOKA PARK

HANUMAN felt a rush of joy as he stood on the high wall for no apparent reason. It was the intangible atmosphere that envelops a completed objective and subtly impacts the committed heart. When he finally arrived at Sita's location, his entire existence throbbed with exulting anticipation for no apparent reason.

It was a warm spring evening. Hanuman jumped to a site where there was a dense cluster of trees since the trees and plants were in bloom. The birds who were resting there were startled, and they flew away making beautiful noises. Deer and other animals were moving around. Flowers fell from the branches and covered Hanuman's body.

Looking at the magnificent form of Hanuman covered in flowers, the creatures in the park assumed that the God of Spring was visiting the grove in the early morning.

The garden was breathtakingly lovely. The sight of beautiful tanks and terraces decorated with gold, silver, ivory, pearl, and coral crystal steps, artificial hills, and waterfalls thrilled Hanuman with excitement. Platforms were coated with gold and silver around some trees. In the breeze, small bells strung from the trees made a melody.

Hanuman climbed to the top of a large, spreading tree with a golden platform around its stem and sat buried amid its leaves.

"If she were still alive and in Lanka," Hanuman thought to himself, "Sita would undoubtedly visit this garden. She preferred this location above all others for isolation and contemplation of Rama. Didn't they say she was fond of groves and trees? She would undoubtedly come here at daybreak to adore the Universal Mother."

He looked around, hiding amid the leaves. He sat on a branch and gazed down. He saw a feminine figure, blindingly gorgeous and gloriously pure, seated on that platform.

She was thin and pale, and she shone like a moon streak at the start of the month's brilliant half. Her beauty sparkled in fits and starts through her darkest depression, like flame through encompassing smoke. She resembled a gorgeous lotus hidden by miry moss, wrapped in a filthy top garment. Her face was swollen with weeping, and she was malnourished. Hanuman saw her as both adorable and pitiful, like the holy word wrenched from its context by unbelievers, like prosperity drowned in underserved ruin, like shattered hope and betrayed faith.

Hanuman firmly stated to himself: "Sita is the embodiment of exquisite sadness. For, see, the gems mentioned by Rama as being on her when she was taken away—all except those she dropped during the flight and which we picked up on the hill—hang unnoticed on the branches of the tree. Rama is seized by a three-fold agony and grief for her suffering, rage for the insult to her, and heartbroken pangs at her separation. He is always in her heart, and she is always in his, and they cannot be separated because they cannot exist without one another."

And as he continued to watch her, his heart jumped back over the ocean in ecstasy, seeking Rama's feet. He returned his gaze to Sita and thought to himself: "It was for the sake of this divine lady that the mighty Vaali, Ravana's peer in prowess, was slain; for her that Kabandha and Viraadha died, and fourteen thousand fierce Rakshasas with Khara, Dooshana, and Trisiras crimsoned the glades of Janasthaana with their gore. It was for her that the glorious Vaanaras dominion was wrested from the valiant Vaali and bestowed to Sugreeva. I crossed the sea, the lord of rivers, and am now here in Lanka to serve her."

Just like a swan could glide across the clean surface of a lake, the moon swam into view and shone brightly as if on purpose to aid Vaayu's son.

Hanuman took another long look at Sita's face, which revealed a sea of care like a heavily-laden ship caught in a storm, peering between the leaves and unsure what to do. The Raakshasis who guarded her were hideous. One had only one eye, while the other had only one ear. Some lacked ears, while others lacked noses. Some had their noses turned sharply upward. Some were bald, while others had strange hairstyles. These hideous animals were armed with spears and other weapons.

And in their midst sat the pale-faced princess, befriended only by her virtue, like an unsupported beautiful creeper on the ground.

It was still dark and early in the morning. The chanting of the Vedas and the morning music of the court bards awoke Ravana from his rest. He remembered Sita as soon as he awoke and began walking toward the park where she was confined.

He entered the palace grounds with his entire entourage, accompanied by perfumed torches and the royal parasol, surrounded by maidens adorned with sparkling jewellery and dressed in spotless white garments. Ravana, like another Manmatha, appeared charming.

Hanuman could hear the roar of the throng and the tinkling of women's anklets as the procession approached the gate. He soon noticed the Rakshasa king approaching. Hanuman quickly buried himself beneath the dense leaves, better than before. Ravana's might and brilliance were breathtaking as he approached Sita. Sita's body shrivelled and trembled at this sight, like a plantain tree in a hurricane.

Ravana approached Sita again, hoping to gain her permission. Sita was coated in dust and wore no jewellery, but she sparkled as if she were wearing all the jewels that a princess must wear. Like a lotus flower tainted by mud, her face was obscured by light and shade. Her state was like being surrounded on four sides by raging fires, like a river that had run dry, like a vessel for a sacrificial fire that had been desecrated, like a cow elephant taken from the herd's leader, seized, and bound as a prisoner.

Sita sat shaking, overcome with anguish and terror. When she noticed Ravana approaching, her heart raced to Rama like a chariot carried by swift steeds. She imagined her defenders far away, despite her fading visage and wasted form. "When will they arrive? Will they ever arrive?" She questioned herself and reflected on God.

Ravana approached her and addressed her. Hanuman hid in the tree's branches and watched what was going down below.

CHAPTER XLIII: RAVANA'S SOLICITATION

RAVANA said to Sita, who was drowning in sadness and clinging to dharma and the thought of her lord: "O lovely one! Why are you afraid of me? Do you realise how much I adore you? Though it is legal for a Rakshasa to abduct another's wife and forcefully possess her, I am a beggar for your love. There is no reason to be afraid of me. I will never touch you until your heart turns to me. No one in the world compares to you in terms of beauty. It is not proper for you to reject magnificent gems and clothes, to sleep on the ground, and to have unkempt hair. Why could someone with so much beauty be sad? Accept me and experience all the world's delights. For your sake, I shall conquer the planet and give it to Janaka. You will be my royal consort. You will rule over all the queens and women in the palace. My wealth and kingdom will be yours to enjoy. My people and kinsfolk will be delighted to serve you.

"Why do you waste your time walking in the wilderness with nasty Rama? How can you love or trust someone who has been stripped of his rights and thrown out of his kingdom and is now wandering around in bark garments? It's even improbable that he's still alive now. In any case, he will never look at you again, let alone approach you. There are numerous attractive women in my apartments. But now that I've seen you, I can't stand the sight of any of them. You will be Queen over all of them and will be grateful for their obedient devotion. We'll travel the world, content in each other's company. With me, you will have unlimited wealth and pleasure. Say only 'yes.'"

Ravana made an earnest plea for love and pity. When Ravana had finished speaking, Sita took a small blade of grass and placed it between them, laughing mockingly and gently saying: "Ravana, set aside all such silly thoughts about me. It is completely inappropriate for you to want me. I can never agree with anything you say. How are you going to persuade me? Don't give in to such foolish and unrealistic wishes and cause yourself grief!"

She then averted her gaze and continued: "How can I become your wife when I am already married to someone else? Do not go against dharma. Consider how closely you keep an eye on your wife to keep them safe from the touch of others. Wouldn't other husbands treat their wives the same way? Remember that other men are just like you. Do not look at another man's wife. True happiness comes from being content with oneself. But if you allow your thoughts to wander to another man's wife, you will be met with sorrow and shame.

"Why do you commit evil and inflict damage on yourself and your people? If you continue in your wrongdoing, this Lanka and its vast wealth will be destroyed, and the enemies you have defeated and humiliated will celebrate. I married Rama, and I can't keep my thoughts and feelings away from him. Listen to me as I talk for your benefit. Don't go looking for your demise. Rama is merciful and will undoubtedly forgive you if you ask his forgiveness.

"I can still hear Rama's bow twanging there. Rama and Lakshmana's arrows will soon arrive in Lanka, and your city will be engulfed in flames. Didn't you come to our hut like a burglar, knowing his power, to steal me while Rama and Lakshmana were away? Can you stand in front of them for a moment, face to face? Will you flee into the mountains to hide? Even so, just as the tree is hit by lightning at the allotted hour, you will perish at their hands. You can't get away." Thus, Sita concluded with a strong warning.

Ravana kept his cool and spoke: "O Sita, doting on this phoney ascetic Rama, you speak foolishly and insult my loving words. I have abstained because I love you; else, you would be dead by now. Two months remain of the time I had given you. Change your mind before they are gone. Come to my bed and be my wife. If you do not comply, you will be taken to my kitchen and cooked for my meal. Beware!"

Sita remained unfazed and responded: "Alas! Alas! Is there no one who can give you sound advice? Rama's punishment is unavoidable. Are you not embarrassed, O wretch, who abducted me while he was away? Your demise is certain. Your horrible fate has compelled you to commit this heinous crime. And yet you are Kubera's brother; you are a legendary warrior; you command an entire four-limbed army. Why should you carry out this heinous act in this heinous manner?"

Ravana's eyes rolled with rage, and he hissed like a snake at Sita.

Seeing his growing rage, one of his young wives, Dhaanyamaali, approached him and hugged him, saying: "King! Why do you bother yourself with this nasty human being that doesn't appear to care about you? She simply does not have the good fortune to be your wife. And what is it about her that makes her so appealing? Why do you waste your time thinking about this insignificant creature? Leave now. Let us have some fun."

She dragged him away gently, and the Rakshasa laughed along with her.

Ravana instructed the raakshasis who guarded Sita to bring her around somehow before leaving the Asoka Park, followed by his retinue. The raakshasis surrounded Sita as soon as he turned his back.

The Princess, who had been brave up until now, shuddered when she saw these hideous creatures who began speaking to her. "When Ravana, scion of a great family and world-renowned warrior, seeks you," one said, "O silly girl, how can you say no to him? What do you believe Ravana is? You should be aware that he is a direct descendant of Brahma. He is the grandson of Pulastya Prajaapati, the son of Brahma, a hero who has fought numerous wars and defeated numerous opponents. How dare you belittle him!"

Another person concluded: "We gave you sound advice. We have done our best, and the rest is up to you. If you refuse his offer, you will undoubtedly perish."

CHAPTER XLIV: FIRST AMONG THE ASTUTE

IF a woman is kept in captivity for an extended period, she may lose her heart and become depressed.

Sita hoped month after month that her lord would find her and come to her aid. Sick of an unfulfilled hope, alone among adversaries, she clung to life only because of her deep faith in Rama's love, which made her believe that he would certainly come.

The raakshasis plied her with what they considered to be well-intended advice. "Won't you take our advice? You are a human with no sense. Your rightful location is in our King's bed-chamber. But because you declined his offer, you are constantly reminded of your terrible husband. He'll never be seen again. Yield to Ravana and be content."

Sita could only cry when she heard these remarks. "What sinful words you speak!" she said. "I can never do what you say. No wife in the race of men would consider abandoning her husband. It is evil for the Rakshasa monarch to want me as his wife. As the sun's brightness is inextricably linked to the sun, so am I to Rama."

The raakshasis gave up on convincing her and murmured to one another, "What can one do with an obstinate idiot like this? It's preferable to feed her before she becomes too skinny from her brooding!"

Another firmly stated, "Let us kill her and distribute her limbs. Get some sauce and some heavy liquor. Let us feast on her, drink, and dance in Nikumbhila's shrine."

Sita sobbed as she heard these horrifying words and saw these horrifying forms. Her physical bravery faltered, and nature took its course. She sobbed like a kid, but her mind was clear, and it was concentrated on Rama.

"Rama destroyed hundreds of Rakshasas in Janasthaana. Why hasn't Rama come to redeem me yet? Why are the warrior princes who slaughtered Viraadha in Dandaka still unconcerned about my fate? It's possible they don't know where I am yet! But how long will Rama be unaware of my presence? How long will Lanka and the Rakshasas be able to survive? Rakshasa widows would be weeping loudly in every house in this metropolis very soon. Ravana and the entire Rakshasa race will inevitably perish."

Thus she reasoned within herself, gradually regaining courage. But soon after, other thoughts invaded her mind, filling her with dread. "Could it be that Rama committed suicide because he couldn't face my loss? That could be the case. Otherwise, how could he have neglected me and left me alone for so long? He is joyful now, and he is with the Gods.

"I must have committed countless sins. How else can I bear all of this and yet live? But something tells me Rama is still alive, or else I'd be dead!" Then another thought entered her mind. "Perhaps he has determined to spend his life in penance and has put all thoughts of me aside. No, no. How could a warrior abandon his duty and take up the life of sanyasa, leaving his wife in the clutches of his foe? What a fool I was to even consider this! The truth is that they have no idea where I am.

"Could it be that Rama has grown tired of me? Is it possible that he has forgotten about me? Fie, fie, fie! What a depraved thought! How can my Rama have forgotten about me? He'll never be able to. And what have I done wrong for him to stop thinking of me? This cannot be the explanation. Perhaps Ravana has performed a ruse and assassinated the Prince."

As a result, her thoughts roamed from one sorrowful thought to another, sinking deeper and deeper into the sea of grief. She concluded that hanging herself was the best option. She could hang herself on a branch of the Simsupa tree with her long braid around her neck.

The Raakshasis were at a loss for what to do after failing to persuade Sita. Some went to tell Ravana about their failure. Some stayed behind to watch over Sita.

Sita, who had decided to commit suicide, unexpectedly began to notice numerous auspicious omens.

Her left eyelids, fingers, and foot all throbbed ominously. Her heart was filled with strange courage once more. All thoughts of self-destruction vanished.

Hanuman, sitting hidden above and watching everything that happened in the grove, pondered his next move.

Hanuman might have thought he had nothing more to do after arriving in Lanka and meeting Sita. But he was not readily pleased. He reflected on himself. "I did what no one else could do: I crossed the sea and discovered Sita. I've observed the Rakshasas' city and taken note of its defences. I've done everything a spy can do without disclosing himself to the enemy. However, the situation here is perilous. Who knows what will happen here if I go back now to tell what I've witnessed to Rama and my king? Sita, unable to stand her anguish, may take her life before Rama, Lakshmana, and the Vaanara host arrive. All of my efforts would be futile. It is insufficient to have seen Sita. I need to talk to her; I need to tell her about Rama and instil hope and courage in her heart so that she can go on living despite everything."

"How do I present myself to Sita? If a monkey appeared and spoke to Sita in this Asoka forest, she would immediately suspect foul play and believe Ravana was performing a new trick on her. She might scream in terror if I came unexpectedly in front of her. The Raakshasis who have been guarding her and have now fallen asleep will be shocked awake and find me. They'd realise I'd come from their enemy and in disguise, and they'd summon the Rakshasas to fight me. Of course,

I'll kill most of them, but the goal of soothing Sita and informing Rama about her would be jeopardised if I were arrested and held prisoner here. This would never be acceptable. King Sugreeva and Rama are eagerly anticipating my homecoming. Even a minor blunder on my part now could spell doom.

"The first step is to prepare a speech for Sita and instil excitement and optimism in her heart." I must approach her in such a way that she never has any doubts about my good faith. So I'll tell her the narrative and virtues of Rama in a beautiful low tone, just for her. Her heart would then be filled with joy and trust, which would replace her distrust."

So he thought, and while still hidden by the tree's branches, he began to speak the sweet words, "Rama," "Rama."

CHAPTER XLV: SITA COMFORTED

HIDDEN among the branches, Hanuman sang the Rama story to Sita in a soft and kind voice: "King Dasaratha managed his country wisely. His army was massive, with chariots, elephants, and horses. He was virtuous and accomplished great things. All of his endeavours were successful. As a result, mankind dubbed him Satya-paraakram. He relished and expressed bliss as the richest of the Ikshavaaku race, king of kings, and ruler of the planet.

"Ramachandra, the eldest of his four sons, had the face of a full moon. Rama was beloved by all because he was wise, virtuous, and a master of the bow. He was the throne's heir. To safeguard his father's honour, he left the kingdom with his wife Sita and brother Lakshmana and lived in the wilderness. He defeated the Rakshasas and protected the rishis there. He annihilated Khara and Dooshana, as well as their vast army. Ravana, enraged, forced a Rakshasa to take the guise of a deer and deceive the princes in pursuit, and in their absence, he forcibly abducted Sita.

"Grief-struck Rama set out to find Sita. He became acquainted with Sugreeva, the Vaanara. Rama assassinated Vaali, the Vaanara monarch, and gave the Vaanara realm to his brother Sugreeva. And Sugreeva dispatched his Vaanara troops to every corner of the planet to find Sita.

"These Vaanara soldiers, who could take any form they wanted, searched the entire planet for the lost Sita. I came here after crossing the sea a hundred yojanas wide after following a clue supplied by Sampaati. And now I see someone whose form, colour, and attributes Rama described as his royal spouse's." Hanuman paused after saying this.

Sita was thrilled with astonishment and happiness as she heard these wonderful words spoken by someone from somewhere. She looked about in all directions, trying to figure out who said such nice things in such wonderful voices and excellent phrasing.

She looked everywhere, up and down, but there was no human figure to match this flawless voice. She only noticed a cute little monkey sitting on a branch above her. Sita saw the son of Vaayu, the Vaanara king's knowledgeable minister, in the form of a small monkey, dazzling like the morning sun.

When Sita saw Hanuman, she thought to herself, "The words I heard, the form I see, they can't be true. I'm just daydreaming. How often has my mind wandered back to the narrative of my Lord? Is it any surprise, then, that I seem to be hearing the story as told by someone? It's not real; it's just a dream.

"They claim that seeing a monkey in a dream portends bad luck for one's clan.

God bless Rama and keep him safe! May God protect Lakshmana from any evil! God bless all my Mithila relatives!

"No, this isn't a dream. And I'm not sleeping. How can one dream if they are not sleeping? This isn't a dream. All of this is true. Could this possibly be a message from my precious Lord? Oh, please let it be so! Oh my God! Please protect me. Perhaps this is Rama's emissary!"

Hanuman descended to the ground and stood before Sita, palms united and head down in homage, glowing with gladness at meeting her.

"Mother, tears are dropping from your eyes like drips from lotus petals," he whispered soothingly. "May I ask who you are, who is resting on the tree trunk, face clouded with grief and tears in your eyes? Are you a Naaga maiden or a goddess? Your body's brilliance makes me wonder if you're mere of earthy origin!

"No, on closer inspection, you appear to be a human woman. Please tell me your true identity. God's blessings! Are you the princess Sita that Ravana kidnapped from Janasthaana? Is my joy in seeing Sita, Rama's adored?"

Sita was overcome with delight. "My kid," she added, "I am Sita, daughter of Videha's monarch and Sree Ramachandra's wife. In Ayodhya, I had twelve years of pure happiness with him. King Dasaratha made plans to crown my husband in the thirteenth year. Then Kaikeyi, his youngest wife, reminded him of the boons he had bestowed long ago and insisted that he proclaim her son Bharata king and exile Rama to the wilderness to redeem his vow. The monarch, bound by pledge, had to give in to her insistence. Rama gave up the throne at his request. I refused to be left behind and went into the forest with my lord. Lakshmana had put on bark garments before me, determined to accompany his brother to the forest and serve him. We three entered the forest and settled in Dandaka. Ravana, the evil-hearted, kidnapped me one day. And he has held me captive in this Asoka garden." In her grief, the powerless princess spoke thus.

Hanuman provided words of comfort to Sita, who was overcome with grief.

"O Videha princess! Rama, the noblest and most powerful warrior, has sent me to you with excellent news. His dear brother Lakshmana, who is always concerned about your well-being, offers his greetings to you through me."

However, when Hanuman took a closer step toward Sita in his joyous attempt to soothe and encourage her, Sita lost the trust created by his words and became suspicious once more. She closed her eyes and moved away from the tree. When Hanuman realised this, he retreated respectfully and stood with his hands clasped in humility.

"I've been duped," she sobbed. "You are, of course, Ravana. You once disguised yourself as an ascetic and imposed on me. You've returned in another disguise, speaking nice words. Why torture me, O Ravana?" So she concluded in her thoughts, and without looking at Hanuman, she sat aside in silence.

Hanuman recognised her concerns and fears. They were normal in someone who had been duped by the Rakshasa. After some consideration, he realised that the only way to gain her trust was to instil hope and joy in her fatigued heart by glorifying Rama and harping on the surety of her rescue and his victory.

"Rama has sent me," he started, "Rama dazzling like the Sun, Rama delightful to look at like the moon, Rama praised by all the rulers of the land, Rama whose words are ever sweet and truthful, Rama whose indignation is ever righteous and well directed."

"While a Rakshasa in the form of a deer enchanted Rama and pulled him away in the forest, you were left alone, and Ravana took you by force. I've come to you at Rama's request to learn about your safety, which is his continual concern. I extend Lakshmana's sincere salutations to you on his behalf. Hanuman is my name. I arrived in Lanka after crossing the sea. I, Rama's servant, crossed the sea to see you by Rama's grace, more than by my prowess. Please do not suspect me. Mother, trust in my statements." Hanuman said this with tears in his eyes.

Hanuman's kind remarks, based on her tremendous love for Rama and faith in him, put an end to Sita's concerns and gave her courage and faith.

"Please excuse my scepticism, O Vaanara friend," she added. "I am prone to unnecessary dread since I have been duped by the Rakshasa and am surrounded by his artifices. Rama's pal and messenger! When and how did you first meet Rama? How did the Prince become acquainted with the Vaanaras? Tell me everything."

Hanuman recited the virtues and appealing traits of Rama and Lakshmana to strengthen her faith. "What mystery is there in Rama being friends with me, my monarch, and the Vaanaras when the entire world lives and finds joy via his loving kindness?" he said.

He went on to describe in detail how the feud between Vaali and Sugreeva arose, how the latter first met Rama and Lakshmana, how they became friends, how Rama promised to slay Vaali and secure the Vaanara kingdom for Sugreeva, how the Vaanaras had picked up and preserved the jewels dropped by Sita, how with mounting sorrow Rama recognised them, how Vaali was slain and Sugreeva crowned, how after

At the end of the story, he placed Rama's signet ring in her hand, which he had brought with him.

Sita joyfully accepted the ring and held it to her eyes. All fear of Ravana's deception and Rakshasa's power had vanished. She had entire faith in Hanuman and a deep love for him. "How foolish was my folly, my kid!" she exclaimed. "How could I have suspected someone like you?"

Vaayu's son told her who he was, who his father was, and what his own power was. "Though I, who enjoy my father Vaayu's kindness, should not sing my praises, I do so now to ease your agony. Vaanara troops will arrive soon to annihilate the Rakshasas and their kingdom. I must first return and inform them of your location."

Then he detailed Rama's anguish at being separated from Sita, as well as the monastic life he led, and Sita's heart melted with loving sadness.

Sita forgot about her pain as she thought of Rama's.

CHAPTER XLVI: SITA AND HANUMAN

"DEAR, dear, Vaanara friend," Sita replied, "I'm not sure whether to rejoice or mourn the news you've delivered. My lord's love for me is the richest honey, yet his sadness over my plight is the most deadly poison." Thus, Sita expressed her feelings and found relief in putting her love and loss into words.

Sita was comforted but also tormented by the realisation that Rama had not forgotten her, but was thinking of her, grieving for her, and looking for her. "We are puppets being pulled by the twin strings of joy and sadness," Sita explained. "This law applies to my lord, Lakshmana, and me. When will he arrive? When will he destroy Lanka, Ravana, and the other Rakshasas, dear Vaanara friend? All of this must be completed within the next two months. Please inform my lord about this. I only have two months left."

Sita continued to speak with tears in her eyes. Hanuman couldn't stand the sight of her anguish.

"Mother!" he screamed, "I'll go right away and fetch Rama back! He will invade Lanka with a massive army. But why should you continue to suffer? Sit on my back if you're willing. I will transport you over the seas and return you to Rama in an instant. I Do not have any doubts about my capacity to do this. Allow me to perform this service, O pure of heart. I can not only carry you and return you to Rama, but I also have the power to tear Lanka apart and toss it and its king at Rama's feet! As I sprang and arrived here, so will I spring and take you to the other shore."

Hanuman continued to speak with affection and zeal. Sita wondered how the little monkey in front of her could ever hope to carry her over the ocean.

Hanuman noticed her scepticism and, to illustrate his abilities, jumped off the platform and began to expand in size. Sita was overjoyed.

"O Son of Vaayu!" she exclaimed. "I recognise your strength, yet it is not proper for you to carry me. Rakshasas will undoubtedly intercept and challenge you along the road. They will attack you with their weapons. Your concern will be to protect me. One cannot be guaranteed victory in a battle, and what would be my fate if you were to fall? And, besides, how could I be certain of retaining my position on your back during the violent convulsions of a fierce fight? I'm afraid I'll slide and tumble into the sea. As a result, you should not attempt to cross the sea with me. Apart from that, Hanuman, stealing me away from the Rakshasas would be a disgrace to my lord's valour. The honour of the Kshatriya race requires that he come and battle, defeat Ravana, and redeem me as the prize of victory. Would Rama have me snatched back if Ravana had stolen me away from him? No, my son, return and bring Rama here with Lakshmana and the

Vaanara army as soon as possible. Let my lord's arrows annihilate Lanka and send Ravana to Yama's domain."

"You are correct," Hanuman remarked, "I will return alone. But what should I say to Rama? What evidence shall I bear of having met and spoken with you?"

Hearing these words, all of her good memories with Rama flooded back to her, and her eyes welled up with tears. As she continued to recall good memories of the past, the weight of her current grief overtook her, and she wept, saying, "What is there that he does not know? Tell my lord that I am embracing his feet. That is sufficient. Lakshmana, his brother born to serve him and a master of arms, stands behind him. Looking at his sweet face, my Lord forgot about his father's death. Dear Lakshmana, the pure-hearted hero, separated from his mother and came away with us, considering me to be his mother. Tell him he should come and relieve my pain."

Sita's eyes welled up with tears as she remembered Lakshmana's heroism and dedicated loyalty. When Rama went hunting the golden deer, did she not insult and curse the unselfish and dedicated friend? The thought of this injustice caused her penitent heart excruciating sorrow.

She didn't want Hanuman to leave, who had come to her and consoled her just as she was about to terminate her life. At the same time, she urged him to get back to Rama and inform him of her situation.

"My kid, here is the jewel given by my mother at my wedding and put on my forehead by the late Emperor," she finally concluded. "Take it as a sign from me and give it to my husband." So speaking, she loosened a knot in her sari, pulled out the precious jewel, and offered it to Hanuman, who accepted it with humble awe.

Hanuman's mind was filled with pride and excitement when he held the jewel.

Rama held a special place in his heart. He had mentally recalled Rama's presence and relayed the happy news of his discovery. Only his body remained in Lanka.

"Dear son," Sita replied, "you must tell Rama what you have learned here, and it will be your good fortune to assist him. Convey my affection to the Prince, as well as to King Sugreeva and the other Vaanara leaders," Sita said again as Hanuman was about to leave. "Tell them that I beg them to assist Rama in saving me from this sea of grief. I hope that you, more than anyone else, will support and guide the Prince in all issues."

"Lay aside your sorrow, lovely princess," Hanuman replied. "Rama, Lakshmana, and the army of Vaanara will descend on Lanka to defeat the Rakshasas and redeem you. Without a doubt."

As he was about to go, Sita asked, "Shouldn't you stay here somewhere for a while and rest? Should you return right away? Your visit brought me great comfort and temporarily distracted me from my pain. When you depart, I'll sink back into my sea of grief. You arrived here after crossing the vast ocean. How will Rama and the rest of the army cross it? Have you considered it?" Doubts attacked her once more.

"Have no doubt, my queen!" Hanuman exclaimed. "Do you believe I am the only Vaanara capable of crossing the sea? Not just Sugreeva, but many of his army members, are capable of flying around the planet. What does the arrow sea mean to them? Do you believe they'd send the best of them as a messenger? Have done with grief, dear lady, since you will soon see me riding on the backs of two great princes. They will exterminate Ravana and his entire race. In a few days, you will witness the two princes standing at the gates of Lanka, bow in hand, slaughtering the Rakshasa host. The Vaanara army will be seen leaping with pleasure over the shattered city.

"Once they get the news from me, they won't waste any time. All I have to do is inform them, and they will begin immediately. Do not give up." Hanuman prepared to go by saying this and bowing deeply.

"Tell Rama and Lakshmana that I am alive," Sita exclaimed. "Make certain that no time is wasted. God bless you."

CHAPTER XLVII: INVITING BATTLE

HANUMAN sat for a time on the top of the garden wall after saying goodbye to Sita, thinking, "What can I do to instil courage in Sita and terror in Ravana and his pals, shaking their arrogant confidence? It would be nice to leave them with a memento of my visit, some sign of what the future holds for them. I must induce dread in Ravana to keep him from bothering Sita in the meanwhile; fear is the only argument they comprehend. As a result, I should do something heinous to frighten them and warn them not to mistreat Sita. Yes, I have to accomplish this before I leave."

He immediately proceeded to expand and assumed a massive form, wreaking havoc on the grove. Trees cracked and fell to the ground, bowers crumbled, and tanks and artificial hills were defaced and destroyed. The picturesque Asoka Park quickly devolved into a shambles from which the deer and birds fled in terror. The slumbering raakshasis awoke, perplexed by this unexplainable sight.

Hanuman sat atop the garden's wall, a massive figure of wrathful terror, waiting for the answer to his challenge. The Raakshasis were terrified at the sight of this foreigner, and some went to inform Ravana. Some approached Sita and inquired, "How did this enormous monkey get here? You should be aware of who he is. Is there anything he said to you? Please tell us the truth. Do not be frightened to express yourself."

"How can I know what is possible in this enchanted world of Rakshasas?" Sita responded by deflecting the question. "This monkey is presumably a Rakshasa, and you probably know more about him than I do."

The Raakshasis fled the park in terror and informed Ravana of what had occurred.

"O, king! The royal garden has been destroyed by a monstrous monkey. It happened during a private conversation with Sita."

Of course, they left off the fact that they had fallen asleep, allowing Sita to converse with the monkey.

"We tried everything we could to gain some information from Sita," they continued. "We asked her who he was, how he got there, and what he said to her. But she refuses to respond. You should capture and kill this beast. Except for the Simsupa tree behind which Sita is seated, the magnificent grove has been utterly destroyed. Its spreading branches have not been harmed. Sita's home was spared by the monkey who destroyed the tanks and bowers. This has to be for a reason. We assume that this is not your average wild animal. It had to have been sent by one of your enemies, either Indra or Kubera. Or is it something to do with Rama? How did this monkey get so close to Sita? He must be a Rama messenger. Send your warriors to catch this monstrous beast."

Ravana was enraged when he learned that his favourite park, designated for his queens, had been demolished. His eyes twinkled as torches, and hot tears streamed down his cheeks like drips of burning oil.

He turned to the bodyguards who stood by him, eager to do his bidding and commanded them to go and destroy the monster monkey right away. Armed with maces, spears, and other weapons, a large force began to carry out the king's orders.

CHAPTER XLVIII: THE TERRIBLE ENVOY

THE Rakshasa warriors were astounded to see a giant Vaanara seated at the garden gate, who grew to an even larger stature and dangerous threat as they approached.

"Oh! Have you arrived yet?" He jumped down and flourished his tail, pounding the ground with it and roaring till the four quarters trembled. He pulled the massive iron rod from the gate and began attacking them all with it. He jumped and sprang in all directions, twirling the iron rod and striking the Rakshasas down one by one. After finishing them, he returned to his position atop the pillared entrance and roared once more.

"Rama will live forever! Lakshmana, long live!" He exclaimed loudly. "King Sugreeva, long live! Oh! Rakshasas of Lanka, your end is near. Rama and Lakshmana, as well as King Sugreeva, have sent me here to destroy you. I'm ready to hurl you to your demise. I saluted Sita and asked for her blessing. And now I'm going to annihilate your city!"

All of Lanka trembled in fear as they heard the thunder of his words. Ravana's ferocious eyes widened in shock and rage when he learned that the warriors dispatched against Hanuman had all been slain.

"What do you mean?" he cried, addressing Jambumaali, the unrivalled warrior and son of Prahasta. And he told him. "Go right away! Punish this monkey and bring it to my attention."

The Rakshasa Jambumaali took his time putting on armour, picking up weapons, and preparing to face his antagonist. Meanwhile, Hanuman was moving around. He climbed to the top of a park temple and stood there, gleaming against the horizon like a second sun that had suddenly appeared in the sky. His shout echoed throughout the city of Lanka, filling all eight quarters. The Rakshasas' hearts shivered with fear. "Rama will live forever! Lakshmana, long live! King Sugreeva, long live! I've come as the King of Kosala's emissary. I've come to annihilate Lanka. I am Hanuman, son of Vaayu, and I have come to completely exterminate Rama's adversaries. I pledged in front of Sita and gained her blessing. Know that I am powerful enough to defeat a thousand Ravanas. I intend to target and destroy the Rakshasas with large rocks and uprooted trees. That is why I have come here!"

The sentries in the temple attacked him with various weapons. Hanuman jumped down and lifted a large pillar that supported the temple. Hanuman slayed the sentries with ease, whipping his enormous weapon around like a willow wand. The temple where the pillar had been removed had collapsed. Sparks of fire flew all around Hanuman as he slammed the ground with the pillar.

"There are monkeys much mightier than I in Sugreeva's army, and they will soon be here," he yelled. "They will annihilate you, your king, and your city, root, and branch. Hasn't your ruler earned the wrath of the Lord of the Ikshvaaku race? Lanka is coming to an end. The Rakshasas will face destruction. The God of Death is on his way to Ravana."

Jambumaali finally arrived. He arrived in a chariot rumbling like thunder, with wide, staring eyes and ugly, uneven teeth clad in crimson, enormous golden rings in his ears, bow in hand, garland around his neck, sword at his hip.

Hanuman noticed the chariot drawn by massive mules. And he prepared himself.

Jambumaali sat in his chariot, bowed his bow, and directed a few arrows at Maaruti, who was seated on the wall. They cut his face and drew blood, which enhanced the attractiveness of his features. It was as if a red lotus had burst out from the heavens. Hanuman was outraged by the wounds and hurled a large boulder at the chariot.

He uprooted a sal tree and twirled it at Jambumaali. Then he drew a massive iron rod from the temple, directed it at the chariot, splintered it, and smashed Jambumaali's massive body into a shapeless mess with no discernible head or limbs.

Ravana was informed of the situation of this conflict. He was gripped by awe. "This is unusual," he thought to himself. "This bloodthirsty beast is not an animal, much less a monkey. It's some new creature concocted by my old foes, the gods, to irritate me."

And he sent mighty commanders and a vast army to catch the beast and bring it before him.

The Rakshasa chiefs rode forth in a swarm of chariots. They charged in full force at Hanuman, who was still stationed on top of the entrance and grinning disdainfully. They pelted him with rocks and huge tree boles, and he grew in stature and fierceness with each dart or arrow that struck him; with each dart or arrow that struck him, he grew in stature and fierceness and ranging all round with energy pelted them with rocks and huge tree boles until all the leaders lay crushed and slain, and the survivors fled in panic and despair.

Hanuman roared in delight after killing or putting to death the entire Rakshasa contingent, and Lanka shuddered at the roar. He returned to his position on the stone battlement over the garden gate.

Fear entered Ravana's heart for the first time after learning of the loss of the force assigned to seize Hanuman and the killing of five of his best commanders.

"Incredibly, a solitary monkey can have such deadly valour and purposeful malevolence," Ravana thought anxiously. "This is certainly a divine plot." But he kept his worry to himself and chuckled mockingly.

He turned to face all of the members of his mighty council. His son, the valiant

Aksha, rose first, eager for war, and the proud father sent him off to face the formidable foe. Aksha, radiant with youth and health, and blazing with tremendous bravery at this opportunity to distinguish himself, rode forth in a gleaming chariot, certain of triumph.

CHAPTER XLIX: HANUMAN BOUND

RAVANA's young kid rode on a golden chariot obtained through tapasya. When Aksha saw Hanuman seated on the stone battlement above the gateway and noticed with approval the exquisite symmetry of his huge limbs and the majestic intrepidity of his expression, he knew he had found an opponent worthy of his steel and collected all his strength and will to do him honour.

Three arrows were aimed toward Hanuman by the young warrior. They struck his body, drawing blood. Maaruti's strength grew, and his face shined with new radiance. He, too, was impressed by the young Rakshasa's abilities.

The confrontation between the two became increasingly heated. Hundreds of arrows emerged from the heavens and struck Maaruti. They fell on Hanuman's body like rain on a rock. Rising in the air, Hanuman evaded the arrows, slipping between the meshes of that lethal network of missiles, and closing a favourable opening with Aksha. Hanuman appreciated Aksha's youthful promise and heroism and was sorry to have to slaughter him, but there was little he could do because the prince appeared to become more and more strong as the conflict progressed, and it was hazardous to take chances with him. Hanuman finally hardened his heart and resolved to destroy the youth.

He charged at Aksha's chariot, smashing it to pieces. The horses were killed. The Rakshasa prince stood chariots on the ground. He rose in the air, bow, and sword in hand, and attacked Hanuman. A massive air war took place. Aksha's bones were crushed and broken in the end, and he died.

Ravana shook with wrath when he learned that Hanuman had killed the prince, but he kept his cool and called his son Indrajit, the conqueror of Indra.

"You've mastered every weapon," he said. "You defeated the Devas and Asuras in combat. You have summoned Brahma and obtained the Brahmastra from him by your austerities. Nobody in the world can stand in your way. The chinkaras I despatched, as well as Jambumaali and our army's five generals, as well as your dear brother Aksha, have all been slaughtered by a dreadful opponent who has ravaged us in the form of a monkey, and it is now up to you to revenge them. Don't underestimate him. Weapons appear to be ineffective against him. Consider carefully what has to be done. Fight with focus and return victorious without allowing your thoughts to stray."

Indrajit, radiant as the gods, revered his father's command and proceeded with boldness and excitement toward the Asoka Vana after getting his blessings.

Indrajit approached Hanuman while riding in a chariot carried by four fearsome lions and twanging his bowstring. His chariot sounded like the monsoon wind.

His lotus-like eyes gleamed with triumph.

Hanuman was overjoyed when he saw the chariot approaching him. Indrajit, a skilled fighter, drew his bow and prepared his arrows for Hanuman. The Naagas, Yakshas, and Siddhas gathered in the sky to witness the impending epic fight.

Hanuman roared and enlarged his stature, even more, when he saw Indrajit. The Rakshasa warrior fired his darts quietly. As in the war between the gods and their cousins, the Asuras, arrow showers began to fall. Hanuman rose into the sky and struck down the sharp arrows with lightning-like speed. His roar made the quarters resound, drowning out the Rakshasa's drumbeats and bow twangs.

The conflict continued with growing fury, leaving everyone in awe. The two warriors were perfect equals in terms of ability and power. Hanuman's strength never wavered, no matter how many times he was wounded. As a result, Indrajit concluded, "My arrows cannot defeat this monkey. That is exactly what my father stated. He can only be bound with the Brahmastra."

The Brahmastra was sent forth by the Rakshasa Prince. The Vaanara warrior was bound and helpless as a result of its touch. Hanuman became aware of what had occurred. "I have been bound by the Brahmastra," he thought to himself. Hanuman had also obtained a boon from Brahma, which he now remembered.

"This will only keep me confined for one muhurta (four-fifths of an hour)," he reasoned. "I am not in any genuine danger. Allow me to witness what the Rakshasas do to me while I am tied and powerless. I might be able to find another job as a messenger here."

He resigned himself to the Brahmastra and lay down on the ground, motionless but in full command of his faculties, as directed by Brahma when he gave him the gift of immortality.

When the Rakshasas saw Hanuman lying helpless on the ground, they approached him and danced with joy, calling him derogatory names and praising their prince, who had before stood at a distance in terror.

"We'll hack you to pieces!" they yelled. "Let us devour him. We will drag him to our Ravana's throne." They yelled in this and other ways.

"This fellow is merely pretending," a number of them feared. "He might get up and attack us." So they took jute and coconut fibre ropes and bound him tightly, exulting: "Now that we have bound him, let us drag him to the Lord of the Rakshasas."

Indrajit was upset because he learned about the Rakshasas' dumb blunder too late and was unable to prevent it.

"Alas!" he exclaimed, heartbroken. "They have undone all of my efforts. These cretins are unaware of the secrets of supernatural weapons. When they use ropes and jute to restrain him, the Astra relinquishes its power. When physical bonds are introduced, the bond of the mantra is broken. Hanuman is now imprisoned merely by ropes that he may cut, and the Brahmastra cannot be utilised again."

Hanuman recognised this and knew he could break free if he wanted, but he welcomed the chance to meet and speak with Ravana and allowed himself to be taken to the king, calmly bearing all their insults and cruelties in apparent weakness. They cursed and abused him, dragged him through the streets, and women and children came out to mock him.

CHAPTER L: LANKA IN FLAMES

His kidnappers carried him to Ravana's court and presented him in front of the King. Hanuman looked at the huge king with wrathful fascination, forgetting the agony and insults he had endured. As he gazed at him on his throne, a pitying admiration for the doomed Rakshasa filled his mind.

Ravana sat there, a figure of dazzling splendour, dressed in golden silk and wearing the regal crown, the gems inlaid in it gleaming brilliantly. His dark physique, illuminated with royal markings, was like a big glowing hill.

"Alas!" exclaimed Hanuman, filled with rage, surprise, and pity. "If this mighty one had not deviated from the path of dharma, not even Indra could have matched him. What a shape, what light, what power! He lost his happiness and surrendered his fame because he trusted the boon he had obtained."

Ravana addressed his ministers while Hanuman was immersed in meditation, saying, "Find out from this vile person who he is, where he has come from, who has sent him here, and why he invaded Lanka. Tell him to tell the truth."

Prahasta questioned Hanuman as the king had directed. "Monkey, don't be terrified! You will avoid penalties if you speak the truth. Was it Indra who brought you here? Or are you Kubera's aide? Whose orders are you following? Speak the truth and you will rescue yourself."

"Neither Indra nor Kubera sent me here," Hanuman remarked directly to Ravana. "My name is Hanuman. I came here to observe the Rakshasa king. That's why I ruined the garden. I've come here as Sugreeva, the Vaanara king's messenger. Ramachandra, the famous son of Ayodhya's king Dasaratha, has become Sugreeva's friend, and murdering Vaali has made Sugreeva king. When Ramachandra, the heir to the Ayodhya kingdom, was living in the Dandaka forest to fulfil his father's pledge, his consort, who had been left alone for a while, went missing, and Sugreeva despatched his servant to search for her all over the globe at the request of Rama and Lakshmana. On my way to Lanka, I came across a good princess. O lord of the Rakshasas, I address you with the deference due to a messenger of a brother monarch. Carrying off princess Sita was a cowardly act that went completely against dharma. If you continue in your evil folly, you will undoubtedly destroy your race. Return Sita to the Prince and beg forgiveness from him. Make Rama your adversary, and you will destroy yourself. Take note of the words of the Vaanara king's modest messenger. These remarks from a brother king are truthful and intended for your good."

Hanuman sounded a harsh warning in a strong and clear voice. When the Rakshasa king heard it, his eyes turned red with rage, and he ordered Hanuman to be slain right away.

However, Vibhishana pointed out that killing a king's emissary would be wrong.

"Kings' law forbids the killing of envoys and messengers under any circumstances. You can have him mutilated, whipped, or branded, but not killed," Vibhishana said.

"What is wrong with killing someone who has sinned so greatly?" Ravana wondered.

"No matter how heinous his offence, it was done at the bidding of others," Vibhishana replied politely. "What is the point of abandoning his royal lords and slaying their instrument, a mere messenger? Let us look for ways to punish those who sent him here. They must be brought here and punished appropriately. If he is killed now, what chance do we have of bringing our true adversaries here? If, on the other hand, he is returned to them alive, they will come here and attack us. They will thereafter face appropriate punishment at your hands."

Ravana concurred. "Very well," he answered, "the most prized item of a monkey is his tail. Set fire to his tail, flog him mercilessly, and put him out."

Hanuman was taken out by his slaves as a result of the Rakshasa king's comments. They wrapped his tail in various rags. As his tail grew in length, they brought more and more old rags and wrapped them around it. They drenched the entire thing in oil and set it ablaze like a massive flaming torch.

Hanuman was led through the streets of Lanka while bound by ropes with his tail ablaze.

"Here comes the burglar who broke into our city!" exclaimed the ladies and children. They mocked him as he was led around by exulting Rakshasas to the tune of pipes and drums across all of Lanka's roads and byways.

The rakshasas told Sita in the Asoka Vana, "Do you know what happened to the monkey with whom you had a secret talk? They have wrapped his tail in oil-soaked linen and set fire to it. His tail is on fire. They're carrying him around town in a procession."

They mocked Sita when they told her the story.

She lit a fire and prayed to Agni, the deity of fire: "O Agni! Be calm to Hanuman; do not damage him if there is any goodness in me and purity."

Hanuman took the blows and taunts and moved from street to street quietly observing everything. To amuse their wives and children, the Rakshasas led him through the city's streets and byways. And he silently recorded all the mysteries of the guarded metropolis for future reference.

"But what exactly is this miracle?" he wondered. "The oil-soaked rags burn brilliantly, but the fire does not hurt and feels pleasant on my tail. The elements themselves appear to be kind to one focused on Rama's mission. Or perhaps Agni is gentle with me since he is a friend of my father Vaayu. Now, I believe I should not waste this unexpected opportunity to instil fear of God in these Rakshasas."

Suddenly, he reduced in size, threw off the chains that tied him, and sprang to the top of a large structure with his burning tail. He grabbed a pillar there and twirled it about, terrifying everyone who saw it.

Then he jumped from mansion to mansion, lighting them on fire. Within minutes, a strong breeze began to blow, and the entire city was engulfed in flames. The Rakshasas and their women and children screamed in terror and fled.

"This monkey is none other than Yama," some speculated. "No, he must be the god Agni," others said. And they all ran away from their burning homes.

Hanuman was glad to see the flames rise, remembering the insults he had received. He sat on the crest of Trikoota Hill, gazing out at the red glow of the burning city, content.

Then he went to the sea and, plunging in, extinguished the fire in his tail before coming ashore.

"Alas! Alas! "What did I do?" He was overcome with emotion. "In my wrath, I've lost my senses. What good are strength, ability, and all other gifts if one cannot control his or her anger? Sita must have died in this big conflagration I've started. My rage-fueled action has completely derailed my entire plan. Unfortunately, there is no fool, no sinner on earth like me. Sita was killed as a result of my fury against the Rakshasas. I must put a stop to my life and my disgrace right now!"

He then heard voices in the skies. The Chaaranas and Yakshas were ecstatic and exclaimed, "What a miracle! Except for the location of Sita, all of Lanka is engulfed in flames!"

Hanuman was relieved after hearing this otherworldly discussion. "Sita rescued herself. She saved me because the flames were kept at bay by her purity and might. How might fire help us honour the goddess of chastity? What damage can fire cause? This fire I started couldn't get close to Sita."

Hanuman returned to Asoka Park with this thought. He saw Sita, who was relieved to see him alive and well under the Simsupa tree.

He bowed before her, ecstatic, and whispered, "Oh mother! I saw you safe and sound. This is your strength, as well as my good fortune. Now permit me to leave."

"You are, indeed, a hero," Sita replied. "Nothing is impossible for you. See to it that my lord arrives soon and defeats the Rakshasas and redeems me. This is something only you can do."

"Be assured," Hanuman said. "Sugreeva, Rama, Lakshmana, and the many Vaanaras will soon arrive. Ravana and his evil legions will perish. The delighted Prince will accompany you to Ayodhya. No more crying. May God bless you." Hanuman then left Sita, comforting her. He proceeded to the seashore and rose into the sky by ascending the magnificent hill known as Arishta.

On the way, he noticed Mynaaka mountain waiting for him. He massaged it gently with his palm but did not stop. He shot straight as an arrow from a bow. He roared as he saw the Mahendra hill and realised he was close to the other shore.

Meanwhile, the Vaanaras, seeing Hanuman flying towards them like a giant eagle across the sky, said, “He has arrived! He has arrived!”

Their hearts had been heavy with concern, and their eyes had been moist. They jumped with excitement now.

“He has undoubtedly succeeded,” Jaambavan predicted. “He wouldn’t growl like this otherwise.”

They climbed trees and hills and waited in awe as Hanuman returned from Lanka, and approached them.

And Hanuman was overjoyed to see his friends covering the mountains and trees. He landed on Mahendra hill amid their joyful ruckus.

CHAPTER LI: A CARNIVAL

THE Vaanaras gathered on the Mahendra peak, overjoyed at the sight of Hanuman, and the veteran Jammbavaan, who welcomed Vaayu's son with great affection, spoke on their behalf. "We'd love to hear the full story of your journey and its triumphant conclusion. We're especially curious about how you discovered Sita. How is she doing now? And, dear Anjana's son, tell us about Ravana's condition and behaviour. We will be able to consider and decide what needs to be done next once we have all of the information."

Hanuman offered mental salutations to Sita and recounted, without omission, everything that happened during the passage and in the city of Lanka; how he searched for Sita in vain in Ravana's palace, how he finally found her in the Asoka Vana, how there Ravana sought and importuned her and was spurned by her, what dire threats he held out, and how the rakshasas teased her.

He told them, with tears in his eyes, what a divinely precious soul Sita was and how nobly she had carried herself. He then described how he destroyed the park and killed the Rakshasa warriors before being bound by Indrajit and brought before Ravana. He described what happened during the interview, and how, as a punishment for his audacity, they set fire to his tail, providing him with a large torch with which he set fire to their city.

Hanuman continued after this detailed account of the events: "So far, our efforts have been successful due to Sita's power of chastity, who is chastity incarnate. When I think of her, I wonder how the Rakshasa could seize and carry her away without being consumed by fire. Ravana, on the other hand, had amassed considerable power through his tapas. What is your advice now? Should we travel straight to Lanka, slay Ravana and the Rakshasa troops, and then return Sita to Rama? It's not as if we don't have the strength to accomplish it. Many of us are capable of defeating Ravana and the Rakshasa hordes. Indeed, I declared out in Lanka, 'I, Rama's envoy and Sugreeva's minister, have come to annihilate you.' But, while we're chatting, Vaidehi, the Goddess of Purity, is a closely guarded prisoner crying for rescue under the Simsupa tree. In her hour of despair, I appeared to her and consoled her with the knowledge of her lord's imminent coming. Consider carefully and decide what should be done next."

Angada, enraged by all of this, leapt to his feet and exclaimed: "I can do it all by myself. And there are a lot of us here, eager fighters looking for a fight. It would be impolite to travel to Rama empty-handed and without Sita after all these days. Let us go immediately to Lanka, defeat Ravana and the Rakshasa army, and return to Kishkindha with Sita."

Jaambavan, the wise old man, protested gently. "No, my prince, it is not right," he said. “We should tell Rama and Lakshmana everything and then do whatever they want. Rama’s goal should be accomplished in the way that he desires. That is sufficient.”

All of the Vaanaras, including Hanuman and Angada, agreed that this was the correct course of action. They then soared towards Kishkindha, rising into the sky.

They landed near the Vaanara king’s protected park. Despite the guards’ warnings, they made their way into it, drank honey, and ate the fruit. They revelled unrestrainedly and damaged the lovely park.

Dadhimukha, Sugreeva’s uncle and custodian of the royal park, rushed to the monarch and complained about the mirth makers’ raucous behaviour.

“Your protected park has been destroyed. The Vanaras that flew south have returned and are behaving erratically in the garden. They pay no attention to what I say. On the contrary, they assaulted and insulted me, drank and destroyed all the honeycombs, plucked and ate all the fruit they wanted, and are now laying senseless as a result of their revelry. All of the trees and vegetation are in ruins. The king should immediately inflict severe punishment on these disobedient Vaanaras.”

Sugreeva recognised the situation right away. “It is apparent, Lakshmana, that Hanuman, Jaambavan, and Angada have succeeded in their search and are celebrating their victory in this way.”

He then turned to Dadhimukha and said, “Send them all here at once.”

Dadhimukha saw the true situation of circumstances and hurried to the Vaanaras to transmit the king’s command.

CHAPTER LII: THE TIDINGS CONVEYED

SUGREEVA's notion was like honey to Rama's ears. They were looking forward to the arrival of the Vaanaras. Within moments, there was a loud commotion in the air, and the Vaanara hordes landed with triumphant yells.

The Vaanaras marched to the presence of their monarch, who was waiting for them with Rama and Lakshmana, led by Hanuman and Angada.

"Seen have I the Goddess of purity, your monarch," Hanuman bowed. "In Lanka, she is secure and well. From here in space, I salute her." And he turned south to offer a reverent salutation.

Hanuman conveyed to the Prince the happy news that Sita had been found and was in good health. Sugreeva and Lakshmana, overcome with delight, embraced Rama.

"Dear Vaanara friends," the Prince of Ayodhya said, "tell me where Sita is. "How is she doing? How did you get a glimpse of her? Please explain everything in full." His eager inquiries piled on top of one another.

The other Vaanaras went to Hanuman, who was standing behind them and requested him to recount what he had seen and done. Hanuman began to recount his story. He had completed a huge feat on his own with unrivalled courage and power, and yet he did not push himself forward into the presence of Prince Rama or King Sugreeva, but gave precedence to Angada and the aged Jaambavan and the others, and remained silent until they requested him to speak.

"After crossing a hundred yojanas of water, I arrived on the southern coast at the city of the wicked Ravana. I observed Sita being held captive and carefully guarded in a garden attached to the palace. She had survived solely on the thought of her lord and the recital of his name. Raakshasis who was cruel and nasty surrounded her. I noticed her laying on the ground, her hair dishevelled and her face darkened with sorrow and care. When I arrived, she had decided to terminate her life to avoid the Rakshasa king's importunities and threats. I began praising your magnificence in hushed tones. I had to gain her trust first, although I was a mere monkey. Then I addressed her. I informed her of King Sugreeva and your alliance. I informed her about your deep sorrow and unwavering devotion. This filled her with sweet grief while also reawakening her hope and determination to live. When I asked for a token to give you, the angel of purity handed me this jewel to give you.

"She begged me to inform you that she would struggle and survive for a month, but then she would die at the hands of Ravana, or she would seek her escape from death. She asked me to offer her condolences to the Vaanara King. Let us immediately think about and plan our trip to Lanka to reclaim the princess." Having said this, he handed Prince Sita's chuda-mani or crest-jewel.

Rama snatched the jewel from Hanuman's grasp and fell at the sight of it, unable to handle the extremes of ecstasy and sadness. "O Lakshmana!" he exclaimed, pressing the jewel to his bosom. "Heroic son of Vaayu, happy are you who have seen Sita," he embraced Hanuman once more. "I can see her in front of me now. You did bring her to me."

"Set aside your grief, my Lord," Hanuman advised, "and consider what needs to be done right now. "Sita questioned your ability to cross the sea with the Vaanara army. I informed her that she had nothing to worry about because, although not the strongest of the Vaanaras, I had traversed it as far as she could see. I told her that I could carry Rama and Lakshmana over the sea on my shoulders and bring them there."

CHAPTER LIII: THE ARMY MOVES FORWARD

"THE deed done by Hanuman, none else in the world could even conceive of attempting—crossing the sea, entering Lanka protected by Ravana and his formidable hosts, and accomplishing the task set him by his king not only fully but beyond the fondest hopes of all," Rama said at the end of his narrative.

And it hurt him to think that he couldn't sufficiently repay Hanuman for the incredible joy he had delivered. "O Hanuman, please accept this embrace as an expression of my heartfelt gratitude for your wonderful service to me."

So speaking, he pulled Hanuman into his arms and clutched him to his breast, his whole being filled with grateful affection.

"Hanuman has indeed created a marvel, Sugreeva," he said. "He entered Lanka, which was heavily guarded by the Rakshasas. He discovered Sita and saved her life by soothing her. He saved my life by bringing back wonderful news about her.

"But how will we cross the sea now? How will our massive army reach the opposite side? We must first cross the sea before we can attack Ravana's city and the Rakshasa army. There is no way I can do it. Our excitement at Hanuman's accomplishment and the excellent news he has conveyed is tempered by concern about our future path."

However, the Vaanara king stated: "What is it, Lord Rama? What is the point of being downcast? Here are my men, ready to die for you and make it our pleasure to carry you and Lakshmana to Lanka. We can do it, without a doubt. You can assume the stronghold fell the instant Hanuman saw Lanka. The feeling of assurance in my heart right now is a good enough omen for me."

Sugreeva had thus reassured Rama and encouraged him to act. Rama and Hanuman then discussed Lanka, the town, the fort, the moat, and other defences. Hanuman described the prosperity of Lanka, the joyful lifestyles of the Rakshasas, their trust in Ravana, and their affection for him. He told Rama about Ravana's army's force and size, the fortress's strength and structure, the sentry's vigilance, the moats, walls and gates, catapults and drawbridges, and the care and thoroughness of all defence systems. He also described how the coast was meticulously secured so that no enemy ship could approach there.

"Yet you may be convinced," he added, "Our Vaanara army is completely capable of conquering Lanka. We have unrivalled fighters like Angada, Dwivida, Mainda, Jaambavan, Panasa, Nala, and Neela among us. We have a massive army. We will fly across the skies and demolish Lanka without touching the ground. We don't care about its mountains or forest defences. We are going to raze the city to the ground. Set the auspicious moment and give us the go-ahead."

At high noon, the army marched towards the southern sea under the triumphal star, Uttara Phalguni. They were met with good omens.

Rama, Sugreeva, and Lakshmana were speaking with one another as they marched. "If only Sita knew we were leaving," Rama replied, "it would inspire her to stay living."

Scouts who knew the route went ahead, keeping an eye out for opponents hiding in ambush. The army was led through areas that could offer food and water to the massive army. The troops moved quickly across mountains and woodlands.

The Vaanaras would sometimes carry Rama and Lakshmana on their shoulders to make the march faster. The Vaanaras' enthusiasm grew with each passing moment. They screamed, leapt, and sported. Rama overheard them speaking to each other, "Ravana will be killed by me! I'm going to meet and murder Ravana!"

Neela and Kumuda proceeded to reconnoitre in front of the troops. Strong warriors were stationed in the rear to protect it from behind. In the centre were King Sugreeva, Rama, and Lakshmana. Rama issued stringent orders that the soldiers cause no harm or suffering to the towns and villages along the way. The marching army made a roar like a sea and filled all eight quarters. The dust they created blanketed the skies.

Rama visited the pinnacle of Mahendra Mountain to survey the sea when they arrived.

"We must now think and decide," he stated, "how the troops will be able to cross the sea. Let us camp and recuperate in the forest till then." Sugreeva then gave the order to the commanders. The Vaanaras set up camp in the woodland near the ocean.

When Sugreeva, Rama, and Lakshmana were satisfied that the entire army had settled comfortably, the two brothers separated.

Rama stated: "People say that if a person loses something important, time will allow him to forget about it and he will no longer grieve. But this is not what I discovered, Lakshmana.' Dejection gripped Rama once more as the thought of Sita and her situation preyed on his mind more than ever.

"When Ravana grabbed Sita and brought her away," Rama sobbed, "she must have yelled aloud, 'Ah my Lord! 'Ah Rama, Lakshmana!' But she didn't see anyone approaching. We did not seek her assistance. My grief grows worse every time I consider the pain she must have endured. She is in considerable pain as she is held captive by the merciless rakshasas. Janaka's daughter, the bride who entered mighty Dasaratha's mansion, lying on the naked ground, surrounded by rakshasas!"

"Rama!" exclaimed Lakshmana, "be free of misery! We will soon crush Ravana, rescue Sita, and return her to Ayodhya. She will enter the city in the form of the goddess of chastity. Give up your anguish. Arm yourself with bravery."

CHAPTER LIV: ANXIETY IN LANKA

THE Rakshasa monarch was embarrassed and terrified at the notion of what Hanuman had accomplished in Lanka. He gathered his ministers and conferred with them.

He began with an apology. "What has occurred is surprising and unexpected. No one has ever been known to enter our city, but this Rama emissary has not only entered Lanka, but he has also visited and spoken with the imprisoned Sita. He has demolished temples and palaces. He has assassinated some of our most feared warriors. He has instilled dread in our people. And this is not going to end here. As a result, we must determine what should be done. You are aware that the king should make decisions only after speaking with his loyal ministers who have a clear vision and are well-versed in statecraft. As a result, I've convened this Council. Let us think about what we should do about it. The monarch has little use for ministers who are not forthright or who, unaware of their ideas, wobble in their ad vocation. The situation at hand is critical. Rama and his army are both powerful. They will, without a doubt, find a way to cross the sea. Think carefully and tell me how we may build and secure our city and army, as well as what efforts we should take to defend ourselves."

Following the king's speech, the Assembly spoke with one voice.

"Wonderful king! Why should you be concerned, knowing that our army and armaments are the most powerful in the world? Where is the opponent that would dare to attack your citadel and who might defeat your army? The entire world is aware of your might. Didn't you attack Bhogavati and defeat the Naaga king? Did you not battle and destroy the strong Kubera and his Yakshas, as well as capture his Pushpaka Vimana and this island of Lanka? How many cities have you not assaulted and taken in the nether region? Varuna's sons and Yama himself have pleaded for your clemency. And who exactly is Rama? Rama and his Vaanara army may be defeated by your son Indrajit alone. Did he not arrest and imprison Indra before releasing him? Rama and his Vaanaras have little chance against such a warrior. All you have to do is order Indrajit to destroy the Vaanara mob, and everything will be finished. Why should you be concerned, wonderful king?" As a result, they spoke highly about their ruler.

Prahasta, the Commander-in-Chief, rose like a vast black cloud. "You, who defeated the Devas, Daanavas, and Gandharvas in battle, why should you, oh King of monarchs, be concerned about these insignificant creatures? True, the monkey came here, caught us napping, and caused us some trouble. This, however, will never happen again. If he returns, I know how to handle him. If you give me the order, I can destroy the whole Vaanara race. You have nothing to worry about from your minor transgression, Sita's kidnapping."

"All of you may stay here with the King," Nikumbha, son of Kumbhakarna, stood and said. I'll go alone, meet and destroy the enemy, and report back to you."

So, one by one, they rose and spoke courageous things to delight Ravana, and then they all stood up together and roared aloud, raising their swords.

Vibhishana, Ravana's younger brother, made them all sit down and spoke to the monarch, hands folded, "Brother, what these people say is beautiful to hear but not true or good to act upon. If you follow these people's suggestions and start a war now, you will destroy Lanka and all of us. We must also consider dharma's requirements. It was not proper, it was a tremendous sin for you to have taken Rama's wife and brought her here. We must first purge ourselves of this vice. What damage did Rama cause us? Rama's actions in the Dandaka forest were genuine self-defence and defence of those who looked to him for security. He only battled and killed those who went out to kill him. His actions certainly do not warrant your kidnapping of his wife. When the guilt is on your side, it is morally wrong to consider battle. Though our strength is enormous, we must evaluate it against the enemy's power before deciding whether to seek or avoid battle. But first and foremost, we must rehabilitate Sita. My advice is to restore Sita, before Rama and the Vaanaras assault Lanka. All of this, dear brother, is for your benefit. We should first correct our own mistakes before moving on."

Vibhishana begged Ravana with bowed hands.

Though Ravana was pleased with the vain-glorying comments of his ministers and generals, he had reservations. As a result, after hearing Vibhishana, he replied, "Let us meet again tomorrow and discuss this matter."

He called the Council to order and then left.

CHAPTER LV: RAVANA CALLS A COUNCIL AGAIN

VIBHISHANA rushed to the king as soon as the day broke. He had given the topic careful consideration and had reached a decision. His brother's welfare needed that he endeavour to convert and save him in some way.

Vibhishana entered the royal palace and stood before the king with his hands folded. Ravana dismissed everyone but the principal ministers and requested his brother to speak.

"My brother and my lord," Vibhishana started, "please forgive me if what I say does not please your ears. My intention is not to flatter you, but to save you from a grave peril while there is still time.

"We have only seen bad omens since you brought Sita to Lanka. Even when the correct mantra is put into the libation, the flame does not spring to welcome it. Snakes can be found in places of worship. Elephants, horses, camels, and monkeys become ill, refuse food, and act strangely. Medicines have lost their effectiveness. Vultures swooping overhead make the augurs nervous. The streets are filled with wild monsters. These omens should not be ignored. Please, please, please return Sita to her husband. Why should we, who have so much to lose, risk anyone's wrath? Let us return Sita to her tribe and live happily." Vibhishana pleaded passionately with his brother in this manner.

Ravana shouted, "Never, never! There should be no mention of Sita being restored to her folks here. This adversary does not inspire confidence in me. I see nothing to be concerned about. You may now depart."

Ravana had no peace of mind despite his uncompromising speech. Sita had not yielded to him, and even his close relatives disapproved of his behaviour. He was agitated, but he convened the Council again, this time with confidence and unconcern. Lust and wounded vanity prevented him from the true path, but he found solace in seeking advice from others. He rode through the streets in a golden chariot driven by noble steeds from the palace to the Hall of Council. Warriors marched in front, behind, and on the sides, brandishing swords and shields and wearing dazzling uniforms. Others followed the chariot on elephants and horses, armed with axes, spears, and other dreadful weapons. Trumpets were blown and drums were pounded.

As the Lord of Lanka, accompanied by his retinue, marched along the royal way, his people bowed their heads, folded their hands, and prayed for victory. Drums and trumpets filled the eight quarters as he walked into the hall.

Ravana sat on an agate throne in Maya's magnificent hall, which gleamed with gold, silver, and exquisite carpets.

Hundreds of devils stood guard outside. Thousands of Rakshasa warriors had gathered in the room in response to the King's summons. Long lines of chariots lined the streets. Each was assigned a seat in the chamber based on his rank.

Hundreds of Vedic priests and chanters arrived and were seated in the hall after receiving marks of respect from the king. Vibhishana, Suka, Prahasta, and others bowed before the king and took their seats. Devoted officers thronged the hall, all courageous and efficient, ready to carry out their king's orders.

The assemblage rivalled Indra's in splendour, and everyone sensed that important decisions were about to be made. Ravana shattered the enormous assembly's expectant silence with a voice as deep and resonant as thunder. "You are strong, brave, and versed in the arts of peace and war," he continued. "You can find a way out of any situation. So, once again, I seek your advice. You are well aware of what I have done. Sita, who was living in the Dandaka forest, was brought here by me. My desire for her is so strong that returning her is inconceivable to me. She has so far refused to comply with my requests and continues to hold out hope that Rama will come here and redeem her. I told her it was an unachievable want and a futile hope. Finally, she requested a year, which I granted her. I'm currently seeking your advice. I'll never agree to sending Sita back and seeking Rama's forgiveness. You, my magnificent warriors, and I have never faced defeat in combat. True, a large monkey managed to cross the water and cause some havoc here. But crossing the water and arriving here will be difficult for Rama and the Vaanara army. And even if they did arrive, why should we be concerned? What chance do they have against us?

"Rama, Lakshmana, Sugreeva, and the Vaanaras are tented on the other side of the sea. Consider how we can defeat Rama and Lakshmana. I should have called the Council sooner. But Kumbhakarna was sleeping, so I waited till he woke up."

Ravana said thus, blinded by passion, concealing his true distress and combining a little falsehood with truth. Sita had not requested a year. She had flatly refused his approaches, but he asked her to rethink and gave her a year to reconsider.

CHAPTER LVI: VIBHEESHANA

RAVANA's younger brother, Kumbhakarna, addressed the assembly: "Wonderful King! You have put yourself at grave risk by disregarding statecraft fundamentals. If you had a grudge against Rama and Lakshmana, you should have confronted them and defeated and slain them before kidnapping Sita. If you had performed in this manner, even Sita would have admired you, and she might have accepted you. You did not contact us before committing the offence and earning Rama's wrath, but now, when it is too late, you seek our advice."

After speaking angrily, Kumbhakarna looked at the king and realised that he was in distress. As sweet as he was strong, he couldn't bear the sadness on his brother's face.

"Let bygones be bygones," he reasoned, "one cannot abandon one's honour." Kumbhakarna had no illusions about the repercussions, but his kind nature accepted them for the sake of his idolised brother. He realised that tearing the heart out of others in the face of impending danger was futile, so he began to say vaunting phrases like the rest: "What you did, and how you did it, could both be incorrect. But it makes no difference. Rama will be slain by me. Do not be scared. One or two of his arrows might strike me. Regardless, I will slay him and suck his blood, and triumph will be yours. Set aside your concern, my brother, and consider other things." He was a proud warrior who loved his brother and his nation, and he chose to die honourably with them.

Ravana's chief counsellor was Prahasta. He encouraged the King by speaking of his unbeatable might.

Ravana became animated and exclaimed: "Didn't I defeat Kubera? Didn't I drive him away and claim Lanka for myself? Who dares to oppose me here? Let's wait and see!"

These statements were praised by the audience.

Vibhishana was the only one who did not applaud. He didn't mind his brother's rage. He believed it was his responsibility to warn him of the danger and wrongs of his methods. He felt obligated to make every effort to save himself from certain death. He got up and said: "You've brought Sita with you, along with doom for yourself and your race. Your first and most important duty to yourself and your people is to return her to Rama. If you do not succeed, we will all perish. This is unquestionable."

"If we confront Rama," he continued, "we will lose. Failure is unavoidable. Our fortune is deteriorating. Let us resurrect Sita, seek Rama's forgiveness, and thereby save our kingdom, our lives, our wealth, and our honour."

At Vibhishana's request, Indrajit, Ravana's son, lost patience and exclaimed: "My uncle's remarks make me feel ashamed. We will never accept his proposal. Are we to be terrified of two insignificant humans? Isn't the entire planet shaking in fear in front of us right now? Vibhishana's advice is an affront to our race!"

Vibhishana responded gently: "You're very inexperienced. That is why you speak in this manner. You are the king's son, and you should be his best friend, but I fear you are turning out to be his worst enemy. And you, ministers who should be giving sound advice, are leading the monarch astray. My Lankan Lord! Do not dismiss anything I say. Return Sita to Rama with honour and ask his pardon. This is the only path; there are no alternatives. We will all perish if we do not take the sole possible path."

Ravana's wrath had become out of control. "I've put up with your nonsense thus far," he yelled angrily "because you are my younger brother Otherwise, you'd be dead by now. I see that a brother is one's deadliest enemy. Everyone knows that envy of brothers causes shame and discomfort to the brave. They conceal their true desire and wait for their opportunity, which they seize without hesitation. The brother grins and talks cheerfully as long as one is safe and prosperous. But when danger approaches, he is ready to flee. If anyone else had said what you have, Vibhishana, I would have slaughtered him right now. Base individual! You are a shame to the rakshasa race!"

Vibhishana, unable to stomach the insult, rose and said: "You may speak freely, my brother. Though you have strayed from the road of dharma, you are still my brother, and I warn you that you are being lured by Yama's noose down the path of destruction.

"Rama's darts are destroying you in my mind's eye, which causes me to talk as I do. You refer to me as your adversary. Defend your city and your life to the best of your ability. God's blessings! I'm leaving. May you have a good life! I believed I could help you in your time of need, but you won't let me. You think I envy you and your possessions. Good advice is rejected by someone whose time has come."

After saying this, and realising that he would have no place in Lanka in the future, Vibhishana renounced all his belongings and rose into the sky, directly to where Rama and Lakshmana were stationed. He was accompanied by four good Rakshasa pals.

CHAPTER LVII: THE VAANARA'S DOUBT

STANDING on the northern coast, the Vaanara chieftains noticed the sky suddenly lit up with a golden brilliance like Mount Meru's top. It was too steady to be a lightning strike.

The forms of five large Rakshasas could be seen in the light. Sugreeva, the Vaanaras' king and commander, looked at them and stated, "There is no question these are Rakshasas from Lanka with hostile intentions."

When the Vaanara warriors heard this, they armed themselves with branches and stones and exclaimed, "Let us go. We will intercept, kill, and bring them down to earth."

Hearing the Vaanaras' comments, Vibhishana showed no fear and cried out from above in a clear voice: "Vibhishana is here before you, the brother of Ravana, the cruel ruler of the Rakshasas." I stand before you as Ravana's brother, who murdered Jataayu and kidnapped Sita and is now holding her captive in Lanka.

"I tried in vain to dissuade him from his evil plans and advised him to restore Sita and seek Rama's forgiveness. All I got in return was scorn and public contempt. As a result, I'm standing here in front of you. I have given up my kingdom, wife, and children to seek service and refuge at Rama's feet. I beg you to alert Rama of this knowledge."

Sugreeva mistrusted the Rakshasa king's brother and reported to Rama: "Vibhishana, Ravana's brother, has come here with four Rakshasa friends seeking asylum at your feet. Consider carefully, you who are knowledgeable in matters, what should be done right now. These Rakshasas are masters of deception. They can turn themselves invisible and perform a variety of other feats. They have all the cunning and bravery of the wicked. They cannot be trusted. These Rakshasas, I believe, were dispatched by Ravana himself.

"Whatever Vibhishana says, we must remember that he is our adversary's brother. He was born into the evil Rakshasa race. How can we put our faith in him? I do not doubt that this is a Ravana scam. It is best to eliminate Vibhishana and his colleagues immediately. If we let him into our camp, he will betray us and return to his people at the earliest opportunity. Allow us, then, to immediately destroy Ravana's brother and his men."

Sugreeva remained in silence, waiting for Rama's response after openly expressing his thoughts at the sight of the Rakshasa.

"You have heard the words of the King who is well-versed in policy," Rama stated to Hanuman and other leaders. "Ravana's brother has arrived and is waiting for us. I'd want to hear your thoughts on this. In times of trouble, one should seek guidance from friends. Tell me without reservation what your hearts desire."

"He has come from our enemy's camp," remarked Angada, the Vaanara prince. "We don't know if he came on his own or was dispatched by our adversary. While it may not be right to reject him outright, it would be risky to accept him without first testing him. Let us at the very least keep a close eye on him and not give him any opportunities for mischief. We can kick him out if his movements are questionable. We will accept him if they are friendly and demonstrate good faith."

"Nothing can be revealed by testing such people," Jaambavan stated. "If he has come here with malicious motives, no test can reveal the truth. Ravana is an unrelenting opponent. His brother claims that he has abruptly broken up with him and came over to us. This abrupt breakup with a brother is difficult to believe. We haven't even crossed the sea yet. What motivates him to seek protection with us when we are on this distant shore? This is all pretty suspicious. They are a treacherous race. I believe we should deny him admission."

Rama then turned to Hanuman the wise.

CHAPTER LVIII: THE DOCTRINE OF SURRENDER AND GRACE

IN answer to Rama's offer, Hanuman stated his thoughts clearly, sweetly, and pregnantly: "Why should you seek our counsel? Brihaspati doesn't have anything to tell you that you don't already know. If admitting Vibhishana is risky, how is the risk mitigated by delay and trial? Furthermore, Vibhishana did not approach us covertly. He has approached us with candour and a specific goal in mind. Some have suggested that his unexpected appearance is strange. But why is that? What is there to ponder if Vibhishana felt disgusted with Ravana and predicted his humiliation and defeat? What's the surprise if he recognised your heroic characteristics and nobility, as well as the surety of your victory?"

"I see no reason to be suspicious of this Rakshasa suppliant's features or speech. His carefree demeanour belies a guiltless heart. I believe Vibhishana has come here sincerely seeking refuge at your feet. And there is nothing unusual about his behaviour. He is aware of Ravana's true weakness. He understands that the Lord of Lanka is doomed to collapse. He is also aware that you have assassinated Vaali and delivered his kingdom to Sugreeva. Given that his true motivation is to secure his sovereignty over Lanka, there is nothing wrong with that, and it is a guarantee that he will be loyal to us. As a result, I believe we should admit him."

Rama patiently listened to the Vaanara leaders' diverse points of view. He was overjoyed when he finally heard Hanuman's comments.

Rama, firm in his dharma, felt satisfaction in Hanuman's words.

"If a man comes as a friend," Rama explained "How can I say no to him? It is a violation of my law. This should be obvious to all of you, my friends and helpers. When a guy surrenders, all his flaws should be overlooked."

Sugreeva, on the other hand, was dissatisfied. He stated: "This Rakshasa has abandoned his brother, whose cause he believes is hopeless. How can one have faith in someone who abandons his brother in his hour of need?"

Rama told Sugreeva: "I see what you're saying. But pay attention. It is natural for kings to suspect their siblings and fellow kings. The exceptions are good kings who have no such suspicions. Most rulers believe that their brothers are envious of them. So it's no surprise that Ravana suspected and insulted Vibhishana. As a result, Vibhishana feared for his safety if he continued in Lanka. As a result, I conclude that he has no malicious intent toward us in seeking safety here. Allow us to speculate that he has his sights set on the kingdom, anticipating Ravana's demise at our hands. There is nothing wrong with this aim. Can we expect everyone to be like our Bharata, Lakshmana?"

Rama fell silent for a minute after saying this, lost in thought of Bharata's altruistic love. Then he said: "Who else in the world is as fortunate as I am? Who among us has a brother like Bharata? What a wonderful father I had! His love for me was so strong that he died when I left for the forest. And who else, my friends, is as fortunate as I am to have friends like you?"

He wiped away the tears in his eyes and returned to the matter at hand.

"I see no value in arguing that Vibhishana will abandon us as he has abandoned his brother. He had no reason to abandon his sibling, and he has no reason to abandon us. We don't want Lanka, and if he does, as is natural, he can only have it through our triumph. From a policy standpoint, rejecting Vibhishana would be a mistake."

"But there is a more compelling explanation. When someone comes to me for help, I can't say no. This is my path. I can never deviate from it. I assure you that if Ravana himself came to me for refuge, I would embrace him without hesitation. So how can I reject his sibling, who has never done me wrong? Bring Vibhishana here."

"Rama, my Lord! It's amazing how the correct path presents itself when you speak!" Sugreeva stated. "I can see now. I'm going to bring Vibhishana. May he, like us, become a cherished friend of yours!" Sugreeva then went to find Vibhishana.

CHAPTER LIX:
THE GREAT CAUSEWAY

RAVANA, on the other hand, did something stupid. He dispatched a scout to entice Sugreeva away from his devotion to Rama. Suka, the Rakshasa, travelled across in disguise and met Sugreeva in private, speaking to him with every semblance of friendly solicitude: "Ravana, the king of Lanka, has sent me because he loves and respects you. He extends his heartfelt greetings. You are a king, and he is another, and it makes no sense for you to stake your high heritage by joining forces with a disinherited prince against an all-powerful king. What does it matter if Ravana sought Rama's wife and abducted her? What do you stand to lose? Consider carefully and select your course. You and your troops must return to Kishkindha as soon as possible."

Sugreeva, on the other hand, was disdainful and firm: "Base individual! Go tell your king that he is not my brother. He is wicked, and as an adversary of my friend Rama, he is also my enemy, and we are on a mission to rid the world of him and his evil gang. He's a fool to think he can insult Rama and still live. Tell him there is no way out, and tell him all of this is coming from me."

When Sugreeva gave this news to the Rakshasa spy, the Vaanaras grabbed him and started roughhousing him, but Rama angrily forbade it and set him free to return the way he came. The spy returned to Lanka and informed Ravana of the outcome of his expedition.

As soon as Rama accepted Vibhishana's commitment, Lakshmana and Sugreeva anointed Vibhishana king of Lanka and performed the abhisheka with seawater. Vibhishana committed constant friendship to Rama, and Rama in turn promised that he would not return to Ayodhya till Ravana was killed.

Sugreeva, Vibhishana, and Lakshmana then discussed how to cross the sea. They decided to start with a prayer to the ocean god and then give their thoughts to Rama.

Rama took their advice and began a fast by spreading darbha grass on the shoreline and laying himself on it, expressing his prayer for a passage over to the king of the sea.

He prayed to the sea god for three days and received no response. Rama then turned to Lakshmana, his eyes burning with rage at the sea-hubris god, and said: "The weak misinterpret civility and kindness for a lack of strength. Mildness is meaningless to them. See how I'm going to bring this arrogant sea to its senses with my arrows, which will not only choke it with the carcasses of gigantic fish but will also dry it up with their foul odour. O Soumitra, bring me my bow and quiver!"

Then, with a bow in hand and rage like the destroying fire at the end of the world, he launched arrows as strong as thunderbolts into the bosom of the sea. These powerful missiles shook the sea to its core, bringing death and terror to all it held, and the afflicted seas soon began to exhale steam in their misery. Rama's fury seemed to be transforming the sea with its infinite waves into a desert of scorching dust devoid of all life. The sea god couldn't take it anymore. He arrived and stood before Rama, shining like the rising sun behind Mount Meru.

With his hands folded, he said: "Ramachandra, my Lord! I, like the earth, air, space, light, and all other constituents of the cosmos, being subject to natural laws. How can I deviate from my nature, which is to be enormous, deep, teeming with waves, and impassable? But this is something I am capable of. Request the Vaanaras to bring boulders and trees to help you build a causeway. I'll agree to it. I'll assist you by receiving and securing the rocks and trees. This is all I can accomplish, and I will also show you the best location for this causeway.

"With you comes Nala, son of Viswakarma, who can build this path: triumph is yours."

Rama, as is his wont, graciously accepted the sea god's apology and offer of assistance. Rama then commanded that they all start working. Thousands of Vanaras jumped right in and began building the causeway.

The Vaanaras went to the mountains and forests and carried boulders and trees to the coast. The larger Vaanaras carried large boulders into the sea. The water splashed up skyward as they dropped. Nala stood and watched over their work. Companies were maintained active by the leaders in charge. When the base of rocks and trees was hard, a dressing of grass and small pieces of wood was used to create a flat surface. The dam builders' noise drowned out the sound of the ocean.

The building was soon finished. The new road sparkled like the Milky Way across the water. Hordes of gods rejoiced above, while hosts of Vaanaras delighted below. The gods and rishis bestowed blessings.

They then proceeded to the causeway. Angada carried Lakshmana on his shoulders, while Hanuman carried Rama. The army of Vaanara crossed the sea.

Malyavan, the aged Rakshasa, tried everything he could to persuade Ravana of the mistake of his ways. He stated: "Your lucky streak has come to an end. You can no longer put your faith in the gods' blessings. Make peace with your adversaries. Take a look at the army that has arrived, a terrifying swarm of Vaanaras and bears. Look at this magnificent causeway that was completed so swiftly. This Rama appears to me to be Vishnu in human form."

Ravana was not amused by such comments. "Your words are like wormwood in my ear," he lamented. "You appear to have joined my adversaries. Aren't humans notorious for their frailty? And he has the help of monkeys and bears! You are terrified of such a man. I am truly ashamed of you. I can't budge in front of Rama.

I can't help myself if it's bad policy or bad ethics. I'd rather die fighting than go to Rama and ask for peace!"

"Believe carefully and do what you think is best," Malyavan replied. And he returned home, with the usual words of thanks: "The King has won! Ravana has won!"

The elderly man was Ravana's grandfather.

Ravana meticulously placed his warriors. He sent Prahasta to guard the eastern gate, Mahaapaarsva, and Mahodara to guard the southern entrance, and Indrajit, his distinguished son who was skilled in the arts of secret magic, to guard the western door, while he decided to guard the northern entrance himself. The strong Viroopaaksha was named the leader of the troops within the city.

He believed he had assured victory by ordering the distribution of his army and chief warriors. As his demise approached, he paid little attention to everyone and stupidly imagined himself unconquerable. To appease the King, the ministers shouted victory and then dispersed.

Rama, Sugreeva, Vibhishana, and others convened a war council. Vibhishana duly presented to the council the information obtained by scouts who had gone out and observed Ravana's plans.

"In terms of numbers, strength, and courage," Vibhishana added, "Ravana's army now mobilised, surpasses that with which he battled Kubera. Still, I am confident in Rama's triumph."

Rama dispersed his soldiers to fulfil Ravana's disposition and assigned tasks to each commander. He gave Neela the instruction to meet Prahasta at the eastern gate. At the southern entrance, Angada was to meet Mahaapaarsva and Mahodara. Hanuman was to meet Indrajit, the maestro of dark magic, at the western entrance.

"Lakshmana and I will meet Ravana, the world's horror, and direct the assault on Lanka. Sugreeva, Jaambavan, and Vibhishana will accompany our main army." The soldiers spent the night on Mount Suvela resting. They took a good look at Lanka the next morning, standing on the mountaintop.

The lovely settlement on Trikoota's summit appeared to be suspended in the air. The Rakshasa troops stood to watch behind the thick fortress wall, which appeared to be another massive wall.

Rama was moved to pity after seeing the huge and gorgeous buildings in Lanka. And he added: "Alas! Because one person, drawn by Time's noose, has committed a transgression, all of this prosperity and the entire Rakshasa race must now be destroyed. Oh, that this noble scion should forget his true greatness and bring death and disaster upon himself and his nation!"

Rama went on: "However, we must now devote all of our attention to the work at hand to win this war and eliminate Ravana. The Rakshasas will try to trick us with various disguises. Allow the Vaanaras and bears to fight in their natural shapes. Only Vibhishana and his companions, like Lakshmana and myself, need to adopt human shapes. Our foes, the Rakshasas, will never take the appearance of a man or a monkey. It would be beneath their dignity for them to do so. We can identify who is who, murder our enemies, and support our allies if we stand together and keep order."

CHAPTER LX: THE BATTLE BEGINS

THE Vaanara army descended Mount Suvela and reached the forest surrounding Lanka.

The scared critters and birds in the forest fled in all directions as the soldiers poured in like a torrent.

Looking up from below at the mountain stronghold and the divinely gorgeous city Viswakarma had built, Rama was overcome with awe and exclaimed: "Oh, the beauty! What riches."

The Vaanaras, for their part, noted the Rakshasa warriors' strength and preparedness for combat, as well as the massive walls and powerful defence engines.

The sounds of drums and trumpets emanating from Lanka, all set for the fight, heightened the Vaanaras' enthusiasm for conflict. Rama had told the army to stand in orderly divisions.

Rama's thoughts turned to Sita. He reasoned that she would have known of his coming with the troops by now, and her gloomy heart would have been awakened. But he said nothing about it and was preoccupied with army preparations.

Sugreeva rushed up into the sky, without warning, and landed on the terrace on top of the tower in Lanka, where he saw Ravana seated in red royal robes, like a thick black cloud seen in the crimson twilight sky. The scar left by Indra's elephant's tusk glowed like a crescent moon on his breast.

"Ravana! You've been caught!" Sugreeva announced. "I am Rama's friend and servant. This is your final day!"

And he sprang on him, knocking off his crown and delivering a powerful blow. For a long period, the two wrestled. Both were wrestling experts. Each had tried every technique of that science. Ravana had exhausted his resources, so he abandoned wrestling in favour of magic, and Sugreeva, sensing this, disentangled himself and leapt back to where Rama was.

The Vaanara commanders, upon seeing Surya's son return, yelled praises and made a tremendous commotion of congratulations at this daring deed, no doubt impulsive and foolhardy, but such as would give the Rakshasas some sense of the opponents they were up against.

Rama was relieved to see Sugreeva had returned safely. Seeing the gushing wounds on his body, he stated: "Sugreeva! This valorous exploit fills me with astonishment and excitement. But what you did was wrong. It is not for a king to take risks. How could you have taken such a risky path so quickly and without consulting anyone?"

Sugreeva admitted his mistake. "True, rushing into war without consulting you was inappropriate. But when I saw the criminal who had insulted Sita, I was overcome with rage and forgot about my responsibilities."

The Vaanara army surrounded Lanka, as Rama had instructed.

Rama summoned Angada and told him: "Prince! Please deliver this message to Ravana. Tell him, 'Great sinner, your doom is near. Rama is waiting for you at the fortress entrance, eager to fight. You have plagued the earth for far too long and perpetrated far too many awful crimes. The time has arrived for the world to rid itself of you. Your sins will be washed away if you come out into the open and fight and die in combat, and you will obtain a position in the world above as a hero. But if you value your life, return Sita to her lord and ask forgiveness. Whatever happens, you are no longer suited to be king. Vibhishana now rules over the kingdom of Lanka. He is deserving of the throne and the protection of his people. If you do not want to surrender and seek safety, have your obsequies performed ahead of time. Bid farewell to all your treasured items in Lanka. Be prepared to die.' Send this message to Ravana, Angada."

Rama directed Angada to convey his message: "Ravana, pay attention. I am Vaali's son, as you are no doubt aware. I've arrived as Rama's messenger. If you value your life, you can plead with Rama for it after a modest surrender, and he never refuses clemency to a suppliant. If everything I've heard about you is accurate, you'll choose to fight, which means you'll die. I would encourage you to say your farewells to your relatives and complete your obsequies personally, as no one of your kind will be left to do so. Last look on gorgeous Lanka!"

Ravana's wrath erupted like wildfire. "Capture him, kill him, the criminal!" he yelled.

Two Rakshasas grabbed Angada at the same time. He ascended into the sky with these two Rakshasas on either side of him, then tossed them down.

He climbed higher and kicked and broke off the king's palace tower as he descended. He then returned to Rama with a single leap.

The Rakshasas were terrified by Angada's feat, but they did not reveal it. Ravana, too, sighed heavily at the sight of the shattered turret. He interpreted it as a negative omen.

Rama gave orders to the soldiers to begin the assault on Lanka as soon as Angada returned.

CHAPTER LXI: SITA'S JOY

SUKA, the Rakshasa scout, went to Ravana and reported: "I completed my work following your orders. My efforts, however, were futile. They were hard on me and made me feel grateful for the opportunity to return. Rama, who enjoyed slaughtering Viraadha, Kabandha, Khara, and others, has arrived with Sugreeva's army. They have discovered the location where Sita is being held captive. The bears and monkeys have crossed the sea and are preparing to fight against Lanka. Oh, Lord! Consider what has to be done, and then do it."

"We may yet escape if Sita is restored," he continued, fearfully, in a muffled voice.

Ravana was furious. "What did you say?", shouted he. "Let no one tell me that Sita has been restored. They who speak in this manner are unaware of my strength. I have the power to slay the gods, the Vaanaras, the Gandharvas, and the Yakshas. Wait and see how this despicable Rama and his army are decimated."

Ravana trusted all he said. He had spent too much time thinking about his prior accomplishments and had grown unnecessarily obstinate.

He then summoned two of his ministers and told them: "Scouts have reported that a big army has constructed a causeway to Lanka and has arrived here. Go, examine the enemy and report back to me with a complete and accurate report on their strength."

As a result, the spies disguised themselves as Vaanaras and arrived at Rama's camp, where they mixed with the other Vaanaras and looked around. However, when Vibhishana discovered their disguise, he apprehended them and brought them before Rama. They begged for their release, claiming that they were only messengers sent by their monarch.

Rama stated: "Display our army to them. Allow them to look around before they return. You Rakshasa messengers, too! When you return to Ravana, tell him, 'The strength you depended on when you brought Sita away will now be tested. Your stronghold, city, and army will be annihilated, and Rama's darts will pierce your skin.' Yes, please deliver this message to your king."

Rama's statements were heard by the spies, who agreed to relay them to their lord. The spies returned to Ravana and stated: "O King! We were discovered by Vibhishana and were terrified, but Rama refused to let them kill us and ordered our release. King! We've seen Rama, Dasaratha's son. He impressed us as being powerful enough to destroy our city and army on his own. We've seen the Vaanaras' bravery and enthusiasm for combat. It is not prudent to risk their lives in a conflict. It appears that Sita should be returned to Rama. Consider what has to be done."

Of course, the advice was earnest and well-intended, but Ravana couldn't hold back his rage. He stated: "Even if the entire world turns against me, I will not succumb to terror. I will not return Sita even if all the Devas, Gandharvas, and Vaanaras band together to resist me. You give me this cowardly counsel because you were battered by the enemy. Hearts of gold! Where can I find a rival who can defeat me?"

After that, he went to his high tower and evaluated the enemy's power. His ministers and officers accompanied him.

"Look!" exclaimed one of them. "Rama is the stately and graceful young man with matted hair and a bow in his hand. Lakshmana, a peerless bowman and Rama's second soul, is the great armed warrior alongside him. And take a peek! Sugreeva stands next to him, wearing Vaali's garland. He is on par with Vaali himself. Vibhishana, your brother, is standing next to him. Such warriors are difficult to defeat. In such a situation, think carefully and take all essential steps to success."

Ravana became increasingly enraged as the ministers lauded the enemy's might. His thoughts took an unusual turn. He assessed Rama based on his personality. He believed that if Sita could be persuaded to surrender to him, Rama would return home humiliated and broken-hearted. As a result, he vowed to make one final attempt using a different technique. He sought the assistance of a Rakshasa sorcerer. "Oh, Lightning-Tongue!" he said, "create a head that looks so much like Rama's that it will fool Rama's closest and dearest into thinking it is his. When I send for you, go to the park where Sita is imprisoned and set it in front of her." The sorcerer consented to do what was asked of him.

Ravana then returned to Asoka Park and attempted to seduce Sita once more. "Your spouse and his soldiers have been annihilated," he declared. "My men crossed the water and murdered Rama and his monkeys while they were tired and asleep. A warrior has brought your husband's head for me to see. Why do you persevere in your stubbornness? Follow my counsel and you will become the queen of Lanka."

Then he sent a Rakshasa to find the sorcerer Vidyut-jiva. The conjurer appeared and placed in front of Sita a head that looked just like Rama's.

Sita was taken aback by the sight and exclaimed, "So, is this my fate?" and burst forth in forlorn sorrow.

Meanwhile, Rama's army was approaching Lanka, and the ministers and generals requested an interview with Ravana immediately. Ravana had no choice but to leave Sita and proceed to the Assembly Hall.

Ravana's presence was required to maintain the sorcerer's illusion. As a result, when he went, the apparition of Rama's head faded like smoke. Sarama, a lady of the royal household appointed as Sita's companion, consoled her by explaining the delusion. She stated: "Rama was not murdered. He has arrived in Lanka at the head of a massive army. They have constructed a magnificent bridge across the sea and are spreading throughout Lanka like a submerged sea. The Rakshasas are terrified. Ravana is only using sorcery to fool you."

Sarama then informed Sita: "Several ministers persuaded Ravana to restore you and save himself by submitting unconditionally to Rama. But he refused to listen to them. Sacred Lady! There will be no harm done to you because Rama will triumph and this evil one will perish."

Even as Sarama was speaking, the sound of the Vaanara army's drums and trumpets reached Sita's ears and filled her with excitement. Ravana's demise was obvious to her. The Rakshasas of Lanka shook in horror when they heard the same sounds.

CHAPTER LXII: SERPENT DARTS

RAVANA was promptly notified that Rama's Vaanara host had enveloped Lanka like a raging sea. In a rage, he climbed the tower of his mansion and inspected the situation. He saw Vaanara troops armed with branches and stones on every side of him. He pondered how he could defeat such a massive invading force.

At the same moment, Rama noticed the Rakshasas guarding the city of Lanka. He could imagine Sita's mournful figure imprisoned within those walls in his mind's eye. He immediately ordered an assault.

'Victory to the Vaanara king!' they yelled. The Vaanara army rushed to the fatal city, shouting, 'Victory to Rama and Lakshmana!' Some threw large rocks toward the fortress wall and the city gates. Others raced on the Rakshasas, armed with gigantic trees ripped up by the roots.

Ravana then dispatched a large force. He told it to go out and murder all the Vaanaras at once. They pounded their drums and blew their trumpets until the sky rang. They attacked the Vaanaras. To fight the Rakshasas, the Vaanaras employed boulders and trees, as well as their nails and fists. Thousands died on both sides. Blood and twisted bodies filled the field.

Aside from this gruelling battle, there were several duels between individual soldiers. Angada faced Indrajit in the same way as Rudra faced Yama. A combat took place between the Rakshasa Prajangha and Sampaati, one of Vibhishana's friends. Hanuman fought Jambumaali, Neela fought Nikumbha, Lakshmana fought Viroopaaksha, and so on. Indrajit's chariot and horses were destroyed, and Angada was struck by Indrajit's mace. Jambumaali struck Hanuman with his weapon, shattering his chariot. The Rakshasas focused their attack on Rama, and hundreds were killed by his arrows.

Vidyunmaali threw darts towards Sushena. The latter crushed the Rakshasa's chariot with a rock. Vidyunmaali charged Sushena with his mace, crushing him to death with a rock. Many warriors fought and died in this manner.

Throughout the day, the combat raged. And the Rakshasas would not cease fighting at night. The fight turned heated. Streams of blood flowed. On both sides, there was heinous bloodshed. Indrajit was attacked by Angada, who slaughtered his horses and charioteer and shattered the chariot. The Vaanaras cheered as they praised their prince's talent and might. All of the army's fighters hailed the Vaanara prince's prowess. Indrajit, like his chariot, lost his temper and turned to wizardry. Making himself invisible, he hurled several darts at Rama and Lakshmana, who was highly irritated by this attack from a foe whose locations no one knew and who seemed to rain deadly missiles from all sides.

Indrajit then launched serpent darts toward Rama and Lakshmana. They couldn't move and were useless on the battlefield since they were bound by them. They exchanged glances, unsure what to do. Lakshmana was devastated at Rama's plight. The Vaanaras, on the other hand, gazed in melancholy confusion.

Indrajit returned to the city after congratulating the Rakshasa troops. He went to his father, triumphant, and reported that the narrative of Rama and Lakshmana was done. Ravana was overcome with excitement. He welcomed his son and extolled his abilities.

When the Vaanara warriors saw Rama and Lakshmana lying low, they believed that the battle was done. When Vibhishana saw Sugreeva standing helpless and lonely, he inspired the Vaanara king. "It is folly to give up hope," he remarked. "Consider Rama and Lakshmana. Their expressions are still brilliant. They are not yet dead. Don't be afraid. They will soon recover from their trance and begin battling."

The leader took courage and did everything he could to keep the men from panicking. The ranks were reformed, each with its chief.

Meanwhile, Ravana had it declared in Lanka that Indrajit had killed Rama and Lakshmana. He summoned his women and told them: "Go immediately and inform Sita that Rama is no longer alive, that the two princes are dead on the battlefield, and that the Vaanara army has been destroyed. Also, to finally persuade her, take her to the Pushpaka Vimana and show her the battleground from above. Allow the obstinate one to observe for herself what has occurred. She will turn to me now that she has no one else to turn to besides me."

The Raakshasis followed the orders. Sita could see the battleground from the Vimaana. Rama and Lakshmana were motionless on the ground, their weapons scattered around them. She was overcome with grief. She felt it was all over and sobbed: "To this end, fate has led me, defying the prophecies of saints and astrologers that I would live as a happy wife, mother, and great queen. These warriors, who had done so much, now lie lifeless, like someone who, after crossing the ocean, drowns in a small pond. Oh, you princes! How did your divine weapons let you down?"

When Sita was in this state of desperation, Trijata, her rakshasi companion, who was looking intently at the immobile figures of the princes, cried out: "There is no reason to be sad, Sita. Your husband and Lakshmana are both alive. They are bound by a charming weapon and are temporarily unconscious. Have faith. Do not be alarmed." Sita's ears were filled with nectar as a result of her remarks. Sita was returned to the Asoka Vana after the Vimaana returned to Lanka.

The power of the sorcery-charged arrows waned with time. Rama sat up and opened his eyes. Despite his injuries, he sat up and restored his strength through willpower. He yelled at his brother, who was laying on the ground: "Alas! What is the point of victory now? How can I return to Ayodhya without you? You were always there to console me when I was down. You are deafeningly silent now, as I face my deepest grief.

"You slayed the Rakshasas with your two hands, releasing showers of arrows. How could death have happened to you? You accompanied me into the jungle, and now I will reciprocate your kindness by accompanying you to Yama's dwelling. I admit defeat. I cannot keep the promise I made to Vibhishana. Oh, King Vaanara! Bring all of your warriors back to Kishkindha. You've put in a lot of effort for me. You have fulfilled all of your responsibilities as a friend. You have my appreciation. But more of you dying is pointless. Return to your hometown. Allow me to expire here." Rama lamented in helpless anguish in this manner.

Then Vibhishana arrived, with a mace. Vibhishana turned to face Rama and Lakshmana. When he saw them injured, covered in arrows, and unable to fight, he burst into tears "It's all over now. What else can you do?"

Sugreeva turned to his uncle, Sushena, and said: "Rama and Lakshmana should go to Kishkindha. I'm going to kill Ravana, reclaim Sita, and bring her there."

Sushena responded: "There are plants that can heal the princes' wounds and restore their health. Some of us know where to look for these herbs. Hanuman has arrived. He will go get the herbs if you send him."

The water and air were shaken up by a powerful wind as they spoke, and the enormous bird Garuda flew into view. When Garuda came, the serpent darts that had encircled Rama and Lakshmana vanished instantly. They were all venomous serpents that had been transformed into arrows by Indrajit's sorcery and tied to the princes' bodies. They took flight when their persistent and feared foe, Garuda, approached. Then Garuda tenderly stroked Rama and Lakshmana's bodies, restoring them to full power. They came up, stronger and more bright than before, and their wounds healed. "Who are you, my benefactor?" Rama inquired.

Garuda responded, "I'm your old companion and close friend. Yours is the glory! Allow me to leave immediately. We'll get to know each other better once the conflict is over." Saying this, Garuda flew away.

When the Vaanaras saw Rama and Lakshmana completely restored and ready for combat, they became enthused once more and continued their assault on Ravana's fortress.

CHAPTER LXIII:
RAVANA'S DEFEAT

RAVANA was shocked to hear, carried by the wind, the happy acclamations of the Vaanaras, whom he assumed were lamenting their vanquished commanders and slaughtered friends. He addressed the Rakshasas who were standing by him: "What has brought the Vaanaras such joy? Something unusual had to have happened. Go figure out what it is."

Some Rakshasas climbed the wall and peeked over it. Returning with fear and trembling, they cried to Ravana: "King! Sugreeva's Vaanara army is attacking the castle with zeal. Both Rama and Lakshmana are still alive. Rama and Lakshmana, like elephants who have broken their bindings, have shaken off the naaga (serpent) darts with which Indrajit bound them, rejoined the army, and are roaring about the field like hungry lions."

Ravana's face sagged. He expressed his concern by saying: "What you say astounds me. So yet, no one has escaped these darts. We are in peril if those weapons are ineffective against these men."

Then, in a fit of rage, he yelled: "Dhoomraaksha, pay attention! Why should I be concerned while you're here? Gather as many men as you desire. Go immediately and destroy these two small fellows, then return swiftly."

Dhoomraaksha was overjoyed and delighted to be singled out by the king. He led a troop of warriors out of the fort and came into contact with the group led by Hanuman who was attempting to enter the western gate. Both sides were slaughtered in the fight that followed. Hanuman eventually killed Dhoomraaksha.

Ravana's rage was unrestrained when she learned about this mishap. "Oh bravest of soldiers, go without delay and destroy these vile fellows," he summoned Vajradamshtra.

Vajradamshtra knelt before the monarch and led a massive army out of the southern gate, where he met Angada.

The Rakshasas, led by Vajradamshtra, fought a bloody battle and slaughtered innumerable Vaanaras. Despite this, the Vaanara force refused to retreat. They murdered countless Rakshasas with boulders and trees. The fighting was fierce on both sides. Angada and the Rakshasa chief eventually fought hand-to-hand for a long time. Vajradamshtra was slain in valiant combat, and the Rakshasas fled in confusion. The Vaanaras surrounded Angada and exclaimed in joy.

Then Ravana gave Prahasta this order: "Send Akampana and allow him to be accompanied by the most terrifying Rakshasas. Allow them to go and annihilate Rama, Sugreeva, and the Vaanara army. Nobody can stand up to Akampana's power and talent."

As a result, Prahasta dispatched an army of Rakshasas led by Akampana. In battle, Akampana lived up to his name by being steadfast and unmovable. He had picked his weapons and warriors with care. As he moved forward, ominous omens met him. But neither he nor his followers paid attention to them. The noise of their challenge was louder than the sound of the water.

A massive battle ensued. Streams of blood flowed. Dust rose and obscured the light, shrouding the earth in foreboding gloom. The bloodshed was massive on both sides. Kumuda, Nala, Mainda, and Dwivida attacked Akampana, who bravely defended himself.

The battle had gone against the Vaanara warriors, who were about to flee when Hanuman appeared. Akampana threw arrows at him, but Hanuman ignored them, taking a massive boulder and throwing it above his head, and hurling it at Akampana. The stone was intercepted by the Rakshasa's darts, which pulverised it to powder. Then Hanuman expanded in size and blazed with dazzling brightness like the sun, uprooting a large tree and attacking and killing the Rakshasa with it. The Rakshasa army was destroyed like a forest in an earthquake, and the survivors fled in terror from the terrible field, which was littered with the dead, and spread the bad news throughout Lanka. The Vaanaras surrounded Hanuman and exclaimed their adoration loudly.

Ravana's emotions dropped when he learned of Akampana's death, but he found strength in his fury and despair, and he began making new plans. He returned to the city's defences and spoke with Prahasta, the commander-in-chief. "This Vaanara siege must be broken. One of us five - me, Kumbhakarna, yourself, Indrajit, or Nikumbha - should take charge of leading the troops out of the castle. Are we supposed to be terrified of monkeys? Why! They used to flee in panic at the mere sound of a Rakshasa's roar. They are ignorant of the science of war. How have they survived all of our attacks?"

Prahasta responded modestly: "Things have unfolded just as we predicted. Long ago, we humbly recommended that it would be preferable to rebuild Sita and establish peace. But I am obligated to obey you. I am willing to give up my life, my family, and everything for your sake. If you choose, I will conduct this excursion."

A massive army was gathered, and everything was prepared for a tremendous endeavour, including the observance of specific rites and sacrifices.

Prahasta then marched out to the pounding of drums. The Vaanaras yelled with joy as they saw the large army commanded by Prahasta emerge from the fortress's eastern entrance, ready for combat.

The Rakshasas descended on the Vaanara army like moths on a flame.

"Look," Rama exclaimed, "there comes forth a Rakshasa at the head of a massive army." What is his name?"

Vibhishana responded, saying: "Prahasta is Ravana's commander-in-chief. He commands one-third of the imperial army."

Then there was a bloody struggle between the Vaanaras, who were armed with stones and trees, and the Rakshasa, who were armed with swords, spears, bows, and axes. Both sides fought vigorously, exchanging stone showers for arrows and fighting in death grips at close quarters, deluging the field with blood.

Dwivida, Durmukha, and Jaambavan killed Prahasta's supporters, Naraantaka, Mahaanaada, Kumbhahanu, and others. Prahasta and Neela engaged in a protracted conflict. Finally, Prahasta charged at Neela, armed with a big iron mace. Neela, for his part, dislodged a large boulder and slammed Prahasta's head against the ground, killing him instantly.

Rakshasa warriors fled in every direction. After this great victory, Neela went to Rama and Lakshmana and told them what had happened, kneeling low. Rama and Lakshmana applauded and congratulated him on his talent.

Some of those who left the battle brought news to the Rakshasa King that Neela, son of Agni, had killed Prahasta. Ravana was overcome with fury and grief. "These Vaanaras have killed my warrior leader," he cried, "who could vanquish Indra and his army of gods. We must not take this lightly. Rama and the monkey host must be destroyed." Ravana then got into his chariot and drove away.

When a new Rakshasa army appeared, the Vaanaras prepared to meet them with stones and trees in hand. Rama was shown the Rakshasa warriors one by one by Vibhishana. "Indrajit is sitting in the chariot, glowing like the rising sun." So he journeyed from one famous fighter to the next until he arrived at Ravana. "The ten-headed Ravana sits in the great chariot, dazzling as the sun."

Rama looked at the majestic and dazzling body with curiosity and pity. "A tremendous warrior, without a question," he continued, "but he is so evil that he must be destroyed."

Ravana slew a large number of Vaanaras. Neela fought bravely against Ravana but was killed by a fiery dart. Hanuman violently assaulted Ravana, and the two fought an equal struggle for a while, but Ravana could not be vanquished and wreaked devastation on the Vaanara host.

Lakshmana and Ravana got into a fight. Lakshmana collapsed unconscious, but Hanuman stepped in and dragged him away to Rama.

Rama then attacked Ravana while riding on Hanuman's shoulders. The Rakshasa king had been severely injured. His golden crown had been shattered. His chariot as well. He stood before Rama without a weapon.

"You may leave now," Rama said. "You fought admirably today. Go away and rest, then return refreshed and armed the next day." And Ravana returned to the city, embarrassed.

CHAPTER LXIV:
THE GIANT IS ROUSED

RAVANA entered the fortress, embarrassed and worried. After some thought, he summoned his bravery and commanded his sleeping brother Kumbhakarna to be awakened.

Kumbhakarna used to sleep for months at a time as a result of a curse, and he had gone to sleep just a few days before the events were last recorded. Ravana directed his ministers to make every effort possible to rouse Kumbhakarna and prepare him for the fight as soon as possible.

"All of my penances have been in vain. It appears like the rishis' prophecy will be fulfilled," Ravana thought to himself, yet rooted in his desire to battle to the death, he gave orders as if certain of final victory: "Let the warriors guard the stronghold on all sides. My brother is soundly asleep. Unaware of my worry, he sleeps peacefully. If left alone, he will not wake up for months. He's only been sleeping for nine days. Immediately rouse him. If he wakes up and goes to battle, the enemy will almost certainly be scattered. Who can stand in the way of my Kumbhakarna? I won't be afraid if he wakes up and fights against my enemies."

Ravana's officers and servants went to Kumbhakarna's palace as a result. They knew he'd be rapaciously hungry as soon as he opened his eyes. So they began by preparing and stacking mountains of food for him. They then produced a great deal of noise by beating drums and blowing conches. Many Rakshasas were fatigued from pushing and shaking the Rakshasa's massive body. The racket they produced with their screams, drums, and trumpets filled the sky and terrified all the birds and beasts of Lanka, but Kumbhakarna slept through it all. The Rakshasas worked hard to wake him up. Elephants were made to tread on his body. They belaboured him with cudgels.

Finally, his eyelids opened slightly, and he brushed them all aside and yawned as if brushing away a mosquito while still sleeping.

Kumbhakarna's sleep, which would have lasted months, was thus disrupted. But before he could figure out why, he started eating and drinking. The masses of flesh and pots of blood and wine that had been prepared for him had been consumed. When his hunger had subsided, the Rakshasas approached him to inform him of the predicament.

Yoopaaksha, Ravana's minister, stated: "We have been vanquished in battle, my Lord, and we are in terrible peril. You'll recall the battle over Sita. The Vaanaras, led by Rama and Lakshmana, have arrived and are storming the fort. They murdered and defeated our army, which had never known defeat. The Vaanara host surrounds Lanka like an ocean. Ravana himself went into battle, but he was forced to retreat after suffering the brunt of the damage. It was our fortunate fortune that he survived."

Kumbhakarna was beyond himself with wrath when he heard this. "I'm going to go destroy this adversary right now. I will murder the Vaanaras and drink Rama and Lakshmana's blood. I'll go and wait for the king when I complete this first."

The ministers were thrilled to hear this venomous speech, but they pleaded with Kumbhakarna to first meet the King and consult with him on what should be done.

Kumbhakarna agreed, washed his face, and went solemnly into the King of Lanka's hall.

When they watched him pass, the Rakshasas gained new bravery and gladness, and they bent low before him and showered flowers on him. He entered the palace and stood in Ravana's presence. Ravana leapt down from his throne and embraced his incomparable brother, overjoyed at his arrival.

"Brother! You have no idea what has transpired," Ravana stated. "You were fast asleep. Rama has become a big threat to me. He has erected a dam across the water that we thought was untouchable, and the Vaanara army now surrounds Lanka like another sea. Our warriors who ventured out and met them were defeated and nearly annihilated. It is now up to you to save us from disaster, and I am confident that you can do it. I am aware of your keenness and bravery in warfare. Go immediately and eliminate these foes, as well as assist us in our time of need and save Lanka."

When Kumbhakarna heard Ravana's anxious remarks, he was inspired to rage against the enemy, but then he remembered the entire incident and Ravana's vain-glorious faith in his invincibility, and he smiled cruelly. He stated: "My brother, the caution we gave you when you came to see us was ignored. You are now bearing the repercussions of your error and transgression. What else can happen when one acts rashly out of lust? If you had wanted to and had the confidence and strength to do so, you should have killed Rama and Lakshmana before seizing her. It is no surprise that when one acts without asking or considering the advice of wise and devoted friends and kinsmen, he finds himself in peril and destruction. Shouldn't a king know who provides him good advice and who gives him badly?"

Ravana was annoyed by all of this scolding. His face reddened with rage, but he kept his cool and said: "Brother! Such discussion has long passed. What I need now is your prowess, not your criticism. What has been done has been done. The question now is what we should do in our current situation. It is now your responsibility to use your strength and expertise to avert the current tragedies caused by past mistakes. If you truly care about me, this is the time to demonstrate it by assisting me rather than criticising my behaviour. Give me consolation from your boundless bravery."

This appeal moved Kumbhakarna. "I don't care," he said. "I am your brother, and I will never abandon you. Rest assured that Rama and Lakshmana are no longer alive. I'm going to scatter and slaughter their monkey army. I will throw Rama's head at your feet, and you will see the Vaanara King's blood gushing on the battlefield. Rama can only approach you over my dead body, which is impossible because no one can vanquish or slay me."

Kumbhakarna's pride grew. "Whoever the opponent is," he yelled, "I will destroy him." In this state, he dashed to the battleground.

The abrupt awakening from deep slumber had entirely disrupted his temper, but once his raging hunger and thirst had been satisfied, he regained his equilibrium and spoke wisdom to Ravana. When he saw Ravana's condition again, fraternal affection and pity overcame him.

Ravana was overjoyed. "My brave fighter! Oh, brother! What a helpful friend I have in Kumbhakarna!" He said, certain that Kumbhakarna would succeed.

Kumbhakarna, armed with his huge spear, was about to march to combat alone when Ravana intervened and dispatched an army to assist him. He adored his brother's large physique with diamonds and clothing and blessed him for saving: "My hero, go! Destroy your opponents and return victorious."

Kumbhakarna, tall and mighty-limbed, was encrusted with gleaming gems. He circled his brother, bowed, and marched out spear in hand at the head of a vast army, amidst the Rakshasas' praise and a shower of flowers and well wishes. When the gigantic shape of Kumbhakarna, a Rakshasa giant, was seen stepping across the fortress wall, the Vaanaras were terrified and began fleeing in all directions. Their chiefs gathered them and put them in battle formation with great effort.

CHAPTER LXV: IS THIS NARAYANA HIMSELF?

Angada rallied the Vaanaras, who reformed in battle order and prepared to meet Kumbhakarna. They threw boulders at him and struck him with severe blows with trees torn by the roots, but he ignored them all with a smirk on his face and continued slaughtering the Vaanaras with methodical cruelty that was scary. Some of them fled to the recently constructed dam, while others attempted to flee by hiding on the seashore and in the woodlands.

Angada had to persuade the Vaanara leaders and troops to re-form and assault Kumbhakarna once more.

Dwivida, Hanuman, Neela, Vrishabha, Sarabha, and other chiefs launched a ferocious attack on Kumbhakarna. But he ignored them all and carried on with his savage killing of the Vaanaras. Angada himself received a blow, which caused him to swoon and fall to the ground. Sugreeva was defeated. Kumbhakarna joyfully took the unconscious Vaanara king towards Lanka. The Rakshasa army exulted and made a joyful roar. Kumbhakarna desired to give the captive Vaanara King to his brother Ravana.

As Kumbhakarna triumphantly carried the unconscious Vaanara monarch across the royal highway, the Rakshasas and their womenfolk, standing on the terraces, showered flowers and poured sandal paste. This, by chance, resurrected Sugreeva. He opened his eyes, puzzled as to where he was and what had transpired. He quickly grasped everything. He then began to bite and shred the ears and nose of the Rakshasa who was carrying him with his teeth and nails. Kumbhakarna was worried and tossed him down, aiming to crush him with his feet. Sugreeva, however, sprang and flew across the sky till he arrived at the location where Rama was.

Hanuman was certain that Sugreeva would return. Hanuman had roused the Vaanara ranks and prepared them for war in anticipation of Sugreeva's departure.

Kumbhakarna, grim and horrific, with torn nose and ears, returned to the battlefield with a massive iron mace like a large blood-red dusk cloud.

Kumbhakarna could no longer be stopped. He started killing and devouring the Vaanaras. The entire army began to vanish in this manner. They tried to scare him away by climbing on his mountain-like body and tearing at it with their nails and fangs, but he shrugged them off like flies. None of the Vaanara leaders could keep him in check.

Lakshmana attempted to hinder his path with his arrows, but the Rakshasa ignored him and pushed ahead to face Rama himself.

Rama aimed powerful darts at the Rakshasa for a long time. The arrow that penetrated the seven sal trees and Vaali's tenacity were ineffective against Kumbhakarna.

Rama wounded the Rakshasa's arms and feet with sharper and stronger arrows, yet nothing short of death could stop him. His legs were severed, yet he wandered around on his stumps and continued fighting his brother's struggle with demoniac ferocity.

Rama finally hacked off his head with an arrow.

The severed head, carried into the sky by the might of Rama's arrow, crashed in Lanka like a hill with its forests aflame. Ravana was informed of the situation.

"Kumbhakarna, your brother, has entered the heaven of killed heroes! He slaughtered thousands of Vaanaras and terrorised Rama and Lakshmana's armies for a long time. But he was eventually killed by Rama himself, and his mutilated body lies like a great tree ravaged by a forest fire. A piece of it has fallen into the sea. Another large section obstructs the fortress's entrance. The severed head, which was flying across the sky, landed in the city and is now laying there."

Ravana felt his own life had abandoned him when the Rakshasas told him this story. He shouted out in anguish and wrath after regaining consciousness: "Oh, great warrior! How could you leave me behind and go to Yama's world? My right hand has been severed! How did Rama slay you, you who no opponent dared to approach in the entire world? What good is this kingdom to me? Why should I cling to life when my beloved brother has abandoned me? Yes, I must torture and slay the man who murdered my dear brother!"

Then he cried, with sudden and useless remorse: "Alas! Why didn't I listen to Vibhishana?"

Trisiras and his sons attempted to calm Ravana.

"What is the use of lamentation?" they wondered. "You who have obtained strength and armour from Brahma, why should you dread or weep?" And Trisiras himself proceeded to the battlefield. Many more, riding on elephants and chariots, excitedly followed him.

A massive battle ensued. Naraantaka, spear in hand, was riding his horse and wreaking havoc on the Vaanaras as he made his way toward Sugreeva. Angada stood up to him and killed both him and his horse.

Hanuman killed Devaantaka and Trisiras, and Neela killed Mahodara. Lakshmana's arrows claimed Atikaaya. However, before they perished, these four had fought like four Yamas, causing massive losses to the Vaanara armies.

Ravana was perplexed when he learned that Atikaaya had died.

"This is amazing! These adversaries have slaughtered one by one my men, solid and mighty like mountains and irresistible like the ocean. My adversaries have emerged from the serpent entanglements with which my peerless son Indrajit had chained them. I have no words to describe this man Rama's strength. Perhaps he is Narayana himself?"

Ravana became depressed as a result of her confusion. He desired that the invading forces not enter the stronghold, and especially not enter the Asoka Vana. He re-supervised the defences and returned to the palace, depressed and despondent.

CHAPTER LXVI: THE DEATH OF INDRAJIT

INDRAJIT reassured his father. "Why should you be concerned when I am still alive?" he asked, gathering an army and leading it on another raid.

He swooped down on the Vaanara army, killing and injuring thousands. They were powerless in the face of his rage. Indrajit's Brahmastra proved powerful against even Rama and Lakshmana, who was bound by it. They were unconscious on the ground, and the Rakshasa prince went immediately to his worried father with the good news.

Vibhishana united the scattered Vaanara leaders and instilled hope and bravery in them.

"Is Hanuman alive?" Jaambavan, who was dead than alive, wandered slowly amid the Vaanaras.

"Yes, I am here," Hanuman remarked as he knelt before Jaambavan.

"My son," the old Vaanara continued, "go immediately northwards over the sea to the Himalayan range. The Herbs Hill is located between the Rishabha and Kailash summits. There are four medicinal plants on the hilltop. Rama and Lakshmana, as well as the Vaanara army, will regain consciousness if you get them here immediately. Their wounds will heal, and they will fight once more. Do this as soon as possible. Only you are capable of accomplishing this."

Hanuman jumped into the air and moved quickly as a result. He arrived at the hill indicated by the venerable Jaambavan, and because he couldn't identify the vegetation, he carried the entire hill back to Lanka.

Even as the Sanjeevi hill approached, Rama, Lakshmana, and the Vaanaras felt the darts slip off their bodies. Their wounds healed, and they got strong enough to stand.

The fight resumed. Sugreeva, after consulting with Rama, chose a few Vaanaras and directed them to enter Lanka and set fire to the city.

They entered the city with torches at about midnight. They attacked, overwhelmed the guard, and set fire to Lanka's palaces and towers. Thousands of homes were burned to the ground. The majestic metropolis has been reduced to ruins.

Ravana was enraged when he saw Lanka being burned down by the Vaanaras and dispatched to the battlefield Kumbha and Nikumbha, the sons of Kumbhakarna, together with Yoopaaksha and other Rakshasa troops.

Sugreeva killed Kumbha, and Hanuman killed Nikumbha in another horrible combat. Makaraaksha, son of Khara, who stood up to Rama, was killed by his flaming arrows. Much more powerful Rakshasas perished. Then, at Ravana's request, Indrajit returned to the battle. He ascended into the sky and vanished. As a result, he fought again, unnoticed by the Vaanaras. Indrajit constructed a Maaya-Sita through necromancy and took her before the Vaanara army, presumably killing her in their presence.

The Vaanaras, duped and appalled, asked themselves, "What good is it now to prolong this war?" They left the field and returned to Rama with the devastating news.

Indrajit gained time as a result of this feat, allowing him to conduct an asuric (demonic) sacrifice. Rama and Lakshmana, like the Vaanara warriors, believed Sita had died and were devastated. When Vibhishana arrived and inquired about what had occurred, they were extremely perplexed and helpless.

He sat and listened to their narrative. "You have been duped," he continued. "Ravana would never allow Sita to be killed. This is just a sorcery trick. Indrajit uses magic to try to defeat you. He has gone to conduct an asuric sacrifice of enormous power, having given up all hope of succeeding through normal means. We cannot defeat him if he completes it. As a result, we should go and impede the sacrifice. Allow Lakshmana to leave immediately and ruin Indrajit's plan."

Accepting this counsel, Rama dispatched Lakshmana, escorted by Hanuman and other Vaanaras, in addition to Vibhishana. They went to the location where Indrajit was preparing to make an offering to bad spirits. The sacrifice was cut short, and a lengthy and bloody conflict began. As he ascended his chariot, Ravana's son fired his arrows. Lakshmana did the same while standing on Hanuman. The combat lasted a long time since they were evenly matched in strength and ability. Indrajit's chariot was wrecked during the battle, and both warriors stepped on the ground and continued the fight.

Finally, Lakshmana used the Indra-astra enchantment and released the fatal arrow by reciting the word Rama. Indrajit's head was cut and fell to the ground, glistening like fire.

Lakshmana then proceeded to Rama. He was badly injured and bleeding all over. He moved slowly, helped along by Jaambavan and Hanuman. Rama had already heard about Indrajit's death.

"This is the end of the Rakshasa race, Lakshmana!" he exclaimed. "You have done it."

Lakshmana stood back humbly, but Rama placed him on his knee, kissed his head, and let out his excitement.

"You have accomplished something unachievable for anyone else. You have taken Ravana's right hand. Who in the world can compete with you, Vibhishana, or Hanuman? You have defeated Indra's conqueror."

Ravana learned of Indrajit's death at the hands of Lakshmana. When he learned that Vibhishana assisted Lakshmana in killing Indrajit, his grief and rage grew, and his tears burned where they fell.

"Oh, my son! O unrivalled fighter! O hero! The powerful Indra has been defeated! Is Death finally victorious? Have you made it to the heaven of heroes? But I shouldn't be sad," he remarked.

But the father's heart would not be denied, and he screamed once more, "The world is now empty for me. Oh, son, you have broken the hearts of your mother Mandodari, your loving wife, and myself. Nothing except vengeance and misery remains for us now.

"It's preferable to destroy Sita, the root of all this calamity." So saying, he went out, sword in hand, ready to kill. When some violent Rakshasas saw Ravana erupt in rage, they rejoiced; but the minister Supaarsva was frightened and appealed to Ravana's better judgement and what was due to himself as a man and monarch.

"How dare you believe such a thing, King!" he exclaimed. "Oh, ten-headed Lord! Are you planning to murder a woman? Will you accept this disgrace and sin? You have mastered the Vedas as well as all of the sciences. You've done a lot of penance. How did you wind up with anything like this? Let us direct our rage onto Rama. Tomorrow is the new moon. Gather all your soldiers, march out of Lanka, kill Rama and Lakshmana, and win. Take Sita next. Put on the armour you obtained from Brahma. Ascend your chariot and prepare for combat."

Ravana believed Supaarsva was correct and that his remarks were appropriate. He sat silently on his seat for a while, immersed in deep meditation. Then, with folded hands, he addressed the commanders, saying, "Go now with all your strength and slay Rama. If you fail, I will go and destroy him myself."

He had never been so kind and humble in dealing with his officers before. This lesson had been imparted to him by adversity. Ravana's army arrived in full force for the great battle, mounted on chariots that sparkled like the hills on the twilight horizon and on the backs of huge elephants and gorgeous horses.

The Vaanaras ripped up rocks and trees and savagely fought the Rakshasas. The Rakshasas countered the attack with similar vigour.

The Vaanaras ran around everywhere, wreaking havoc on the Rakshasas, their chariots, and their beasts. Each Rakshasa was surrounded by Vaanaras and killed. The Rakshasas, too, did not spare the Vaanaras, killing tens of thousands of them.

Rama drew his bow and unleashed a hail of arrows on the Rakshasas, destroying their army like a blazing fire. Because of the arrow shower, they couldn't see Rama. Their terror summoned a swarm of Ramas, who dealt death in all directions.

Numerous elephants and horses were killed. Thousands of chariots were shattered. The Rakshasa army was crushed, except for a few survivors who fled to Lanka.

Rakshasa women clung to one another in Lanka, lamenting aloud that Ravana's stupidity had brought this enormous misfortune upon them.

CHAPTER LXVII: END OF RAVANA

EVERY home in Lanka was filled with sobs. Grief, shame, and hatred raged in Ravana's chest like a roaring sea. He had thus far despatched his commanders and men in detachments, and despite their valour, they had been thoroughly decimated. This resulted from his strong belief in his invincibility and contempt for the enemies. As a general, he was inattentive and reckless, but he was brave, and finally determined to fight himself and with his single power to defeat the enemies, he started. He was confident in his prowess and the efficacy of the boons he had obtained, and he rode forth on his holy chariot, carried by eight horses and loaded with all sorts of weaponry, escorted by a division of Rakshasa chariot warriors.

The sun appeared to be hidden by an unexpected eclipse when Ravana issued from Lanka, and filthy birds and monsters of the night shouted at large with strange ill-omened screams; nevertheless, Ravana drove out to battle followed by Viroopaaksha, Mahodara, and Mahaapaarsva.

The great Rakshasa warriors that pursued Ravana were slain by a lethal flight of arrows and chunks of rock, and Ravana now found himself confronted by Lakshmana, who attempted to obstruct his further progress. Forcing his way past Lakshmana, Ravana charged Rama with all the rage of anger and vengeance he could muster, attempting to overwhelm him with a hail of arrows.

Rama easily deflected these arrows with his own, striking Ravana repeatedly but failing to penetrate his armour. Thus they fought, these supreme bowmen, each intent on destroying the other and employing increasingly potent secret-power missiles, while the gods in heaven marvelled and admired. Neither hero had ever faced a foe like this before, and on both sides, adoration was mixed with rage.

Rama pierced every limb of Ravana with his darts. Despite this, he did not fall.

Meanwhile, Maatali brought his master Indra's chariot to the battleground for Rama's use.

Indra, the God-King, has sent this to you for your use," Maatali stated. "Be glad to ascend this chariot and destroy Ravana, the gods' enemy!"

Rama bowed to the gods before circumambulating and ascending the celestial chariot. Then began a fierce battle.

Ravana collapsed unconscious from his wounds, and his charioteer gently escorted him off the battlefield.

When Ravana regained consciousness, he was furious with his charioteer for bringing him off the battlefield and insisted on being returned to face Rama. The gruelling battle resumed. Every astra encountered another. The two chariots travelled and the two warriors fought in unusual ways for a long time, while both armies watched with breathless adoration and terror.

The charioteer, Maatali, whispered into Rama's ear: "The end of the Rakshasa is near. Do not postpone any longer. May I bring up Brahma-astra?"

Rama cast the incantation and dispatched the Brahma-astra. Though the Rakshasa's ten heads had previously been severed, they had grown again, perplexing Rama. The Brahma-astra, releasing flames, approached Ravana and broke the secret of his invincibility, which was enshrined in his chest.

The bow then slipped from Rakshasa's grasp, and he fell from the chariot and lay stretched on the battleground.

The gods blew their horns. Rama and his chariot were surrounded by a shower of flowers from the heavens. Rama was encircled by Lakshmana, Vibhishana, Jaambavan, and other soldiers who were overcome with delight and love.

When the first flush of triumph faded and Vibhishana gazed at his brother's body, the natural call of blood and recollections of boyhood days when Ravana and he had loved and played overcame him, and he erupted into lamentations over his lost sibling.

"Oh, warrior!" he exclaimed. "O brave and illustrious King of Kings! Your massive arms are now powerless on the ground! You, self-willed and misguided, surrounded by evil advisers, would disregard my warning! The worst-case scenario has now occurred! You received what you have sown, and here you lie on the bare ground, O once-mighty Rakshasa monarch!"

Rama responded to Vibhishana's lament: "Ravana fought like a true warrior and died as a hero! Death has cleansed him of his crimes. It does not call for grief. Ravana has arrived in Heaven."

Rama cleared Vibhishana's mind and ordered him to perform the burial ceremonies for his late brother.

Rama stated: "It is now up to you, his brother, to perform the ceremonies. All animosity ceases with death. Even I, his former antagonist, can properly execute his obsequies. Isn't your brother also my brother?"

Ravana's palace women gathered in the field to grieve. They led the queen Mandodari, who resembled the goddess of grief. The crowned Queen and Ravana's adored wife were in complete despair.

"Indra, King of the Gods, dared not face your wrath," she exclaimed. "At the sight of you, the Rishis and Gandharvas fled in all directions in terror. And now a mere man, a forest wanderer, has brought you down! My lord, my lord, I warned you a long time ago. Did I not tell you that this Rama is no ordinary human, but someone bigger than Indra, Agni, or Yama, whom you could never defeat? Did I not say this when we learned he murdered your brother Khara in Janasthaana? I learned the truth when Hanuman broke into Lanka, the impenetrable castle, and destroyed it. I asked you not to arouse their wrath, but you refused.

"Why did you look lustfully at chaste Sita? This was the insanity that led to your death! Sita and Rama are now reunited and happy after their brief separation, but you have irrevocably cast me and our race into the depths of sadness. What do I do now? I had a Lord of Lanka as a lord! I had a son who had defeated Indra. They have abandoned me, and I am now a defenceless widow with no friends or a place to live!"

Sobbing, Mandodari collapsed over Ravana's body and passed out.

CHAPTER LXVIII: THE END

In a beautiful ceremony, Vibhishana was crowned King of Lanka. The new Lord of Lanka arrived at the Vaanara camp and bowed low in front of Rama.

Then Rama told Hanuman, "With the King's permission, enter Lanka and inform Sita of what has occurred." Hanuman obtained permission from Vibhishana and travelled to Asoka Vana to inform Sita of the news.

Sita's delight was indescribable.

"Why, mother," Hanuman inquired, "don't you speak?"

"What can I say, my son?" she replied. "How can I pay back my debt to you? Your intelligence, chivalry, and humility are all yours. Nobody on the planet can compare to you." Her eyes welled up with feelings of thanks and affection as she stated this.

"I wish to slaughter these wicked ladies who tormented you," Hanuman murmured to Sita as he glanced at the raakshasi women who had guarded her. "Please grant me leave!"

"No, my son," she replied. "Who in the world is without blame? It is the role of noble spirits to be compassionate toward all individuals, sinners, and saints alike."

"These Raakshasis, however," she went on, "carried out their master's orders. What is their fault? Their ruler is no longer alive and has paid the price for his wrongdoing. Punishing these Raakshasis now is unjust."

Hanuman's sole words of reverent admiration were that what she said was only fit for Rama's wife.

"What message am I gonna deliver to Rama?" he inquired.

"I am excited to be in his presence," she replied. "That's it."

Hanuman returned to Rama and described his visit. Rama's face had darkened for some reason, and he had fallen into a brown study with dull eyes. He turned to Vibhishana a bit later and said:

"Ask Sita to bathe and dress before bringing her here."

When the message arrived at the Asoka Vana, Sita replied, "I'd rather go as I am."

"Not so, dear lady," Vibhishana responded, "the Prince's orders must be followed."

Sita proceeded to the camp after a bath, bedecked in jewels, and sitting in a palanquin.

Rama awoke from his trance as he heard Sita's arrival. The events of the past rose like waves, beating against his psyche and causing it to erupt in a flurry of humiliation, pain, and joy.

They thronged around Sita's palanquin as it passed through the large concourse of Vaanaras, causing chaos. It was exacerbated by the Vaanara leaders' attempts to shove them aside to make room for the palanquin.

"Let no one is kept away," Rama urged. "These loving Vaanaras have stood and suffered in my place. Sita will be thrilled to see me surrounded by such kind people. No one should be pushed away."

Rama's expression revealed a peculiar mental shift. Nobody, not even Lakshmana, could understand what he was saying.

Sita stepped out of the palanquin, her eyes downcast, and walked towards Rama. "Aryaputra," she wailed, unable to speak further.

"I have slain the enemy," Rama declared. "I have found you. As a Kshatriya, I have fulfilled my responsibilities. My vow has finally been accomplished."

"I fought this bloody war to fulfil my obligations as a Kshatriya, not just because I was attached to you. It gives me no delight to receive you back now, for doubt surrounds you like a gloomy cloud of smoke."

"What do you want to do now?" he said. "You must live alone because we cannot coexist. You may remain under the care of any of our relatives or acquaintances. How can a Kshatriya reclaim a bride who has spent so much time in a stranger's home?"

Sita turned to face Rama. Her eyes were on fire.

"You have spoken unworthy words!" she exclaimed. "They have been heard by my ears, and my heart is broken. Your rage appears to have damaged your comprehension. My lord has forgotten about the family from which I came. Janaka, the great seer, was my father and raised me. Is it my fault that the evil Rakshasa seized and imprisoned me? But, because this is how you see it, I just have one option."

"Fetch the faggots, Lakshmana, and ignite a fire," she added, turning to Lakshmana.

Lakshmana, who had been observing Rama's behaviour with dismay and wrath, turned to gaze at Rama's face, seeking his orders, but Rama did not reply "No" or show any signs of softening.

Obeying Sita, Lakshmana lit a large fire, and the princess circled her lord, eyes locked on the ground, exclaiming, "Ye Gods, I bow before you. Oh, Agni, you recognise my purity and will accept me as your own!"

She jumped into the flames with these remarks. And, a marvel of marvels! The lambent flames were packed with celestial images as all the gods gathered there, and Brahma said, "Narayana! Mighty God who went in human form to defeat Ravana! Isn't this your Lakshmi?"

Agni, the God of Fire, arose from the flames in his own body and brought Sita to Rama, her garments and jewels unharmed and unbroken.

"Who am I?" Rama asked Brahma. "All I know and can tell you is that I am Rama, Dasaratha's son. You know who I am, where I come from, and everything else; it is up to you to inform me."

Rama regarded Sita as pure as fire after saying this to Brahma.

"Do you think I didn't know about your unquestionable purity? The purpose of this ordeal was to appease the masses. They'd say it if it wasn't there, wouldn't they? That Rama, blinded by love, acted with surprising weakness and violated the rule of well-bred men."

With those words, he brought her to his side.

Then Dasaratha descended from heaven and blessed the Prince on his lap. He exclaimed to Sita, "My child! Please forgive my son. Forgive him for the damage he did you to preserve the world's dharma. May God bless you!"

Indra granted his gift, and the Vaanaras who died fighting for Rama were resurrected.

Rama and Sita, being reunited, ascended the Pushpaka, which swiftly took them in the air to Ayodhya with their allies, the Vaanara soldiers, and Vibhishana.

"Look there!" he said as they flew through the sky, "there is the causeway made by Nala! Look there, that's Kishkindha," he continued again, "where I met and befriended Hanuman and Sugreeva." And Rama showed Sita the places where he and Lakshmana had roamed and told her about his amazing experiences.

Ayodhya was submerged in a sea of ecstasy. Rama and Bharata crossed paths. Kaikeyi and her hunchback maid had devised and constructed schemes for Bharata's sake. But today, as Bharata bowed at Rama's feet, he felt a thrill greater than anything they had intended for him. What kingly crown could ever compare to the bliss found at Rama's feet? What kind of power could bestow the grandeur that was now Bharata's for all time?

Bharata's penance was over now that Rama had been crowned King as his father had intended, and his heart was filled with delight.

Rama, filled with love for Hanuman, handed Sita a pearl necklace to wrap around Hanuman's neck. As she did so, he noticed a beautiful smile grace her face. What else could Hanuman want?

Vasishtha received the new King and Queen and fixed the hour for the coronation, interrupted fourteen years before.

GLOSSARY

Agneyaastra: A missile charged with an invocation to the God Agni (Fire).

Aryaputra: 'Noble prince'; a classical form of address by wife to husband, betokening love and respect combined.

Ashrama: Hermitage.

Agni: The God of Fire.

Amaravati: The city in heaven where Indra has his abode.

Aruna: The God of Dawn, first son of Kasyapa Prajapati and Vinata. He was born lame. Aruna was the elder brother of Garuda. Aruna is the charioteer of the Sun God.

Astras: Miraculous weapons whose power lay in the invocations with which they were charged.

Asuras: Enemies of the Gods.

Avatar: Incarnation.

Bala, Ati Bala: Two invocations to obviate hunger, thirst, and sleep.

Bhogavati: The capital of the Serpent King in the nether world.

Brahmana: The first of the four castes devoting their lives to study and teaching and the performance of religious ceremonies.

Brahma: The Creator, one of the Trinity.

Brahmastra: The most powerful among Astras. See Astras.

Brahmachari: One who is in the first of the four stages in a Brahmin's life, the stage of study and practice of a disciplined life.

Brahmarishi: The highest type of sage.

Brihaspati: The preceptor of the Devas, the planet Jupiter.

Chaitra: The month falls in the second half of April and the first half of May.

Daanavas: Sons of Danu and Kasyapa Prajaapati, enemies of Devas.

Darbha: A species of sacred grass used for religious rites.

Deva-Lok: The celestial regions.

Devas: Celestial beings, sons of Aditi and Kasyapa.

Dharma: Duty as laid down by religion or custom.

Gandharvas: A Class of semi-divine beings. Celestial musicians.

Garuda: The bird king who is Vishnu's vehicle.

Guru: Aachaarya, preceptor.

Hari: One of the names of Vishnu. The second of the Hindu Trinity. Other names are Krishna, Mukunda, Maadhava, Kesava, and Narayana.

Ikshvaaku: King of the Solar race from whom the name came for the race of Solar kings.

Indra: The chief and the king of the Gods.

Indra-Astra: Missile charged with an invocation to Indra.

Jaambavan: Leader of bears in the army of Sugreeva.

Jamadagni: A great sage, and father of Parasurama.

Kaamavalli: A name that Shurpanakha gave to herself.

Kailash: The abode of Shiva.

Kalpaka: A tree that was issued out of the Ocean when it was churned by Devas and Asuras. A celestial tree that grants any wish to people who are under it.

Kekaya: A country northwest of Kosala, the place where Bharata's maternal grandfather ruled. West of modern Punjab.

Kinkaras: Soldiers, personal attendants.

Kshatriya: The second of the four castes.

Kubera: God of Wealth.

Kusa: A kind of grass used in religious ceremonies

Lakshmi: The Goddess of Well-being-wife of Vishnu.

Malyavan: The aged Rakshasa grandfather of Ravana.

Malyavati: A stream flowing by the foot of Chitrakoota Hill.

Maaruti: Name of Hanuman, the son of Marut, the Wind god.

Manmatha: The God of Love.

Mantras: Scriptural verses, incantations.

Maya: The architect of Asuras.

Meru: A fabulous mountain around which the Sun is supposed to revolve.

Naaga: Semi-divine serpents.

Narayana: Vishnu.

Nandigama: A village near Ayodhya where Bharata lived and ruled Ayodhya as a deputy of Rama.

Nikumbhila: A cave and grove in Lanka where oblations were offered to Kaali.

Paarijaata: A celestial flowering tree.

Payasam: A sweet preparation of milk and rice.

Parasurama: The sixth incarnation of Vishnu who curbed the growing arrogance of the Kshatriyas.

Pinaaka: Bow of Shiva.

Pushpaka Vimana: Aerial chariot of Ravana which originally belonged to Kubera. Sitting in this chariot, one could obtain anything he or she desired.

Raajagriha: The capital of the Kekaya country.

Rakshasas: Evil-minded strong beings similar to Asuras.

Raakshasi: Feminine of Rakshasa.

Raghu: An ancestor of Rama. He was the king of the Solar race.

Rishabha: A peak in the Himalayas.

Rishi: A sage who has undergone severe austerities.

Rudra: Shiva.

Sanyaasini: A female recluse, feminine of Sanyaasi.

Sarama: Wife of Vibhishana. She and Trijata were the friends among the Raakshasis that Sita had during her incarceration in the Asoka Vana.

Sarayu: A tributary of the river Ganges on the North bank.

Siddha: One who has attained special powers through penance. A class of heavenly beings.

Shiva: One of the Hindu Trinity.

Surya: The Sun God.

Sukra: The Guru or aachaarya of the Asuras, the planet Venus.

Tamasa: A river flowing into Ganga.

Tapas: Austerities and penances.

Tapasvini: One who does Tapas or penance.

Tapasya: Power obtained through Tapas or penance.

Trivikrama: See Vaamana.

Vaamana: The fifth incarnation of Vishnu to curb the power of Mahaabali. Vaamana became a Trivikrama of huge stature who measured Earth and Heaven in two steps.

Vaayu: The Wind God who was the father of Hanuman.

Vaidehi: Another name for Sita.

Vaishnava: Appertaining to Vishnu or worship of Vishnu.

Varuna: The Lord of the Ocean.

Veda: Scripture. It is in four books-Rig-Veda, Yajur Veda, Saama Veda, and Atharva Veda.

Vidyut-jiva: 'Lightning Tongued', a Rakshasa sorcerer.

Vinata: Mother of Garuda.

Vishnu: See Narayana.

Viswakarma: The celestial architect.

Vritra: An Asura killed by Indra.

Yagna: Sacrifice, a religious ceremony accompanied by oblations.

Yakshas: A class of celestial beings.

Yama: God of Death.

Yojana: A measure of distance almost equal to nine miles.

Yudhaajit: Son of the King of Kekaya. Brother of Kaikeyi.

Yuvaraaja: Prince-Regent.